INSIDE OUTSIDE

Also by Russell Galbraith

Fiction
George Square 1919

General
Destiny's Daughter: The tragedy of RMS Queen Elizabeth
The Hampden Story

Biography
Without Quarter: A biography of Tom Johnston

A Biography of Tam Dalyell

INSIDE
OUTSIDE

The Man They Can't Gag

RUSSELL GALBRAITH

MAINSTREAM
PUBLISHING

EDINBURGH AND LONDON

FOR THREE GENERATIONS:
HETTY, ELAINE, NATALIE;
AND FOR YVONNE

First published in Great Britain in 2000 by
MAINSTREAM PUBLISHING COMPANY (EDINBURGH) LTD
7 Albany Street
Edinburgh EH1 3UG

ISBN 1 84018 367 5

A catalogue record for this book is available from the British Library

Typeset in Stone Print and Unconform
Printed and bound by Butler and Tanner Ltd, Frome and London

ACKNOWLEDGEMENTS

Thanks are due to Sir David Attenborough, Tony Benn, Lord Biffen of Tanat, Robert Brown, Dr Tom Carberry, George Cunningham, Lord Ewing of Kirkford, Michael Foot, Diana Gould, Lord Healey of Riddlesden, Nigel Hepper, David Hoddy, Sir Bernard Ingham, Neil Kinnock, Allister Mackie, John Muir, James Ovens, Gareth Boyd Roberts, Lord Robertson of Port Ellen, Lt Col Aidan Sprot MC, Lord Steel of Aikwood, Professor Alan Thompson, Ken Waddell, William Wolfe, Senior Minister Lee Kuan Yew and Lord Younger of Leckie. Also, Sybil Cavanagh, Jean Cordner, Bob Cuddihy, Jamie Fergusson, James Hastings, Paul Koh, W. R. McKay, Isla Robertson, Janet Royall, Kathryn Seren, Ted Williamson and Yeong Yoon Ying. In addition I would like to record my appreciation of the facilities available at the Public Records Office at Kew, the British Library's national newspaper archive, the Mitchell Library, Glasgow, the West Lothian Local History Library and the National Trust for Scotland. Everyone at Mainstream deserves my thanks but I am especially indebted to Deborah Kilpatrick, Caroline Budge, Bill Campbell and Peter Mackenzie. Tam Dalyell, a famously busy man, committed himself to many hours of interview without complaint. Kathleen Dalyell offered crucial support and encouragement. At no stage did either of them attempt to interfere with my plans for the book or influence its content. Principal sources, in addition to Dalyell's own writings, are named as part of the main narrative and a select bibliography appears at the end.

CONTENTS

ONE

THE ALCHEMIST

When the century turned, Tam Dalyell had been a Member of Parliament for almost 40 years. In all that time, he had never served as a member of any government. His presence on the front bench had been fleeting when compared to all the years before and since – yet his name at least is probably as well known as that of any minister, outside the seven men and one woman who, during his years in the House of Commons, made it to the pinnacle of power: 10 Downing Street.

Dalyell's virtues, according to his own assessment, include a 'hide like a rhinoceros'. To one interviewer he admitted: 'I am very unembarrassable'. The fact that he doesn't blush easily has been a useful quality, considering the twists and turns of his long parliamentary career: Dalyell was the last MP to be brought before the House of Commons and reprimanded by the Speaker wearing a black cap; and on five other occasions he was ordered to leave the chamber for calling one Prime Minister a liar.

Dalyell has always been that rare creature, a driven 'issue' politician. Faced with a hostile House of Commons, he once observed: 'You have got to have mental tenacity and guts, intertwined with a kind of vanity and egotism, which leads one to believe that one is right when all others are out of step.' It is a quality which doesn't always endear him to his colleagues. Roy Hattersley, a former deputy leader of the Labour Party, thought him 'a zealot who is obsessed with the inconsistency which made him famous'. George Robertson, Secretary of State for Defence at the time of the Balkans war, commented bluntly: 'If we'd listened to Tam's advice the Argentinians would still have the Falklands, Saddam would still have Kuwait, and the refugees would still be in Macedonia and Albania. That's the ultimate proof of the pudding'. Tony Benn, another Labour heavyweight, disagreed. He thought it was a mistake for people to dismiss Dalyell as 'old hat, because very often the old hats turn out to have been the first ones to identify what later becomes the conventional wisdom. There's a solemnity and authority about the way Tam presents a case,' Benn went on. 'There's no muck-raking, no scandal, no abuse, no desire for publicity or headlines: he has contempt for all that. He hasn't even got an office in the House of Commons. I don't know where he works. None of the trappings of power interest him in any way at all. He is totally unbribable. But he exercises judgement. And his judgement is usually confirmed by history, which is a very unusual quality among Members of Parliament.'

The fact that Dalyell is prepared to admit: 'I cannot disguise that the opinion of the cognoscenti matters to me', is no more contradictory than several other aspects of the man. George Younger, who clashed furiously with Dalyell, first as Secretary of State for Scotland and later as Secretary of State for Defence when Mrs Thatcher was in Downing Street, described Dalyell as 'a breaker with convention, an instinctive rebel, not particularly in a left-wing or a right-wing sense, he's just a rebel. Much of the time he's right and pursues causes we can all appreciate,' Younger added. 'Quite often, though, he gets it utterly and completely wrong. But that's the nature of such activities. You can't be right all the time.'

When he arrived in the House of Commons, Dalyell's old friend from Cambridge, John Biffen, Chief Secretary to the Treasury in Margaret Thatcher's first cabinet, thought he was 'very difficult to typecast'. Biffen said: 'The Labour Party at that stage was full of people who were typecast. You had the whole of the Bevanite overhang and the CND arguments continuing, as well as disagreements over Europe. People were being slotted right across the spectrum. Tam was never slottable.'

Tony Benn considered Dalyell 'predictable in the sense that he's a signpost and not a weathercock. You always know if you go back to the crossroads Tam will be there, pointing, distinct from the weathercocks who are blown by the opinion polls. On the other hand, he's unpredictable in the sense that you don't know what issue he's going to focus on. And that combination of being predictable on his principles and unpredictable on the issues he's going to raise gives him a great deal of strength.'

This tendency, together with his 'wonderfully brooding and unpredictable presence' appeared to unsettle journalist Kenneth Roy. Writing more than a quarter of a century after Dalyell first arrived at Westminster, Roy noted: 'One never knows quite what he is going to say next, or how he is going to say it, or sometimes even why.' The former Labour leader, Neil Kinnock, took the view MPs like Dalyell – who could be 'brilliantly terse, often forensic, occasionally bewildering' – were 'the grit in the parliamentary oyster. And there would be damn few pearls without them,' said Kinnock.

It was during Kinnock's leadership that Dalyell told Kenneth Roy: 'I think you've got to be very careful about the terms 'right' and 'left'. I mean, what am I? One of the most vehement members of the Parliamentary Labour Party for getting the army out of Northern Ireland, and therefore on the far left. On the other hand, an unreconstructed, constant pro-European Community man, which puts me on the extreme right. And where does my strong support for the nuclear industry put me? On the right, I suppose. But I am also shoulder to shoulder with the left in favour of a wealth tax. This categorisation is very difficult.' Roy assured his readers: 'In the days before television, he would have made a barnstorming actor-manager, shocking and delighting the provinces . . . Instead he has been treading the boards at Westminster for the last quarter of a century, a one-man show of undiminished bravura in the midst of so much dreary ensemble playing.'

Among earlier newspaper attention, Robert Brown, writing in *The Guardian* on 3 September 1968, found 'he talks seriously but dresses so unstylishly that he was married in a sports jacket and kilt'. Dalyell's wife Kathleen offered no complaint. 'It was a very nice jacket,' she said. 'Tam didn't think there was much point buying something he'd only wear once.'

Robert Brown, a serious Labour thinker who helped launch the short-lived breakaway Scottish Labour Party along with Jim Sillars in 1976, and a leading political journalist of the period, acknowledged that the Americans would call Dalyell 'an oddball, and not just for the socialism that followed Eton and Cambridge'. He suspected the young Dalyell was 'originally artless as a politician. Certainly, he sees himself as an open-natured man. But subtleties have developed that to some people seem devious, and he does not make friends easily enough to have his eccentricities casually explained. In political company,' added Brown, 'Tam's morality is often uncomfortable.' Commenting on his subject's 'zest for perfection', the same writer suggested with wry good humour: 'If cradled in medieval times, he might have dedicated himself to the quest for the elixir of life or for the alchemy to turn base metal into gold.'

Dalyell found no difficulty in separating what the leadership might deem right or expedient from what he perceived as his duty to the Labour Party, particularly that part of it based in his own constituency. His constituency chairman, Allister Mackie, insists: 'As far as he's concerned, ours is the only opinion in the Labour Party that counts. He is an absolutely unique character, totally unpredictable, quite different from any other MP I've known, and a great electoral asset.' The former Liberal leader David Steel, now presiding officer of the Scottish Parliament, agreed: 'If you took all the Members of Parliament of the last 30 years and deleted those who had been ministers, I think you would find Tam would probably come out on top as an example of an effective parliamentarian. He has been a model of tenacity, pursuing campaigns like the *Belgrano*. I felt very sympathetic towards him on this, especially after the Thatcher cross-examination on television by Mrs Diana Gould. I think then I realised we hadn't been told the whole truth about what happened. On devolution I think he has been consistently wrong. But time will tell.'

The diarist Woodrow Wyatt saw Dalyell as 'an amiable crank'. Mrs Thatcher, he told a visiting American journalist, was not Dalyell's 'kind of girl'. Surprisingly, perhaps, considering the severity of his attacks on her personally, there were occasions when Mrs Thatcher looked on him kindly, according to John Biffen. 'I think,' said Biffen, 'he always inspired a great measure of affection because he was seen to be a very genuine person. But, like many crusaders, at times he allowed the cause to run away with him and with his judgement.'

Away from Westminster, another experienced Dalyell watcher, James Ovens, a retired miner who was present when the old Etonian was originally selected as the Labour candidate in West Lothian, observed: 'I sometimes wonder, if he had used that searching mind on the Stock Exchange and the banking system with the same enthusiasm he put into all his major campaigns, he might have made a tremendous contribution to the domestic affairs of the Labour Party. I thought he was right over the *Belgrano*. But I kept asking, why isn't the Labour hierarchy supporting him?'

According to Michael Foot, leader of the Labour Party during the Falklands war: 'One of the great virtues of the House of Commons is that we have MPs like Tam, who stick to their own views through thick and thin, and whom everybody knows is absolutely honest. I think it's very important to have individual MPs with the guts and the knowledge to be able to operate in this way. The procedures of the House of Commons should protect such people even when they are in a tiny minority, or a minority of one.' Foot continued, 'Nobody can match the way Tam operates. In my time, when he was either criticising or in revolt against the party leadership, I was sympathetic to his views.'

Dalyell parts company with the present administration over what he perceives as Tony Blair's 'demeaning of parliament' and 'dismantling the machinery of the party, and downgrading the National Executive Council.'

Previous Labour governments, headed by Harold Wilson and James Callaghan, were much more concerned with what we think of as traditional Labour values.' But he denies there is any personal antagonism between him and the present leadership. 'We're just on a different planet,' Dalyell explained. 'I am completely against spin. And I am absolutely contemptuous of the acting part of Tony Blair. One thing I have never done in my life is talk in slogans. There are two different kinds of slogans. The kind of slogans this government uses are meaningless: "Fairness for all!" "The Third Way!" "The people's this, the people's that!" "Full employment" is a definite statement of what you want to achieve. "Votes for Women" is something concrete. But all this use of abstract nouns! We desperately need tough, serious answers to serious questions, rather than this awful soundbite presentation. When Harold Wilson was Prime Minister, he would make a speech every three or four weeks in the House of Commons, sometimes at inordinate length, and he could be interrupted. When did Tony Blair last make a speech in the House of Commons, except following the Queen's Speech, when he is required to present his legislative programme?'

Asked by the *New Statesman* to place 12 Labour leaders in order of merit, Dalyell put Tony Blair at the bottom of the list. 'They printed the fact that one person among those canvassed put Tony Blair twelfth without printing my name,' said Dalyell. 'But that person was me. They could have printed my name if they had wished. It wouldn't have bothered me.' What does bother him considerably, though, is his perception that the Prime Minister has been trying to operate like a President, without the necessary checks and balances. 'My objection to the way he is demeaning parliament isn't just a question of *amour-propre*,' Dalyell insisted. 'It's a question of democracy. What we are seeing under Tony Blair is the first presidential government, even more so than Margaret Thatcher's government. As I told a meeting of the Parliamentary Labour Party, with Tony Blair present, any Prime Minister is entitled to his chums. Harold Wilson and James Callaghan both had inner circles, but the people surrounding them were all elected. Tony Blair's inner circle wasn't elected by anybody. When we discussed the debacle of the European elections, I told the Prime Minister I thought he bore a certain responsibility in the matter. You could've heard a pin drop after I said this,' Dalyell added. 'The room which had been rather bubbly went silent. I warned him that people would work hard for a Labour government or the Labour Party. I wasn't so sure they'd work hard for a napoleonic Blair presidency. and after I'd told him this he said in the wind-up, looking at me directly and speaking quite nicely, 'Tam, I am not Napoleon!' Unabashed, Dalyell continues to insist it's nonsense to suggest that the Labour Party owes its victory at the last election to Tony Blair and the attractions of New Labour. John Smith would have won the election without compromising. The majority would have been just as large. And it would have been a far better government with John Smith in charge. John Smith was of the Labour Party. Tony Blair is not.'

TWO

RELATIVE VALUES

Tam Dalyell was born at 9 Randolph Crescent, Edinburgh, on 9 August 1932. His father was Percy Gordon Loch, an adventurous and widely travelled soldier who pursued a remarkable career in India and the Middle East, helping to sustain the Empire before and after World War I. 'He was,' said his son, 'one of those absolutely incorruptible Edwardian Anglo-Indian civil servants, who followed his father, grandfather and great-grandfather into the Indian Civil Service. Albeit old-fashioned.' Dalyell added, 'he was a man of considerable probity'.

William Loch, Dalyell's grandfather, had been the British Resident in Nepal. His first wife, Edith Mary Gibb, daughter of the vice-Chancellor of Bombay University, died in childbirth, leaving Percy, aged three, and a newly born infant, the future Lieutenant General Sir Kenneth Loch, Master General of Ordnance and head of the British Council. William Loch, with two young children needing care, remarried. 'Edith Orde Wingate, my adored step-grandmother,' said Dalyell, 'was part of the well-known Wingate tribe. She was an extremely tough, nice lady, prepared to raise two small boys who were not her own. When my grandfather became ill he wrote to the Viceroy, asking for leave to go back to Britain for treatment. Curzon, who was a shit, denied him twice. The third time he just went. But he was dead within two months.'

Percy Gordon Loch was educated at Cheltenham, his brother at Wellington. Sandhurst followed. 'They were both awarded King's cadetships, which were available to anyone whose parents had served the Empire,' said Dalyell. Commissioned in the North Staffordshire Regiment in 1905 at the age of 18, Percy Gordon Loch joined the 97th Infantry of the Indian Army the following year. His first posting was Multan, then 'the farthest frontier of the British India Empire', in what is now east-central Pakistan. Located on the main southern route into India from Afghanistan, it was a commercial and military centre of great importance to the Raj. His father, William Loch, had been present during the siege and capture of the city in 1849, in a war against the Sikhs. The young subaltern's family connections proved useful when he managed to obtain an appointment as private secretary to Sir William Willocks on the 1910 Irrigation Survey of Mesopotamia. 'While working with Willocks, the great Victorian-Edwardian water engineer who dammed the Tigris and the Euphrates, my father siphoned off money to help his friend Leonard Woolley, the archaeologist,' said Dalyell. 'It was a highly dicey thing to do. But his initiative appealed to the British Resident in the Persian Gulf, Sir Percy Cox, who decided my father should join his staff as a likely young man. Cox was very grand,' Dalyell continued. 'He was the pro-consul in the Gulf in the way that Milner was the pro-consul in Egypt. It was Cox who drew a line in the sand and created Kuwait. Before the war he virtually ran the whole of Mesopotamia, which was administered through the Indian Political Service. Things were a bit different after the war. The seige at Kut-el-Amara delivered a tremendous blow to British military prestige.'

The seige was the direct result of a failed military advance on Baghdad, which had been advocated by Cox following the capture of Basra in November 1914. On 8 December 1915, a mixed garrison of British and Indian troops was surrounded by a strong Turkish force led by General Khalil Bey. Shortly before the Turkish bombardment began, Major General Charles Townshend of the 6th (Poona) Division of the Indian Army informed his men: 'The honour of our mother country and the Empire demands that we all work heart and soul in defence of this place.' All attempts to relieve Kut-el-Amara failed. On 29 April 1916, Townshend surrendered.

When World War I started, Percy Gordon Loch's knowledge of Mesopotamia earned him a place on the General Staff, assessing intelligence reports from Turkey, Persia and Arabia. Two years later he renewed a century-old family connection with Bahrain: in 1816 another ancestor, Francis Erskine Loch, had helped to conclude the first treaty between Britain and Bahrain, when the ruling Sheik was persuaded to let his country become a British protectorate. There was an admirable perspicuity about the job title bestowed on this latest Loch to leave his mark on the desert sheikdom, Political Agent. Percy's main task was to maintain good relations with the cunning and legendary Ibn Sa'ud, whose continued goodwill was critical to Allied operations throughout the Middle East. Loch remained in Bahrain for two years practising diplomacy, before the grey men of the Indian General

Staff, who charted his life from faraway Simla and ultimately Whitehall, decided it was time for a change. His next posting was Kuwait where, according to his version of events, he initiated a policy of purchasing all available supplies, regardless of cost, to prevent them reaching the enemy.

Percy Loch's diplomatic career continued after the war with his return to India where, for a period of five years, he served in the Foreign and Political Department of the Government of India at Simla and Delhi. Six years after the war ended he was appointed First Assistant to the Resident at Kashmir, and then Political Agent at Gilgit, a remote town on the north-western frontier, within sight of the Himalayas. Relations between Britain and the Soviet Union were strained and the Foreign Office in London feared there could be trouble on the Gilgit frontier. During a long period of service at Gilgit, the curious and energetic Percy Loch 'travelled over 7,000 miles in the mountains, entered a number of little known valleys and crossed many high passes'. According to one account of his Kiplingesque adventures among the local tribesmen, one remote pass, an awesome 17,000 feet above sea level, had been crossed only twice before by Europeans. It was a dangerous and lonely existence. 'He talked a lot about the hardship of life on the frontier,' said Dalyell. 'You had to be extremely self-reliant in those days. You also needed a good relationship with the *sepoys*. If you didn't succeed in gaining the trust of the Indian soldiers, you could be in great trouble.' Percy Loch believed he possessed 'mediumistic powers to an unusual degree'. However, after indulging in what he mysteriously described as 'some experimenting', Loch deliberately refrained from cultivating his gift. As he later told family and friends, 'In the unsettled and lonely circumstances of service in the East it seemed an unwise thing to do.'

Loch, who married Eleanor Wilkie-Dalyell of The Binns in 1928, remained in India for another three years, occupying various senior governmental posts, including Chief Commissioner of Coorg at Bangalore and President of Administration in Rewa, where he was credited with reorganising the Rewa State Army and equipping it with modern weapons. Shortly after the birth of his son, he returned to Bahrain accompanied by his wife. 'It was considered unsafe to take European babies to the Persian Gulf because of the water,' Dalyell explained. 'So I remained in Scotland with my grandparents, living at The Binns. I didn't know much about it then, of course, but later I regretted not going with my parents to Bahrain. If I had, I might have learned Arabic. My parents were both good linguists. At one stage when my father thought he was going to Tibet, he learned Tibetan.'

Percy Loch and his wife remained in Bahrain until 1937. His role was to provide 'political advice to the Sheik of Bahrain and, at the same time, report anything of importance to London. He was very much the British presence in that part of the world.' Dalyell counters any suggestion that his father was a spy with the admission: 'He had close links with the intelligence community, certainly. And he was of that kind of disposition. But if he was a spy, then everyone working for Sir Percy Cox was a spy. People like him and Gertrude Bell and Freya Stark were all mixed up together, travelling widely in the Middle East, doing what they could for the good of the Empire.' T.E. Lawrence had been part of the same circle. 'They didn't like him,' said Dalyell. 'They thought he was a man of enormous vanity and ego. I once entered a prize competition, I think at Eton, and the set book was *The Seven Pillars of Wisdom*. My parents were very disapproving. They didn't tell me not to do it, but they didn't like the idea at all. They thought he was a fraud.'

Five years after his son was born, Percy Gordon Loch retired. A year later he adopted a new name. With the death of her father Major Sir James Wilkie-Dalyell in 1935, Eleanor Loch had inherited The Binns, a historic and ancient estate 20 miles west of Edinburgh, and its attendant title, a baronetcy originally created in 1685 to honour General Tam Dalyell. Rare among Scottish honours, the baronetcy of The Binns can be continued through the female line, although in the absence of a male heir, the title is considered dormant. The name derives from the twin hillocks which dominate the 215 acre estate. A natural and attractive location for a house, with splendid views of the Forth and Fife, evidence exists of settlement there as early as 1476.

Starting with Thomas Dalyell – 'a merchant adventurer to the northern seas' – the present castle has been home to the same family for almost 400 years. In 1601, Thomas Dalyell consolidated his position in Edinburgh society by marrying an aristocrat, Lady Janet Bruce, the daughter of Lord Kinloss. Two years later, following the Union of the Crowns, he accompanied King James V1 to London as deputy Master of the Rolls. The Binns was acquired as the family home in 1612. Thomas Dalyell and his wife spent the next three decades improving the property. As a succession of tradesmen tackled the various tasks and the house changed and grew around them, the couple's young son approached manhood – and lasting notoriety as General 'Black Tam' Dalyell, scourge of the Covenanters.

Following the execution of Charles I on a scaffold erected in Whitehall on 30 January 1649 General Dalyell swore 'to cut neither his hair or his beard' until the monarchy was restored, as a token of respect for the deceased sovereign. Twenty years earlier Dalyell had been a prominent figure in the disastrous expedition to La Rochelle, headed by one of the King's favourites, the Duke of Buckingham. During the bloody aftermath of Charles's execution, Dalyell appeared in Ireland fighting against Cromwell, and at Worcester in the final battle of the Civil War. Here he was captured, and imprisoned at Dudley Castle before going to the Tower. 'This might have been the end of him, except he escaped,' his considerably less troublesome descendant recalled proudly more than 300 years later. 'Once when I went there on a parliamentary visit, the Keeper of the Tower showed me a list of all the people who had escaped over the years. As you can imagine, it wasn't a very long list. But there was his name, Dalyell, Tam, 1653.' The present Master of the Binns added: 'Having somehow managed to reach the continent, and carrying letters of introduction from his friend the Prince of Wales, he travelled to Russia where he fought against the invading Turks on behalf of Czar Alexis, father of Peter the Great. During this period, Alexis captured Smolensk and conquered a large part of Lithuania. General Dalyell ended his service with the Czar commanding a fort at Smolensk. As this was the gateway to Moscow, it was an important appointment, which shows just how much the Czar trusted him.'

With a presentation sword from the ruler of the Russians in his luggage, Dalyell returned to Scotland to begin a new career as Charles II's notorious henchman in his religious war against the Covenanters. This was an ugly period in Scottish history. As the historian and prominent Labour politician Tom Johnston noted in *The History of the Working Classes in Scotland*, ministers who preached without licence from a bishop and parishioners who absented themselves from church on Sundays were declared guilty of sedition and subject to heavy fines, as well as branding, exile and imprisonment.

Charles had been prepared to subscribe to the Solemn League and Covenant when it suited his purpose, to obtain the Scottish Crown, in a ceremony at Scone on 1 January 1651. Similarly, the ferociously loyal General Dalyell and his father could be counted among those who had previously subscribed to the idea of religious freedom. However, any statute passed by the Lords of the Articles who, with the suspension of the Scottish parliament, governed Scotland under the watchful eye of the King's Commissioner, commanded his support.

Appointed commander-in-chief in 1666, this 'wicked old mercenary' began a campaign of terror against the Covenanters, earning himself a letter of commendation in the King's own handwriting and the everlasting hatred of many of his countrymen. According to one account of the period, 'So ill was his repute among the Covenanters that they averred that he was wont to roast his prisoners in the stone-vaulted kitchen at The Binns and play cards with the Devil on the marble-table still preserved there.'

Dalyell's day of infamy was 28 November 1666. A small force of Covenanters had been cornered at Rullion Green, on the lower slopes of the Pentland Hills, outside Edinburgh. This huddled band was all that remained of a courageous uprising in Galloway a few weeks earlier, when a bloody encounter between 2,000 'gaunt, desperate peasants and preachers' and a contingent of government troops headed by General Sir James Turner ended, surprisingly, with the General being captured and the Covenanters marching boldly on Edinburgh. Finding the gates of the capital securely closed against them, the Covenanters retreated to the surrounding hills to rest and consider their next move. Shortly before sunset, Dalyell and his small army, who had been following the Covenanters at a safe distance, pounced.

According to John Prebble in *The Lion in the North*, although the Covenanters 'fought bravely, singing the 78th Psalm, they were scattered in the dusk. More than 100 prisoners were taken, of whom two-thirds were sent to Barbados. The rest were hanged, ten of them on one gibbet in Edinburgh and the others before their own doors in their own country.' They were later described by Lord Rothes, the King's High Commissioner in Scotland, as a collection of 'damned fools and incorrigible fanatics' for not renouncing their faith. It is a matter of lasting debate whether or not General Dalyell ordered his men to treat the defeated Covenanters lightly, saving many of them from the sword. His family claim he was so outraged by the severity of the court's judgement that he resigned his commission. Nevertheless, Dalyell's loyalty to Charles never wavered. It was in service to the King that he raised the first troop of the Royal Scots Greys at The Binns in 1678. Three years later the regiment increased in size, with the addition of two more cavalry troops to aid the Royal cause. Nearly 300 years later, by which time traditional cavalry had been replaced by tanks and armoured vehicles, the Founder's 11th generation grandson joined the regiment as a less-than-distinguished conscript, a failed officer cadet, confined to the ranks for the whole of his national service. According to his former commanding officer, Lieutenant Colonel Aidan Sprot, 'He wasn't cut out to be a soldier, unlike his famous forebear.'

The 'old Muscovite' would no doubt have been vexed that his namesake didn't naturally aspire to be a leader of men in battle. At the very least, it appeared to question the lasting quality of whatever warlike gene distinguished him in his age-old trade. It hadn't been established then that the commander-in-chief of the world's most formidable military machine was the product of a different branch of the same family tree – and a direct descendant of the Laird of The Binns.

Magdalin Monteith, granddaughter of the man legend had it played cards with the devil, left Scotland for America in 1728 to join her youngest son,

Thomas Monteith, in Rappahannock County, Virginia. Like so many of her people before and since, the adventurous Magdalin was attracted by the opportunities available in the fast-developing colonies of the new world. Her eldest son, James Monteith, stayed behind to enjoy his inheritance: the baronetcy of The Binns. He also followed the family tradition of changing his name to Dalyell to maintain the connection between title, name and house. Four years later, a letter from his brother in Virginia informed him of Magdalin's death. It also brought news of his marriage into a family of plantation owners in Virginia. 'A portrait of Magdalin Monteith hangs in The Binns,' said Dalyell. 'Her emigration to America is well-documented. But we wanted to learn more about Thomas Monteith and the later generations of the family in America. Through the Genealogical Society of New England, we met Gareth Boyd Roberts of Boston. He knew all about Thomas Monteith and what had happened to his descendants. But he didn't know about his mother Magdalin and the fact that she was a granddaughter of General Tam Dalyell of The Binns until we told him.' Gareth Boyd Roberts, author of *Ancestors of American Presidents*, confirmed: 'A large quantity of antiquities relating to this has been extracted from The Binns. There weren't many baronets or peers, or the brothers of baronets and peers, who emigrated from Britain to America. Thomas Monteith was certainly one. Three or four generations after he married in Virginia, part of the family moved to Missouri. Harry Truman was born in Independence, Missouri, on 8 May 1884. The line from Thomas Monteith to Harry Truman is absolutely certain. Likewise the fact that the present Tam Dalyell of The Binns would have been a sixth or seventh cousin of the 33rd President of the United States.'

General Tam Dalyell's bible, sword and jackboots were among the mementos of the family's variously esteemed and long-haired ancestor which awaited Eleanor Loch and her husband and son when she inherited The Binns. It suited them to keep possession of the famous old house. But they also recognised the lasting importance of continuing the ancient link between The Binns and the Dalyell family name. It was a curious and unusual dilemma, answered finally by Percy Gordon Loch's offer to change his name and that of their son to Dalyell. 'It didn't really affect me at all,' said Dalyell. 'For a start I was quite young. Also, because I lived at The Binns with my grandparents, I was always known as Tam Dalyell. I suppose if I had been older, and had been using the name Loch, then things would have been different. It might have seemed a little odd to my friends at school.'

As a small boy, Dalyell was shy and serious-minded. According to one contemporary: 'I had the impression he was probably over-protected at home. I remember seeing him at a party, clinging to his nanny's skirt. He was the sort of chap other boys tend to pick on, a bit of a butt, really.' His education began at St George's in Edinburgh, now 'a famous girls school. But then it took boys,' said Dalyell. 'A few years ago I attended a reunion there. I think there were about 150 ladies present and only two men, me and one other. The women thought it was very brave of us to attend!'

His spell there was followed by another brief period attending Edinburgh Academy, before the outbreak of war and the nearness of the central Scotland industrial belt to The Binns encouraged his parents to evacuate him to safety in rural Moray. 'While living on a farm at Tulloch Gribbon, I became unwell and was taken to hospital in Grantown-on-Spey,' said Dalyell. 'The medical staff wanted my parents' permission to remove my appendix. When they couldn't locate them they went ahead anyway. They were very nervous about it. I learned later the operation was performed by a doctor assisted by a vet, more vet than doctor, I think. But if they hadn't acted immediately there would have been no more Tam!' His recovery coincided with another change of school. This time Tam headed south, following the traditional route for children of the prosperous and socially ambitious Scottish aristocracy – the low road to England. His destination was the fashionable Harecroft Hall, an exclusive preparatory school 'for the sons of gentlefolk' three miles inland from Seascale, on the Cumbrian coast. 'It's a beautiful location, a lovely old manor house, set in some 15 acres of rhododendron woods, on the edge of the Lake District,' said the present headmaster, David Hoddy. 'There were a dozen prep schools in the area before the war. Harecroft Hall is the sole survivor. In Tam's day the school catered for about 40 boys, all boarders, with perhaps seven boys in each class.'

School fees were 60 guineas a term. The uniform was a salmon pink blazer with a matching cap, monogrammed HH. The pink blazer was discontinued following David Hoddy's appointment as headmaster seven years ago. 'These days, dressing boys in pink isn't a particularly good idea,' said Hoddy. Making them walk about in public wearing a cap bearing the initials HH during World War II attracted trouble of a different kind, according to Nigel Hepper, world famous botanist, school historian and former pupil. 'Local lads we encountered on the bus used to mock us,' said Hepper, 'saying it meant Heil Hitler. I seldom wore it on the bus after that. It was embarrassingly bright pink and easily marked.' Added Hoddy: 'Originally everyone was served at table by maids wearing black and white uniforms. That stopped with the war, when the girls were called away for service in the land army and the boys had to start looking after themselves. But the school prided itself on the fact that the children were well fed, despite the war. The school owned two cows, which meant there was no shortage of fresh milk. There was also a plentiful supply of fresh eggs and there was always a barrel of apples at the back door for the boys to help themselves.'

In addition to normal periods of study, the governors believed in providing an exacting routine of running, including regular excursions to the slopes of Scafell and Great Gable. 'It was a pretty tough school,' said Nigel Hepper. 'Every day we were made to take part in games, regardless of the weather. It didn't matter if there was rain, snow or ice, we were still required to go running. You'd often see lots of small boys, strung out for miles across the Cumbrian countryside, struggling to return.' At one stage, according to David Hoddy, a shotgun was a practical feature of the headmaster's study. 'Any child was allowed to take four shells and go out and shoot something which would be dressed and plucked for tea. The health and safety authorities, not to mention the police, would suffer a minor hernia and crucify us if that sort of thing happened today.'

Dalyell's reputation as a campaigning MP depends to a large extent on his ready access to a wide circle of expert knowledge. 'If there's something he doesn't know, he knows who does,' said one observer admiringly. Aged eight, in the garden at Harecroft Hall, he stayed close to Nigel Hepper, three years his senior. Hepper was a future assistant keeper of the Herbarium at the Royal Botanic Gardens, Kew. 'Nigel was in charge of the school garden,' explained Dalyell. 'He was always going out into the countryside on his bike or pony to collect flowers and plants. The material he collected then is now part of a huge millenium project into the effects of global warming. It was Nigel Hepper,' added Dalyell with a satisfied smile, 'who taught me how to grow radishes.'

At Eton, Dalyell's contemporaries included Hugh Campbell, heir to the Thane of Cawdor, and Gregor Murray, a future Duke of Atholl and the only man in Britain permitted to maintain a private army. In his obituary of Murray, written for *The Independent* more than 50 years later, Dalyell explained: 'This goes back to an honour awarded by Queen Victoria 250 years ago, very much against the wishes of her government. No small part of Whitehall's displeasure may have been due to the fact that the day the colours – and the resultant right to bear arms – were presented to the family was the 100th anniversary of the arrival of the men of Atholl to join with Bonnie Prince Charlie in the final and disastrous attempt to put the Stuarts back on the throne. From their place of honour on the right of Prince Charles Edward's line that day, the Atholl Brigade charged with such effect that the 1745 rising hung in the balance. Even after a century, Queen Victoria's mandarins felt that to give such men back their guns seemed more than a touch imprudent.'

Dalyell also delighted in recalling how the diminutive Hugh Campbell, then Viscount Emlyn, once interrupted preparations for a school production of Macbeth with the shrill announcement, 'Shakespeare and his witches got it wrong, sir! The Macbeths were a junior branch of the Campbells and never were Thanes of Cawdor.' When the senior master responsible for the production demanded to know what made him so certain of his facts, the youngster squeaked, 'Because, sir, my Dad is the Thane of Cawdor.'

Douglas Hurd, future Foreign Secretary, and Nicholas Ridley, another Thatcher luminary, were also at Eton with Dalyell. A prolonged and serious exchange in the House of Commons, involving Dalyell and Ridley, was reduced to laughter years later when someone on the Tory benches cried out: 'He was the minister's fag at Eton!'

'Fortunately for me,' Dalyell observed later, 'I was never Nicholas Ridley's fag. I say fortunately,' Dalyell explained, 'because Ridley was rough with his tongue and cane on those whom he considered less than perfect.' He was also an outstanding artist, better than his grandfather, Sir Edwin Lutyens, in the opinion of Wilfred Blunt, who taught art at Eton. Observed Dalyell: 'I suspect he rather enjoyed the intense dislike of the small boys in the house, as he certainly enjoyed the intense fury – and dislike – of most of the Parliamentary Labour Party, and a good number of his own colleagues on the Conservative benches in the House of Commons'.

Dalyell considered his old school friend 'the most intellectually arrogant boy I ever knew at Eton, and the most arrogant MP I ever knew in the House of Commons.' Ridley's ministerial career ended ingloriously, following an interview in *The Spectator* in which, as Secretary of State for the Environment, he claimed European union was a German plot designed to rob Britain of its sovereignty. His remarks inspired a cartoon of Chancellor Helmut Kohl, complete with Hitler moustache, on the magazine's cover. Ridley resigned soon after it appeared.

Dalyell enjoyed his years at Eton. His fag was Jacob Rothschild, of international banking fame. 'I was,' he maintained, 'superbly well taught. No doubt about it. The headmaster was Sir Robert Burley. Everyone called him Red Robert. I liked him very much. I was also extremely fortunate in having as my "modern tutor" René Peyrefitte, a 27-year-old Sorbonne intellectual on secondment to the school from the University of Montpellier, who spoke to us in nothing but French and vouchsafed often that he found the British class system "*tout-à-fait extraordinaire*". I was a very spoilt young man. But I also worked very hard.'

It was, perhaps, an early indication of his nonconformist spirit that he preferred soccer to cricket, rugby or the Eton 'field game'. Dalyell's passion for football is genuine and long held. He will interrupt a discourse about a parliamentary visit to Portugal to extol the virtues of Eusebio, the great Benfica forward. Following a visit to Brazil, one of his main topics of conversation was the enormous skill displayed by the once great Rivelino, 'probably the best inside forward I ever saw'. Nearer home, his boyhood hero was Tommy Walker of Hearts and Chelsea. In an obituary tribute written for *The Independent* on 19 January 1993, Dalyell recalled: 'Walker was born of a shale-mining family in Livingston Station, a village in West Lothian, now swallowed up in the New Town of Livingston. Shale miners had a vigorous loyalty to one another, and this was a quality which Walker displayed to his fellow players, both on the field and as a manager.'

Walker played at a time, Dalyell noted, when it was safe for a 13-year-old boy to squeeze into the terracing of a crowd of 137,000 at Hampden Park, Glasgow. Dalyell witnessed his hero's return to the Scottish team in a match against England after an absence of six years, much of it spent in India with the Royal Corps of Signals. Early in the match Walker started the move which ended in 'the diminutive Hibernian winger Jimmy Caskie putting the ball past Frank Swift. The Hampden Roar exploded as never before or since.'

Like every other boy of his age leaving school in the immediate postwar years, Dalyell was now liable for military service. Emmanuel Shinwell, Secretary of State for War in the 1945 government, had been obliged to replace vast armies of civilians who fought in the war, and now wanted to go home, with fresh peacetime recruits. The Labour government, with Clement Attlee as Prime Minister, firstly imposed compulsory military service of a year, then 18 months, then as the war in Korea escalated, two years. A number of employment categories were declared exempt including clergymen, miners, merchant sailors, seagoing fishermen and agricultural workers engaged in essential food production. Otherwise, all young men fit enough to pass a compulsory medical examination were liable for service. 'Opposition to the measure,' observed Trevor Royle in his 1986 account of the national service experience, *The Best Years of their Lives*, 'was mainly confined to those who thought that, *ipso facto*, conscription was a bad thing, and to those who believed that compulsory service would weaken the effectiveness of the armed forces'. When the National service Bill was introduced in the House of Commons in March 1947, the pugnacious Shinwell looked on angrily as a large group of Labour MPs defied the Whip and voted with the Liberals against his proposals. It was this rebellion which forced the government to reduce the amount of time which the authorities intended young men should spend in uniform between leaving school and starting their careers, from 18 months to a year. But it was a short-won victory for the rebels: within a year, Shinwell's original demands had been met.

Two years later, Kim Il Sung, with Russian and Chinese support, crossed the border between North and South Korea and Dalyell's distant kinsman in the White House demonstrated that the *Truman Doctrine* meant what it said: the United States would resist the spread of communism anywhere in the world. For those awaiting call-up in Britain, the result was an additional six months away from home in their roles of soldiers, sailors and airmen, ready to defend Britain's diminishing 'Great Power' status.

Aged 18, Dalyell followed the example of thousands of other youngsters the length and breadth of the country, calling voluntarily at his local branch of the Ministry of Labour and National Service to sign the necessary papers and await a medical examination. Three categories of fitness were deemed suitable for military service: Grade Four covered anyone who was judged physically or mentally incapable of serving in any of Britain's armed forces. Dalyell passed Grade One and looked forward to becoming an officer in the Royal Scots Greys.

A portrait of his great ancestor, General Tam Dalyell, hung in every mess. Many of his friends assumed a commission would be automatically forthcoming. Dalyell appeared to confirm their faith in his latent military abilities when he passed 'highly' into OCTU from the first War Office selection board he attended. However, his luck was about to change. 'It was at Mons that things started to go wrong,' he said. 'I acquitted myself well during the first part of training. Then I was sent to an organisation known as D squadron. Because my name was first out of the hat, they made me the first troop sergeant. And I made a complete hash of it, one way or the other!'

During training on Salisbury Plain, an armoured car went missing under his command. Half a century later, with an agonised chuckle, Dalyell recalled: 'It turned up eventually, behind some hill. But the whole thing was a bit of a fiasco and I was returned to the unit. I'm not whinging about it,' he added. 'But I think I was quite unfairly treated by one particular individual, a captain in the Royal Tank Regiment, who appeared to believe I thought I had an automatic right to the Greys because of my ancestor. I wasn't like that, even in those days, I really wasn't. But this particular officer was very much prejudiced against the cavalry. When I finally joined the Royal Scots Greys, not as an officer but as a trooper in Germany, a lot of the officers who attended Mons appeared to take the view of there but for the grace of God go we!'

Added Dalyell: 'A lot of it was my own fault. But other people had been equally incompetent and got away with it'. He believes that his failure to obtain a commission in the family regiment affected his parents more than himself. 'I think they were both pretty disappointed,' he said. 'But my father was very good about it. He told me not to whinge, just to get on with it. So that's what I did.'

As his boyhood friend George Younger, commissioned in the Argyll and Sutherland Highlanders and a future Secretary of State for Defence, recalled: 'He undoubtedly had a bit of a rough time when he was called up into the Royal Scots Greys. It couldn't have been easy, with his background. I don't think he was popular with the other cadets. They gave him a pretty rough time. I remember talking to him about it once and Tam simply grimaced and shook his head, as if it was something he'd rather forget.' Almost half a century after the event, '22424588', Trooper Dalyell, described his service in the family regiment as 'a toughening experience. I soon learned that if you become a trooper in a cavalry regiment your ancestor founded, and everybody knows it, then you either adapt by developing a very thick skin or you cave in. I developed a very thick skin.' In fact, his arrival at the regimental barracks at Luneburg in Germany surprised everyone. His squadron commander, Major Aidan Sprot, who later commanded the regiment, explained: 'We didn't realise who he was at first. We just saw the name on a list of people joining: Trooper Dalyell. His mother was still alive, so he wasn't yet Master of the Binns, and important in his own right. It wasn't until later we realised who he was. I don't remember how we found out'.

Dalyell soon discovered that his fellow troopers were drawn from all walks of life. 'This was no ordinary crowd of jocks,' he said. 'People came from all over the country, including the south of England. We were all part of one of the leading tank regiments in the British army, handling some of the most expensive equipment available. Before anyone was allowed to join the Royal Scots Grey, they were well and truly sifted. This meant the average intelligence of the troopers and NCOs was, to put it bluntly, above that of most infantry regiments.'

His attempts to make friends in the billet were greatly assisted by his ability to speak German – and an unexpected talent for dealing on the black market. 'I used to receive regular supplies of coffee from home and head for some of the less salubrious parts of Hamburg to sell it,' Dalyell explained. 'When some of the other chaps, including a few sergeants, heard what I was doing they asked me to do the same for them. Once, whilst on manoeuvres we were getting a bit low on rations. I found this farmhouse and the old couple who owned the place took a shine to me because I spoke German, and let me buy a large ham with some of the proceeds from my last visit to Hamburg. I was known as Tam the Ham after that. On another occasion I landed in trouble when my insatiable curiosity took me to Cuxhaven. I was spotted photographing the submarine pens and reported to the military police. The regiment made all sorts of excuses on my behalf: that I was just curious and all the rest of it, and somehow managed to rescue me from a hell of a lot of trouble. But I was ordered to stop my black market activities immediately. I think they were worried that if anything else like that happened, it would embarrass the regiment.'

Dalyell's talents as a soldier were less evident. 'I think he would be the first to admit he wasn't cut out to be a soldier,' said his old squadron commander, Aidan Sprot. 'But he had to do his two years, like everyone else. I know he was deeply hurt because he failed officer training. It says a lot about the man that he was prepared to join us as a trooper. Some of the soldiers probably hadn't heard of General Tam Dalyell before they joined the regiment. But everyone is told the regimental history soon after they enlist and they would have certainly learned about General Tam and The Binns and the raising of the Greys in the days of Charles II. They might have been surprised to learn he was related to Trooper Dalyell, but I am sure they all knew about it.' Sprot added: 'I remember one occasion when I was seated in my office and I heard someone arriving in the office of the squadron sergeant major next door. He did all the usual things sergeant majors do when they receive an unexpected visit from a trooper: shouting at him to stand to attention, speak up, all that. Then I heard Tam say, in his lovely, rather drawly voice, that when the regiment returned home he hoped the sergeant major would come up to The Binns and see the regimental relics. And then I heard the sergeant major getting to his feet and saying in a quiet, very respectful voice, "Oh, sir, that is very kind"!' Sprot laughed. 'I mean, can you imagine, a sergeant major talking to a trooper like that? It was the most delightful episode. And it's typical of Tam.'

Dalyell believes his general good standing was enhanced by his decision to take a whipping rather than face a charge when he incurred the displeasure of a senior sergeant. 'We spent a lot of time on manoeuvres on Luneburg Heath,' Dalyell recalled, 'and on this occasion something went wrong with the gyro on one of the tanks. Two of us were ordered to fix it. We did, but we also skived off to play tennis before the troop sergeant returned to check it. When he arrived and found us gone he was absolutely furious. We could, he told us when we saw him next, either go on a charge or take six of the best straight away. I immediately dropped my tennis shorts, lowered my bum bags, which everybody wore, and put my head under the desk to await punishment. He fetched his riding whip from next door and gave me six of the best. Then he gave my friend the same. God, it hurt! Afterwards, Dalyell explained, 'there was a sort of code that you didn't complain. I'd been told by my father not to whinge. The upshot was that because I took it like a man, people thought I was gutsy.' Dalyell disclosed that it wasn't a story he told often. 'I don't think I've talked about it in nearly 50 years,' he said. 'The truth of the matter is, although I think it would be denied, in those days when some of the subalterns did something wrong, they were likewise whipped by the 2ic. We are talking, remember, about 50 years ago. That sort of thing would be unimaginable today. My father's reaction, when I told him about it, was "That's exactly what we did on the north-west frontier!" My mother simply laughed. It was the sort of thing Anglo-India expected.'

His former squadron commander, Aidan Sprot, disclaimed all knowledge of the incident and denied that whipping was a common form of punishment in the regiment. 'I would have thought such a punishment highly unusual,' he said. 'Of course, many things happened in the ranks that the officers didn't know anything about. I mean, one would be an awful fool if one couldn't do something without being found out by the officers. I dread to think what happens throughout the army without officers knowing.'

Dalyell was deeply affected by his period of national service in the Royal Scots Greys. He distinctly remembers one occasion, following 'ugly news' from Korea, when the regiment was stationed at Luneburg, a few kilometres from Stalin's armoury. Lieutenant-Colonel Douglas Stewart, addressing the assembled soldiery, left none of them in any doubt that 'war would be terrible'. As part of training, Stewart regularly arranged visits to Belsen where troopers could be 'taught the lurid facts of the concentration camp. Stewart believed,' wrote Dalyell in an obituary tribute to his old CO, 'that he had an obligation not to leave the next generation in any doubt as to what he and others leading the spearhead of the British Army had found in 1945. His actions began the process by which I became an ardent European, determined that a European war should never occur again.'

Dalyell's association with the regiment continued long after his national service ended and the Royal Scots Greys amalgamated with the Dragoon Guards to form the Royal Scots Dragoon Guards (Carabineers and Greys). He is an honorary member of the officers' mess and, according to Aidan Sprot, 'takes a great interest in it, attending all sorts of functions. I think everyone in the regiment respects him. He was worried, at the time of the Falklands crisis, that his open stand against the war might damage his relations with the regiment. I told him not to worry, that we all knew he had his own ideas. I am sure that politically, he must be the opposite of his great ancestor, General Tam Dalyell. One must assume that the present Tam, being Labour, is a bit to the left. The way General Tam behaved, cutting off people's heads and things, he must have been ultra-right. The great thing about the army, politics never enter into it.'

THREE

ALMOST A TORY

Demobbed from the Royal Scots Greys at the end of his national service, Dalyell bid a not-too-unhappy farewell to his life as an ordinary trooper and set out for Cambridge, where he began developing a serious interest in politics – as a Tory!

His lifelong friend, John Biffen, a future leader of the House of Commons, introduced him to the Cambridge University Conservative Association. Dalyell, never one for half measures, became chairman. Said Biffen: 'Tam was a keen Conservative, very much what I would call a "conscience Tory", interested in social affairs. His views weren't necessarily all that popular within CUCA but they were clearly and genuinely held. He was extremely amiable, with a pleasing personality. I rather approved of his views and I liked him as a person. I didn't much care for right-wing Conservatives in the university context. So, as I was about to graduate, I decided Tam was my man and arranged for him to succeed me as chairman. I don't think he was all that happy in the job.'

What he later described as 'a hall of scholarly fame' greeted Dalyell on his arrival. It was a special privilege to take the History Tripos at King's College in the 1950s, Dalyell claimed. His supervisors were 'John Saltmarsh, who in himself encapsulated a Medieval Fenman, the clever Arthur Hibbert, the formidably young Noël Annan, the razor-sharp Dr Eric Hobsbawn and Christopher Morris.' Among the lecturers who made a lasting impression on him were Dom David Knowles, Herbert Butterfield, T.F. Smail, Brian Wormwald and Geoffrey Elton who introduced him 'to the mechanics of government and the mechanisms of power.'

Elton believed that being the only Cambridge don who had been turned down by Oxbridge as a student 'gave him a different perspective'. His public persona was 'disagreeable, if stimulating and challenging. He paid no obeisance to Cambridge doubt and diffidence.' Elton took a special interest in the civil service. Shortly before his death on 4 December 1994, he bemoaned proposals for performance-related pay and promotion in the civil service. Elton wanted to know, if such circumstances prevailed, who would give 'powerful, cantankerous, strong-willed rulers unpalatable advice'. Dalyell observed: 'He drew a convincing parallel – Elton's parallels were often convincing, but seldom succinct – between Henry VIII and Mrs Thatcher, concluding that until his last year his hero, Thomas Cromwell, had managed matters with greater skill than Lord Bancroft, Sir Anthony Acland and Sir Douglas Wass.'

Before he even arrived at Cambridge, when he was still serving with the Royal Scots Greys as part of the British Army on the Rhine, a letter arrived for Dalyell in Christopher Morris's 'minute handwriting, courteously recommending a long book-list, headed by Motley's *Rise of the Dutch Republic'*. Morris's special interests, according to Dalyell, were the political thought of the Tudors, and Hobbes, Locke, Montesquieu, Rousseau and ecclesiastical history. 'Morris believed,' remarked Dalyell, 'that his future pupils should take the opportunity of national service to get the historical classics under their belts. Even by the standards of Cambridge Fellows, Morris himself was enormously widely read, and would recommend books, tailored to the needs of individuals as he perceived them.'

Professor Austin Robinson was another important influence during Dalyell's Cambridge years. Shortly after he arrived in the House of Commons, as MP for West Lothian, Dalyell told Hugh Gaitskell: 'Austin Robinson taught me a lot, and I admired him greatly.'

'In that case,' replied Gaitskell, 'you may be of some use to the Labour Party in Parliament.'

In an obituary of Robinson, written for *The Independent* on 11 June 1993, Dalyell claimed: 'It was Gaitskell's opinion that Austin Robinson and Alec Cairncross would be the two most useful outside economic advisers to an incoming Labour government in 1963 or 1964. Alas, one result of Gaitskell's untimely death was that we were to have six years of Tommy Balogh, to be seen without fail behind Wilson's shoulder at the Huyton 1964 count, and ensconced in the Downing Street Inner Office. Substitute Robinson for Balogh and the whole history of the Labour government of 1964–70 would have been different and better.'

Noël Annan, a Fellow of King's College since 1944, caused 'something of a sensation' when he was elected Provost of King's 11 years later, aged 39.

Described by *The Times* as 'the epitome of the Great and the Good' following his death on 21 February 2000, Annan instilled in his students the belief that 'if you hear the call to make your country a better place, you have a duty to obey it'.

Dalyell's own political conversion to Labour wasn't 'a road to Damascus thing'. As he told Kenneth Roy: 'I had a lot of left-wing friends. We used to go to each other's meetings.'

As his political mentor at university, John Biffen, recalled: 'Tam was very intense, definitely on the left of the Tory Party at Cambridge. He immersed himself in social issues like education and the health service. Everyone else tended to worry about economics and foreign affairs. Our contemporaries included Geoffrey Howe, Douglas Hurd and Patrick Jenkin. In the rather presumptious way one behaves as a student politician we all had labels and spent a good deal of time trying to work out what we would do when we were running the country, years before the call came.' Biffen added: 'As students we took our politics very seriously indeed. The absence of cynicism was commendable. We invited speakers from right across the political spectrum. They were all given a fair hearing. People didn't engage in any sort of rowdiness or yah-booing. We heard a wide range of opinions. I'm not sure if that would be true today.'

In a review of a Cambridge Union debate on the motion: 'That this house fears militarism more than pacificism', published in *Varsity* on 21 February 1953, Dalyell congratulated his friend for delivering 'a first-rate debating speech' on the theme 'Pacificism justifies the interpretation that this country is weak'. Dalyell could have been addressing his attention to another time and place, barely a decade in the future, however, with the general criticism: 'If a floor speaker is conscious that he has an attentive, but not necessarily sympathetic, audience, there can be little doubt that he will make a more profitable speech than if he is faced by those who like to put on an air of studied boredom.' It couldn't be a pretty sight, Dalyell maintained, 'especially for distinguished visitors, to see members on the front bench lounging and yawning as if they were alone in their bedrooms.'

Biffen was surprised when Dalyell switched his political loyalties. 'I thought Eton and Cambridge graduates would be natural Tories,' he said. 'I didn't think of them becoming Labour politicians.' It didn't escape Dalyell's notice that few of his contemporaries from a similar background had been exposed to life in the ranks as he had serving as a trooper. And he was, he discovered, an intervener by nature. 'It wasn't so much that I changed, more that I should never have been a Tory,' he said. 'What happened at Suez was part of it, of course. But I was also struck by what seemed like the Conservatives' incompetence to handle big problems like Scottish unemployment and the Third World. I thought there had to be planning.'

An early appraisal of Dalyell's career, written for *The Guardian* by the distinguished Scottish journalist Robert Brown, maintained: 'To him society should be purposeful as well as classless. Politics are to ensure that people get value for money and a better deal. Tam is against any government that squanders Britain's fiscal and manpower resources on defence indefensibles, when so many other ways exist of being socialist, scientific, humane and wise.' The writer added: 'His parliamentary role is self-imposed. It is to keep Labour on the right lines on the big issues – science, technology, education, sport. These are his chosen specialities, charting their deeps for MPs with less aptitude or time to be so well-informed on them. Tam has the intellect as well as the instinctive arrogance needed for the task. It means he goes straight to the experts, asking tirelessly and becoming expert himself.'

John Biffen offered the intriguing suggestion that his old friend might have made 'a sort of Rab Butler-type Tory' if he hadn't deserted the Conservative Party for Labour. But he also believed Dalyell had made the right decision: 'His temperament was such,' said Biffen, 'that I don't think he would have found it at all congenial to have stayed in the Conservative Party.'

On his return home, it didn't take Dalyell long to become a familiar figure in Scottish Labour Party circles. His previous incarnation, breathing the Tory-poisoned-air of Eton and Cambridge, ensured he was someone people talked about, a minor grade political celebrity, instantly recognised, endlessly assessed. To many older members, especially those who numbered amongst the we-despise-all-toffs brigade who swelled the Labour ranks, he appeared strange – an unlikely recruit to the socialist cause.

John Biffen visited The Binns shortly after leaving Cambridge. 'His mother was very supportive of Tam's activities and all the work he was doing on behalf of the Labour Party in West Lothian,' said Biffen. 'But you could see she was pleased to meet friends from an early stage in his career. I think Tam had been introducing her to all sorts of people, non-university people from the Labour Party in Scotland, who were very different in social terms from what she was used to.'

Another prominent parliamentarian, David Steel, spent two summers working at The Binns as a summer holiday guide, working for the National Trust. 'I thought Tam was rather a strange young man,' said Steel. 'His whole experience was quite different from mine. He had been to Eton and Cambridge. He had been in the Tory party, and then converted to Labour. And he lived in this grand house with his mother who was a genial eccentric, some of whose traits Tam inherited. I always considered it a strange coincidence that after I worked at The Binns, my father became minister of St Michael's, Linlithgow, the church where Tam and his mother worshipped. It is also strange that when I first met Tam he was a prospective Labour candidate for a constituency called Roxburgh, Selkirk and Peebles – with which, at that time, I had absolutely no connection.' He added: 'It was my job as a guide to take parties round the house, telling them tales of Bloody Tam, showing people the various relics, that sort of thing. I developed a technique for dealing with disruptive children, ushering them quietly outside, as if the tour was headed in that direction anyway. Tam's mother used to tease me about this and tell me she would often find dejected people who had been expelled outside the house. She claimed there was one occasion when Tam was sunbathing in the nude in some secluded corner of the garden and a group of people appeared, despatched by me. I don't remember this at all, but Mrs Dalyell insisted it happened!'

In the smoke-darkened rooms of the Labour Party the sincerity of Dalyell's views, and the level of his commitment, withstood the closest examination. He quickly displayed an appetite for hard work. From his earliest days as a teacher, Dalyell proved an active member of his union, the Educational Institute of Scotland. His performance as a candidate in the 1959 general election also attracted praise.

This was the year Harold Macmillan 'cruised to victory' on the slogan 'You never had it so good.' Labour, with Hugh Gaitskell as leader, began their election campaign expecting to win. Their principal opponent's posturing on the world stage didn't worry them. In the event Labour's confidence proved to be a false high, probably exaggerated from the start, considering that 'the average Briton was noticeably better off after three and a half years of Macmillan's leadership and it would have taken a remarkable *volte-face* on the public's part to unseat him,' as historian Philip Ziegler claimed.

Held during one of the worst periods of the Cold War, Macmillan's campaign was clearly influenced by his decision, a few weeks before he called the election, to don the mantle of world statesman and fly to Moscow to confer with the Soviet Premier, Nikita Kruschev. In a speech to 800 members of the Chartered Accountants Students Society of London, the hero of El Alamein, Field Marshal Viscount Montgomery, praised Macmillan's

35

initiative and claimed the most important issue of the election wasn't pensions, rents, purchase tax or unemployment – it was peace. The peppery brasshat left his audience in no doubt that he believed the only way to ensure peace was to return Harold Macmillan to Downing Street. In a glowing endorsement of Macmillan's good work in going to Moscow – 'He did it, nobody else!' – Montgomery contended grandly, 'We see at long last the promised land of peace, coming into sight.' Britain's desert hero also emphasised his opinion that it would be 'madness' to change the management of the country at the general election. 'I would go further and say anybody who votes Labour in this coming election should be locked up in a lunatic asylum.'

Those who returned fire included William Connor of the *Daily Mirror*, the man who began his first column after the war with the words, 'As I was saying when I was interrupted, it is a powerful hard thing to please all of the people all of the time.' Connor condemned the old Field Marshal's comments as 'elementary Sandhurst stuff, as subtle as debagging'. Lord Hailsham, a member of Macmillan's government and a noisy contender for the leadership when illness obliged Macmillan to retire four years later, chortled: 'These fighting men have a colourful way of expressing themselves.' His own remark that 'a man who votes Labour should have his head examined' wasn't intended to be taken literally, Hailsham explained. Rather, it was 'intended to represent the general estimate of their mental capability'.

Labour's official response was left to Morgan Phillips, the General Secretary. 'If Labour voters had been locked up in a lunatic asylum when the Second World War began, our Field Marshal would have been left without an army,' he stormed.

Macmillan's supporters claimed his journey to Moscow paved the way for a historic meeting between Kruschev and the US President, Dwight Eisenhower, at Camp David. The summit between the two most powerful men on earth coincided with the UK general election. However, his role in begetting the arrival of Kruschev in the United States failed to stimulate US interest in Macmillan's own political future. As Alistair Cooke reported, whenever he attempted to raise the topic of the British election with a large and miscellaneous acquaintance, the usual response was 'raging apathy'.

In fairness to Macmillan, and anyone else with a hankering to exaggerate Britain's importance in the United States, there was no shortage of competition in areas of special interest to Americans at that time. High above the earth, the Russian space craft Lunik III headed for the moon. Officials from the US Space Agency and the US Department of Defense were forced to admit that America was trailing the Soviet Union in space. Russia, said a spokesman, 'has a solid advantage over us in the field of rocket propulsion'. To the complacent American public in general this was bad news, barely improved by the same spokesman's qualified assertion that 'In all other fields, including inter-continental missiles, we can match and perhaps outperform them.'

There was never any question of Dalyell, a novice candidate appearing in his first general election, winning in Roxburgh, Selkirk and Peebles against a strongly entrenched Conservative candidate, Commander C.E.M. Donaldson, MP for the constituency for the past nine years; or, in a three-way contest, even coming second. 'Historically it was one of only two seats in Scotland where the Labour Party had never overtaken the Liberals,' said David Steel, the former Liberal leader, who represented the constituency for 32 years, after a by-election victory in 1965. 'The historic demise of the Liberals and the rise of the Labour Party happened everywhere except in the Borders and Orkney and Shetland.'

Dalyell had been the sole contender at the final selection conference when others in the Labour Party, with more right to the nomination, ducked the challenge. His determination to attain acceptability among his new-found comrades was such that he was willing to adopt the role of suitor in a hopeless cause. It also provided an opportunity to test a theory he was developing in private about first-time candidates. 'I believe Labour candidates should not be selected for safe or winnable Labour seats unless they have fought in a hopeless or marginal constituency first,' Dalyell later stated. 'This is for a very practical reason. No one can be certain about how they might react to the test of elections until they have actually been involved in it. And not only does one find out about oneself,' Dalyell maintained, 'but the Party finds out about the candidate.'

On any judgement, for Labour at least, the Borders constituency which he now pursued clearly qualified in the 'hopeless or marginal' category. In the previous election Commander Donaldson, who commanded the Canadian Fleet Manning Depot at Greenock during the war, won with a majority of 7,170, attracting nearly 48 per cent of the vote. Barely 20 per cent of the electorate favoured the Labour candidate, who finished third: 3,426 votes behind the second-placed Liberal.

Campaigning in his first general election, Dalyell's background probably proved useful in gaining attention in an area famous for its old families and grand houses, although the label he carried never proved popular with the majority of voters living there. 'The fact is,' said David Steel, 'no Labour candidate ever really fought the seat seriously before. And, as anyone who knows him will confirm, Tam is very serious about everything he does! Also, it's fair to say, he was up against an absentee MP. Commander Donaldson followed the old Scottish Tory tradition – the constituency was simply the place that sent them to Westminster. He was resident in London. John McCormick, the Liberal candidate, wasn't a fit man and was quite unwell when the election was called. This enabled Tam to make a good deal of the running both before and during the campaign. You can be sure, he wasn't just going to turn up for the election and treat it as a hopeless seat. He worked very hard at winning over quite a long period of time. And that showed in the final result.'

Hard-pressed reporters, seeking an angle in an otherwise dull contest, responded with predictable glee when they discovered that the polite young man with the aristocratic background and blue-chip education, representing Labour, used a bicycle to cover the constituency, one of the largest by area in the country. In the months ahead of the election, held on Thursday 8 October 1959, Dalyell and his bicycle were a common sight on border country roads as he visited farms and towns, and a good many villages, stubbornly pushing the Labour cause. As the *Glasgow Herald* noted with characteristic disdain: 'Mr Dalyell has not spared himself in covering the constituency, but his hopes of coming second in the race must remain slim.'

Dalyell blamed Hugh Gaitskell, the Labour leader, and his 'needless promise on tax' for the final rout. No one expected Gaitskell, in a speech at Newcastle barely a week before polling, to provide an astonishing hostage to fortune with a promise to the electorate not to increase 'standard or other forms of income tax so long as normal peacetime conditions continue'. He followed this three days later with an additional pledge, issued from Transport House, to remove purchase tax from essential goods.

A new and costly National Superannuation Scheme, masterminded by Richard Crossman, which aimed eventually to provide the average wage-earner with a pension equivalent to half pay at 65, had been a central plank in Labour's election strategy. 'The blunt fact was,' observed Dalyell, 'that an adequate subsistence pension for all could only be financed by increased taxation, or by increased insurance contributions, or else by a sensible balance between the two. The foolish and completely gratuitous pledge given by Gaitskell, the weekend before polling day, that a Labour government would not increase taxation, damaged belief in Crossman's scheme. The electors were sceptical about financial matters, including pensions, from that point on, and many were diverted from their original intention to vote

Labour.' Suddenly, as historian Ben Pimlott noted, 'Gaitskell, the model of integrity, was transformed by the ravenous press into a shameless offerer of bribes.'

The final count showed a 2.7 per cent drop in the Labour vote from 1955. Harold Macmillan remained in Downing Street with a majority of 100 seats. Among those ranged behind him in the new Parliament would be the Tory candidate for Roxburgh, Selkirk and Peebles, Commander Donaldson. His winning margin and share of the vote was increased at the expense of 'King' John McCormick, fighting as a Liberal but probably better known in Scotland as a pioneering figure in the nationalist movement. This was McCormick's sixth attempt to win a seat at Westminster, beginning at Inverness in 1931, when the National Government, headed by Ramsay MacDonald, confirmed its grip on power and Labour was reduced to an ineffective, squabbling parliamentary rump.

Dalyell finished his first parliamentary contest in third place, bottom of the poll. As the final figures showed, however, it had been a creditable performance, with Labour's share of the vote up from the last general election. 'In fact,' said David Steel, 'Dalyell obtained the highest Labour vote ever in Roxburgh, Selkirk and Peebles. The redrawn constituency was created in 1955 and abolished in 1983. When the Labour Party was looking for a candidate to fight the 1964 general election, it was a relief to know Tam had moved on to other things, like West Lothian! Following his performance in the 1959 election,' Steel continued, 'I reckoned my job at the next general election would be to squeeze the Labour vote down to its previous level or less. Nothing less than an internal realignment of the constituency was required if we were to defeat the Tories. This meant siphoning off a lot of Tam's support, and that's what happened over two elections, first in 1964 and then a year later in the by-election which followed Commander Donaldson's death. By then Labour obtained less than half of the vote Tam achieved.'

The political map of Scotland looked a good deal different, when Dalyell first pitched for a seat in the House of Commons from how it appeared, as the twentieth century approached its end. In 1955, with Anthony Eden as Prime Minister, a majority of the popular vote in Scotland favoured the Tories, giving them 36 Members of Parliament against 34 representing Labour. This time round, the electoral trend shifted noticeably north of the Border: Macmillan's supporters won 31 seats in Scotland against 38 for Labour. 'Despite the extent of Macmillan's victory, and the depths of Labour despair, that was the year,' reflected one observer, 'when the Tories' march to a Westminster wipe-out in Scotland began.'

AN IMPOSSIBLE DREAM

FOUR

AN IMPOSSIBLE DREAM

Dalyell had been discouraged by his father before going to Eton from following a career in the Indian Civil Service, a Loch family tradition. 'He took the view that I had to make up my own mind about what I wanted to do with my life,' explained Dalyell. 'He would give me the best education he could and then it was up to me. But he also thought the family had had enough of India and that the British presence in India wasn't going to last in the way it had for generations.'

Instead, Dalyell opted for life as a dominie. A teacher training course at Moray House, Edinburgh, which included a probationary attachment to the city's Boroughmuir Secondary School, was followed in 1956 with an appointment to Bo'ness Academy, a few miles from his home at The Binns, as a fully registered teacher. Bo'ness, the medieval Borrowstouness, was the Roman settlement at the east end of the Antonine Wall, the barricade between the Forth and Clyde estuaries and the ultimate northern boundary during the heyday of the Roman occupation. A study of the town by the anthropologist Professor Frank Girling of Leeds University, which attracted Dalyell's attention, 'made a convincing case that Bo'ness people were perhaps the most ethnically Roman in Britain'.

James Watt had worked in the town at the start of the industrial revolution, as Dalyell enjoyed telling his pupils; sometimes adding the fine historical detail, in the interests of local pride, that for years the place where they lived had once made most of the manhole covers for the sewers of Britain. It troubled his socialist instincts that the foundry where the covers were made was now closed, like two other foundries in the neighbourhood and several other important industries, including a local pottery, famous for its mass-produced white china, and a ship-chandlers which suffered when much of its business from the inter-war years moved to the Far East.

Dalyell's enthusiasm for football, and his willingness to devote a large part of his free time to the task, made him an unlikely, but readily available, team coach. 'Because I lived so near by, and was interested, I was useful as a coach and referee,' explained Dalyell. 'I was also able to persuade a few professionals to come along and help.' Due largely to his efforts, the team hit a winning streak: 'They were scoring as many as 15 goals in a game,' local journalist Ken Waddell recalled happily. 'No doubt about it, this was Tam's team, he was in charge! He picked the team and decided tactics. They were highly organised. Tam made the boys think teamwise. And of course, because they were winning all the time, they were soon the talk of the town. Suddenly, 1,000 people were watching a schools match at Bo'ness Academy on a Saturday morning. I was getting orders from the *Edinburgh Evening News* and the *Edinburgh Evening Dispatch* to send them reports of the game. You can imagine the effect on the town. People were absolutely delighted.' It was a rewarding experience for Dalyell. 'We went through round one, round two and round three of the Scottish schoolboys intermediate shield. Then we played Airdrie Academy in the fourth round, won that, won the semi-finals and in the final beat Penilee, the huge Glasgow comprehensive. I was absolutely delighted with what the boys managed to achieve.'

A visit to Russia, Sweden and Denmark, aboard the ship school *Dunera*, brought the team fresh glory. 'They won every game, playing against bigger, older boys,' Ken Waddell, who reported on the tour for *The Linlithgowshire Journal and Gazette*, recalled. 'We docked in Leningrad, Stockholm and Copenhagen, played a game in each port and won them all.'

Dalyell spent four years at Bo'ness, starting in 1956, addressing the wider problems of his chosen profession. Young teachers, he concluded, weren't treated with sufficient respect within the educational system. 'I find it quaint,' said Dalyell, in his maiden speech as a Member of Parliament, delivered on 10 July 1962, when he was still under 30, 'that I am supposedly fit to represent 59,000 electors in this House of Commons and yet, two months ago, under the system, I should not have been considered fit to interview a couple of parents at my registered class.'

Dalyell believed that teachers generally, and headmasters in particular, wasted far too much time on administrative chores which could be passed on to others, leaving them to concentrate on improving the educational well-being of their pupils. The business of running a school and being a teacher were two quite different professions, Dalyell argued. He found it strange that 'a man who has been a successful teacher of algebra or French for a quarter of a century' should suddenly find himself transferred to a totally different occupation. 'Is it really imperative that headmasters, who are highly skilled and successful teaching practitioners, should be tied up with milk returns and lengthy telephone calls to education offices, often about nothing in particular, and should sometimes be called on to act as taxi-man to wee Jeanie who decides that she is feeling ill and wants to go home?' Dalyell demanded. He proposed the introduction of a completely new profession to help reduce the problem – the School Administrative Service, with 'promotion and rates of pay comparable to branches of the Civil Service'.

There was also a role for retired teachers within the system, Dalyell suggested. They could be hired to give special coaching to marginal pupils at the request of their headmaster, either in school or at home. A good many youngsters would reap the benefits of such a scheme. And he knew a number of retired teachers 'who would welcome it, not chiefly on financial grounds, but on humane grounds, because they would feel that the world still needed them'.

It was typical of Dalyell's approach to a complex social problem that just as he believed it would be beneficial to extend the professional life of elderly teachers, he questioned the wisdom of raising the school leaving age for all pupils. The main problem, according to Dalyell, was convincing 'non-academic young men, who may be from three to five years past puberty, that schooling is worthwhile'. A good deal of time had been spent arguing over what subjects non-academic pupils should study, in theory at least. 'The real difficulty,' observed Dalyell, 'is finding a way to persuade them to study anything at all.' Dalyell believed that teaching non-academic 'boys' in their final year was no job for a woman. Any increase in the school leaving age simply exacerbated the problem. In 1960, he maintained with characteristic frankness: 'No one disputes the ability of women teachers to do a first-class job with academic pupils who are definitely working towards some specific educational end. What is in question is the ability of women teachers to handle the ever more bulky louts who line the back rows of our classrooms, who believe they have little in school to work towards, and no academic challenge.'

These were the lives he hoped to improve with his first major public campaign: the case for ship schools. It was important to remember, Dalyell argued, that the country's future prosperity would depend to a large extent on people who were by nature non-academic. One 'outstandingly sad fact' he discovered during his years as a teacher was that pupils who failed at the 12-plus stage saw their hopes gradually fade away. 'Their keenness diminishes,' wrote Dalyell. 'Teachers, being only human, tend to give more of their attention to brighter classes. The keenness of the pupils who have qualified for the non-academic stream diminishes further. A vicious circle has started.' Dalyell proposed a system of ship schools as the ideal means to occupy the last critical six months of a pupil's time at school, especially non-academic pupils who could be a source of serious trouble in an overcrowded classroom. 'The claim is,' he explained in his 1960 book *The Case for Ship Schools*, 'that a new type of challenge in the form of doing well on a ship school course would produce a response, and serve to raise pupils' expectations of themselves, and of what they were capable of doing. The vicious circle could be broken,' Dalyell maintained, 'by the completion of a successful ship school course, if only because it would restore to them some of their self-respect and self-esteem. Having succeeded once, and broken the spell of the inferiority complex, a pupil might even wish to take up the academic thread once more.'

The purpose of ship school courses, Dalyell believed, would be 'to encourage pupils to think out a different set of certainties than those which have so far governed human relations between countries.' Trumpeting the cause of internationalism, over nationalism he declared: 'The hope is that a ship school course would help pupils develop in a wide moral sense, beyond the capacity of the present generations and devote their energies to wider causes than we have known.'

His hopes for the ship school project, and the scope of his ambition, provide a useful insight into Dalyell's political attitudes across a wide range of subjects shortly before he emerged on the national scene. Dalyell believed firmly that world problems couldn't be solved within one single culture. 'In these days when biological warfare makes small countries without a large industrial base potentially as strong as the USA or the USSR, the need to use force between peoples, still felt as a basic instinct by many individuals, must be countered,' he warned. The modern military concept of 'overkill' encouraged Dalyell in the belief that 'large scale warfare and suicide have come to mean the same thing. And if Cyprus and Suez are to be taken as lessons, they must tell us that small scale wars used as an instrument of British policy are no longer likely to be successful.'

Dalyell's proposal, in its complete form, was startling in its vision. He hoped it would lead to an international scheme, supported by all the major governments, leading to total disarmament and world peace. 'The ideal behind the ship schools suggestion,' wrote the young Dalyell, 'implies more than simply a breaking down of national barriers; it is an attempt at the constructive harmonisation of the policies of the states represented on the ship school course, because with a positive will to harmony, so much that is new and exciting could be done to make the world a fuller, healthier place; besides, it is more satisfactory to have a positive reason for implementing something such as ship schools rather than doing things on the basis of preventing some bogeyman evil, such as the possible dangers of national barriers.'

Easily and predictably, Dalyell's ideas could be dismissed as unworldly, or just plain daft, by people of a less optimistic nature or anyone with a jaundiced view of human behaviour. Someone of a less determined disposition might have been discouraged by the findings of Professor Seymour Harris of Harvard University who calculated that $8 billion dollars withdrawn from US government defence spending resulted in the loss of one million jobs. He responded to Dalyell's appeal for comments on the suitability of the scheme with measured calm: 'Since the spending of the Pentagon in 1959 was in the region of $46 billion, it will be appreciated that this might involve unemployment among breadwinners of five million plus in the USA, with global consequences for all peoples.' Dalyell countered: 'The political split, and the Cold War, are such enormous historical entities, that the imagination boggles at the hypothetical implications for the world if they were suddenly removed.'

Writing in 1960 Dalyell claimed: 'Economic and social conditions have changed so radically in the short span of years since the end of the war that there now exists a different society with different wants from 1945. Part of the reason why these new educational wants have not received much publicity has been that the more articulate members of both political parties usually send their own children to private schools where the wants that ship schools would most urgently satisfy, are normally taken for granted.'

Dalyell acknowledged that the cost of his proposals, at 1960 prices, would be enormous: the running costs alone would amount to no less than £80 million a year. But he was unfazed by the prospect of screaming headlines and unremitting criticism of his proposals. 'Costs,' he argued strongly, 'are relative and must be seen against the background of the world in which it is proposed to make expenditure.' It was true that the sum he proposed was larger than the entire allocation to the University Grants Committee in 1959. But it was not a great deal larger, claimed Dalyell, than the recent annual subsidy paid to poultry farmers. It was also worth remembering, he continued stubbornly, that 'a cool £65 million had been squandered on Blue Streak without any return whatever'.

It offended Dalyell that in Britain, like America, expenditure on 'the production of alcohol, TV crime films and bath salts' basked under the superior reputation of the market, being profitable; while expenditure on 'more hospitals, better roads, increased educational facilities and other public sector outlay, such as ship schools', was cast as evil because they implied higher rates and higher taxes. 'It is a value judgement,' wrote Dalyell, 'that if a choice has to be made, more and better educational facilities are preferable to more and better bath salts, and to more and longer motor cars. But it would be a mistake to suppose that a decision to devote a notably high proportion of the increase in wealth to educational facilities rests merely on this sort of value judgement: that more schooling is better than more bath salts, or that poetry is better than Benthamite push-pin.'

Dalyell thought he saw signs that the contradiction between heaping up more private goods and having unsatisfactory public services was beginning to dawn on people. 'Now, in all probability, that the spin drier is theirs, as are the washing machine, the TV set and the radiogram, they have reached that level of income where the education of their children begins to take priority over the extra gadget that some advertisement is trying to persuade them to buy.' But he also acknowledged gloomily: 'Of course, the trouble is that a ship school programme would never look practicable even to a sympathetic politician, at any given moment in time. The arguments for postponement will always look strong.'

In fact, the first ship school sailed from Britain a good deal sooner than Dalyell, with all his heady optimism, expected.

It began with a far-reaching change in UK defence strategy East of Suez: in future, troops would travel by air instead of by sea. The purpose-built, 517-foot-long troopship *Dunera*, built at Barclay Curle's on the Clyde in 1937, was declared surplus to defence requirements. Its owners, the British India Steam Navigation Company, received £5 million in compensation from the Ministry of Defence. 'Fortunately,' Dalyell recalled with gratitude, 'being seafaring men and not accountants, they wanted to fulfil their obligations to their crews'.

It also helped that the British India Steam Navigation Company had been involved in a similar exercise more than 20 years earlier, when four troopships, the *Neuralia*, the *Nevasa*, the *Dunera* and the *Dilwara*, had been employed to take parties of schoolboys on eight-week summer cruises outside term time. It was this example which inspired Dalyell in his wider ambitions. Then, however, the boys occupied accommodation designed for troops, sleeping in hammocks.

Dalyell, who had been attracting attention with his proposals for ship schools, and who enjoyed a family connection with the British India Steam Navigation Company, was invited to attend a meeting of educationalists aboard the *Dunera* at Southampton to consider a suitable scheme. Dalyell later maintained it was this meeting, held on 4 November 1960, which 'determined the path of future development'. The main outcome was an assurance from the Ministry of Education that if the scheme went ahead, pupils would be allowed to participate during term time. On the strength of this, and promises from a number of local education authorities, the *Dunera*'s owners agreed to meet the costs of converting the vessel to accommodate a new category of passenger; including classrooms and dormitories for both boys and girls.

The first departure was from Greenock during April 1961. Clive Harston, 'a tall, cheerful, authoritative figure', had been appointed Director of Studies with Dalyell as his deputy. Harston combined 'teaching experience in several parts of the world with 18 years as a staff colonel in the army.' Dalyell admired his 'meticulous organisation and his capacity to foresee and circumvent trouble.' As the first Director of Studies aboard the *Dunera*, he 'always tried to be fair to pupils, but often reflected that an early discovery by young people that life itself was unfair was a salutary experience'. Years later, Dalyell commented: 'Truth to tell, Harston's military approach did not go down well with all teacher party leaders. But Harston was in his element and quite superb with tough teenage boys.'

Following the Southampton meeting it had been left to Dalyell, supported by 'salesmen' recruited from the ship's owners, to persuade the authorities that the idea was 'neither a joyride nor an excuse for pupils to miss a fortnight's school, but a serious educational experiment.' Dalyell expected the scheme to appeal more to boys than girls. 'In fact,' he recorded later, 'the ratio was about 5:3 in favour of the girls. Maybe they found it easier to get into their father's pockets, I don't know. But the difference was very marked. It may be, of course, that girls are more adventurous!'

The cost of a ten-day cruise was fixed at £28 for the first year, with teachers travelling free as party leaders on the basis of one teacher to fifteen pupils. In addition, the ship carried 120 fare-paying passengers, who were charged between £50 and £60, depending on cabin size. 'Apart from the commercial reasons which make it necessary to fill the cabin accommodation with passengers rather than teachers,' Dalyell explained in *Ship School*, his 1962 account of the *Dunera*'s activities, 'it is an excellent arrangement for other adults to join the cruise. If they want peace, they do not bother us, and we do not bother them. If they want to take part in activities such as deck tennis or water polo with the pupils, they are very welcome. They are equally welcome to attend lectures and join shore excursions. Many cabin passengers have voluntarily told us that cruising in the *Dunera* is infinitely better, for the life and happiness that ripples through the whole ship from the children.'

Strict rules of behaviour aboard ship contributed greatly to maintaining order at sea; although a late night disturbance in one of the boys' dormitories in the first night out required a firm response. Dalyell ordered everyone involved to go to a classroom, where he made them copy down the ship's fire regulations. 'It was a simple enough punishment,' an amused Dalyell recounted years later. 'But it evidently rankled, judging by the number of times I have been accosted on the London underground and told, "I know you! You're the geezer from the *Dunera* who made me write out all those blasted fire regulations!"'

The greatest source of worry for the adults in charge centred on trips ashore. Dalyell imagined a situation in which he was 'closeted with Interpol in Amsterdam or Lisbon, searching for a youngster who had gone astray. Mercifully, such fears have proved illusory.' Writing in 1962, he could report: 'On no single occasion has one pupil among 10,000, carried to 57 different ports, been late for the ship. As a teacher who spent most of his timetable teaching junior secondary pupils, I would hardly have believed such a record possible.' The fact this record was maintained was due at times to the resourcefulness of the children involved. On one occasion, in Copenhagen, as the ship was making ready to depart, 'up drove a well-upholstered cadillac, flying the proud flag of the United States' ambassador, and out stepped three small girls, who thanked the immaculate chauffeur with dignity. Apparently,' explained Dalyell, 'they had missed their way, entered a building above which fluttered the familiar stars and stripes, and asked for help from Uncle Sam!'

Dalyell completed more than a dozen voyages aboard the *Dunera* as deputy Director of Studies. Ken Waddell, who accompanied the ship to the Baltic as a reporter, judged that Dalyell was very popular with the children on board. 'I think a lot of them regarded him as slightly eccentric,' Waddell added. 'They probably thought they could take a rise out of him. But they all loved him. They thought he was a super guy.'

Ship schools never achieved the status of Dalyell's youthful, exuberant dream. But the scheme he did so much to promote lasted more than 20 years. Between them, a total of four ships – the *Dunera*, the *Devonia*, the *Nevasa* and the *Uganda* – carried more than 1,000,000 children to ports throughout Europe and parts of northern Africa. It ended with the Falklands war when the *Uganda*, the last in a well-remembered line, was requisitioned as a hospital ship and ordered to the South Atlantic. A thoughtful Dalyell observed: 'I'm prouder of the role I played in the ship school scheme than anything else I've ever done.'

FIVE

WINNING THE MINERS

With his performance in the Borders, Dalyell proved he could withstand the rigours of an election campaign and bring out Labour's core vote. Having enjoyed the campaign, he had also satisfied himself that he would like to try again: if the opportunity presented itself, he wanted to be an MP. There was a chance that at the next election he might be adopted in a winnable seat. No one could foresee a by-election on his own home ground, West Lothian, before then. Dalyell was in the Mediterranean working as deputy Director of Studies aboard the school ship *Dunera* when a message from his mother delivered the surprising news that he was one of several nominations to succeed the late John Taylor. Deputy chief whip in the Labour opposition at Westminster, Taylor had been MP for West Lothian for more than a decade, winning for the first time in 1951 and retaining the seat with a slightly fluctuating majority through two elections. His death before the age of 60 was totally unexpected, and followed a visit to Tanzania where he became ill and on his return home 'simply withered away. It was tragic,' said Dalyell.

Dalyell's nomination by the Kinneil branch of the National Association of Colliery Oversmen, Deputies and Shot Firers (NACODS) surprised everyone, including himself. 'It turned out an elderly miner, who had the nomination in his gift, was grateful to me for the way I encouraged his grandson, who was a pupil at Bo'ness Academy and was a keen footballer. Also, it emerged that Abe Moffat, the extremely powerful and able President of the Scottish Miners, wanted the nomination for someone in his office at Hillside Crescent, Edinburgh. That's how things were fixed in those days,' remarked Dalyell, 'these days too, for that matter!'

Obtaining the NACODS nomination made Dalyell a serious candidate. 'I wouldn't have got very far without it,' said Dalyell. 'Although I had been an active member of the Labour Party since leaving Cambridge, a 29-year-old former Etonian from The Binns was hardly your obvious Labour candidate in West Lothian. Then people heard that Abe Moffat was absolutely furious about my name going forward for selection. And delegates who wouldn't have given me a second look thought: Well, if he has that effect on the dreaded Abe, he must be a man of considerable substance! If I had been nominated by the Bo'ness Coop, or whatever, things might have been different. But here was a mining trade union putting my name forward, at a time when there were six pits in the constituency.'

James Ovens, a retired miner who attended the 1962 selection conference as a delegate, explained: 'The West Lothian miners could send as many as 46 delegates to the selection conference to choose a candidate. I was one of the delegates from the Riddochhill colliery. We had been mandated to vote for Kellahan, the official NUM candidate, who had the support of Abe Moffat at the miners' HQ. You weren't supposed to be there to play at politics. You were strictly mandated on behalf of other people at every stage of the vote, unless your candidate happened to be knocked out, in which case you enjoyed a bit of freedom to manoeuvre.'

The conference was held on the afternoon of Sunday 6 May 1962. There were 133 delegates present. The meeting was chaired by Crawford Morgan with Will Marshall, the legendary, power-broking secretary of the Labour Party in Scotland, seated alongside. 'The atmosphere was lively but nothing untoward,' said James Ovens. 'These meetings were always wonderful, with very lively minds, very intelligent guys present.'

Six candidates contested the selection process. In addition to Dalyell and Abe Moffat's favoured candidate, Dan Kellahan, they were Mrs Olive Taylor, from Hemel Hempstead, widow of the previous MP, who had been unpopular in many quarters because of his long periods of absence from the constituency, Arthur Houston, a teacher in Cumbernauld, Thomas McGregor, an engineer from Edinburgh, and William Ferrier, the Provost of Armadale. 'Willie Ferrier would have made a perfectly good Labour MP,' said Dalyell. 'But he suffered from his association with Armadale Town Council. Shortly before the selection conference there was a *cause célèbre* in Armadale when the council exchanged the town piano for a crate of whisky. A lot of people were very angry about it. They wanted to know what happened to the piano. It was terribly unfair on Willie.'

Each candidate was allowed 15 minutes to address the delegates and 10 minutes to answer questions. 'I often make bad speeches,' Dalyell remarked dolefully. 'But on this occasion, I made a good speech. At any rate, I led on the first ballot.' James Ovens reported: 'Tam shone out a bit. He was a Cambridge graduate, a confident speaker. There was only one other man I thought might win, and that was McGregor. Kellahan was an ordinary guy, and he couldn't express himself as well as Tam. Tam had a good command of the English language. Working class people are always fascinated by that type of intelligent speaker; whether they're saying anything of substance or not doesn't matter. If they are intelligent and have a command of the English language, that's it.'

On the first ballot the vote divided as follows: Dalyell 44; Kellahan 30; McGregor 27; Houston 16; Ferrier 11; Taylor 5. 'This meant,' said Ovens, 'that under the rules of the selection process, Mrs Taylor was eliminated.' Following the first vote, according to Ovens's detailed record of the day's proceedings, 'one of the delegates left the meeting. This reduced the number of those present and entitled to vote to 132.' The second vote showed Dalyell on 47; Kellahan 33; McGregor 28; Houston 16; Ferrier 8. 'This time,' said Ovens, 'the last pair, Houston and Ferrier, were eliminated.'

Three down, three to go: Dalyell, who had been leading from the start, Kellahan, who carried Abe Moffat's powerful endorsement, and McGregor, the man from Edinburgh, who many observers believed would win in the end. 'If Dan Kellahan had been eliminated at this stage,' Dalyell admitted, 'I think Tom McGregor would have been awarded the nomination.'

In fact, the third vote concluded surprisingly, with Dalyell drawing further ahead: 57 delegates opted for the man from The Binns, compared to 39 for Kellahan and 36 for McGregor.

'It was now a straight fight between Dalyell and Kellahan,' said James Ovens. 'Six votes decided the issue. There were people on our delegation who didn't vote for Kellahan. I wasn't one of them. We were mandated to vote for the miners' candidate, and that's what I did. But I know there were others with a similar mandate who voted for Tam because he impressed them.'

Dalyell elaborated: 'There was also a problem with Dan Kellahan's age. Some of the miners thought that 63 was a bit elderly for anyone to be starting in parliament, with or without Abe Moffat's endorsement.'

The final result of the selection conference was Dalyell 69, Kellahan 63. Dalyell was now the official Labour candidate for West Lothian. As journalist Kenneth Roy later observed: 'Thus the young man from the big house, with the top drawer accent and the Etonian education, emerged as one of the unlikeliest standard-bearers of the Scottish working class.' However, as Dalyell himself recorded: 'From the moment the result of the ballot was announced, no MP could have had greater kindness or more help from the mining community in Scotland, and from the officials of the National Union of Mineworkers. When I think of what they were being asked to swallow, in the shape of an Old Etonian, with many views they did not share, I cannot speak warmly enough of the generosity of a generation that is now largely departed.' Five candidates presented themselves to the West Lothian electorate at the by-election on 14 June 1962 – a plethora of choice for a constituency which had become accustomed to deciding the winner in a straight fight. It had been a simple choice between Labour and Conservative candidates since 1950 when, as David Douglas, writing in the *Glasgow Herald*, observed: 'Home Rule and Communism alike disappeared in the dust of lost deposits'. Given five candidates, the same writer noted drily, 'Short of anarchy everyone should be able to find at least one set of views with which he is in broad agreement.' Added the urbane and clear-minded Douglas: 'Since the Scots are not a politically unstable people, and the West Lothian folk in particular have already earned the respect of all the candidates for their common sense and general hard-headedness, it is tempting to regard the outcome as a foregone victory for Mr Dalyell. At 29 he is the youngest, though not the least experienced, of the current aspirants, all of whom are under 40.'

The last time Labour had failed to hold West Lothian was in 1931. This was the year the second Labour government 'sagged at its knees and fell dead', as Tom Johnston, Lord Privy Seal in the departing cabinet, and future Secretary of State for Scotland in Churchill's wartime coalition, described the aftermath of one of the worst financial crises in the nation's history. In the same year, the former hero of the left, Ramsay MacDonald, formed his ill-remembered National Government in partnership with the Tories and the Liberals.

More than a quarter of a century later, in addition to Dalyell, the candidates were Ian Stewart, who polled 18,083 votes on behalf of the Conservatives at the 1959 election, trailing the Labour candidate, John Taylor, by 9,371; David Bryce, who represented the Liberals; Gordon McLennan, appearing for the Communists; and a Scottish Nationalist candidate with strong local connections, William Wolfe.

During the campaign, Dalyell upset the formidable Will Marshall, general secretary of the Scottish Labour Party, by forecasting that Wolfe, who was in his third year as County Commissioner for the Boy Scouts movement in West Lothian, would attract nearly 10,000 votes. 'Will Marshall thought I was mad,' said Dalyell. 'He told me he had been working under the mistaken impression that I was a person of good judgement. Now he studied me carefully before announcing, with all the authority of his considerable reputation, that if I believed nearly 10,000 people were about to vote

Nationalist in West Lothian, then I didn't have the judgement to be a Labour MP!'

Unemployment, as always in Scotland, was high on the list of campaign issues, as the candidates soon discovered. The far-reaching Toothill Report of 1962, commissioned by the Scottish Council (Development and Industry), showed that unemployment in Scotland between 1953 and 1959 averaged 3.1 per cent, in comparison to 1.6 per cent for Britain as a whole. In the area covered by the West Lothian constituency at the time of the by-election, unemployment averaged 3.9 per cent. Jobs were being lost at a disturbing rate at the Bo'ness docks, as well as in boatbuilding and chemical processing.

Of enormous importance, the shale oil industry, once a world leader, had ceased production a few months earlier. The continued presence of the industry had been the sole reason for keeping Baads Colliery in operation. According to one report: 'When it closed, 1500 men lost their jobs. The fear of other pit closures remains.' Shale mines were generally shallower than coal mines, explained Dalyell, but they could be 'even more dangerous, through gas, damp and the brittle nature of the shale, which could cause severe injury'. The industry owed its existence to the pioneering work of James 'Paraffin' Young, a Glasgow-born industrial chemist, who opened his first processing plant, using cannel coal to produce paraffin, in 1850. His initiative made Bathgate home to the world's first oil refinery. Young's process yielded profits as high as 92 per cent – an industrialist's dream! Later, he discovered it was possible to substitute shale for cannel coal – and shale was available in almost unlimited quantities beneath the soil of West Lothian. Barely 20 years after Young began work at Bathgate, 97 oil companies were established in the area. And, a century after Young first patented his discoveries, the West Lothian shale oil industry was busy manufacturing high-grade aero-engine fuel and industrial wax – until the day it closed.

Dalyell's involvement in the 1962 by-election campaign was due in part to the support of the dying National Union of Shale-oil Miners. 'It was,' he said, 'one of their last acts as a union. Now the pink-coloured bings, a familiar feature of the West Lothian landscape, are all that remain of a once-great industry.'

Investment in the coal industry was also in steep decline, falling massively in Scotland as a whole, from £16.9 million in 1959 to £11.7 million a year later, as shown by the Toothill Report. Two-thirds of the population of West Lothian were dependent on mining for their livelihoods: there had been a tradition of mining in the area since the reign of Alexander III. Job prospects within the constituency, according to various reports, were worse than before the giant BMC plant opened at Bathgate. Around 1,200 workers were already employed at BMC with the prospect of an additional 4,000 jobs at some future date. The area also hoped to benefit from the opening of the Forth Road Bridge in 1964 and the creation of Livingston New Town.

Dalyell proposed introducing a National Industrial Planning Board and an extension of public ownership to reduce unemployment. 'If old industries are to close down,' he declared, 'they must be replaced by new ones. Elect me,' he promised in the course of a diligent door-to-door campaign, 'and I will take it as an order to get weaving in search of new industry for the county.'

Dalyell's appearance and manner, together with his methodical style of knocking on every door in every corner of the constituency, were clearly having an effect on the campaign – or at least, as long as the final outcome was unknown, on the journalists sent to cover it! An anonymous reporter from the *Glasgow Herald* offered an account of his meeting with an unusually poetic West Lothian resident. '"Did you really see Tam?" a man in Linlithgow said to me, in the same kind of tone in which Browning once asked, "Ah! Did you once see Shelley plain. And did he stop and speak to you?"' This unlikely exchange was inspired by the idea that while the 'five contestants race around the county, wound up, according to one theory, by their agents in the morning, pointed in the correct direction and given a push, Mr Dalyell seems to be holding the travelling record'.

In fact, the man responsible for ensuring Dalyell made the best possible impact on the voters in West Lothian judged him 'the perfect candidate. Tam took nothing for granted'. John Muir, a veteran campaign fixer who organised the 1962 by-election for Labour, explained: 'It was our job to win the election. The politics were left to the candidate.' Dalyell, according to Muir, was 'an organiser's dream. There was nobody else like him. He worked day and night. There's nothing big-headed about him, like there is with a lot of candidates. If you had something to say, he listened!'

Long before opinion polls and other detailed surveys aided by computers charted the daily ups and downs of a campaign-in-progress, a 'good register' was an essential part of an organiser's guide on how a constituency was thinking. 'There would be a team of people, with the candidate as the focal point, and you'd go along a street knocking on doors,' John Muir said. 'There was no easy way to do it – accurate information was absolutely essential. There would be a card for every house. We'd knock on a door and ask whoever lived there if they would be voting Labour. Depending on what they said, you marked them down yes or no. If someone appeared to be swithering over their vote, you'd send in the candidate to persuade them. It was his job to make them vote for us. At the end, you added up the yes votes and that told you whether or not you were going to win. West Lothian was very much a mining constituency, and Tam was anything but working class, but he was marvellous with people. His sincerity shone through, both on the doorstep and at public meetings.'

Reporters claimed that Dalyell, on his marathon door-to-door canvassing trips, had been mistaken for the Unionist candidate. *The Scotsman* credited John Marshall, the enterprising SNP agent, as the original source for a long-enduring tale that in Bo'ness children playing in the street had been heard singing, 'Vote for Tory Tam, the Labour man!'

Neither Dalyell or his SNP opponent, William Wolfe, realised they would also become candidates for a place in the *Guinness Book of Records*: the 1962 West Lothian by-election proved to be the first of seven parliamentary contests to feature the pair, to the delight of uncommitted observers who thought, on at least one occasion, that Wolfe would win. Wolfe, a chartered accountant by training, and a future leader of the SNP, was a political novice when he and Dalyell faced each other for the first time. 'I had never taken part in political activity of any kind,' said Wolfe. 'We hadn't the foggiest idea about canvassing. But it was the most publicised SNP campaign, to date.'

Wolfe's general political philosophy had been well and truly aired in a letter to the *West Lothian Courier* on 21 February 1962, in which he described Scotland as a separate nation with its own history and traditions, outlook and economy. Scotland, wrote Wolfe, could be a self-governing nation again, with no loss to herself or the world. Size was no barrier. Four months later, in his appeal to the West Lothian electors, Wolfe insisted unconditionally: 'Put Scotland First!' Later he claimed: 'I treated my audiences, and the electorate generally, as patriotic Scots looking for a solution to their communities' problems and to Scotland's problems in a political way that was honourable and likely to be effective. I always assumed that they believed in the continued existence of the nation. I dealt with economic matters and avoided left-versus-right arguments.' Dalyell, considered by many people (in his later career especially) as a constant critic of the Nationalists, maintained: 'I got on astonishingly well with Billy Wolfe. We were never personally abusive at any stage of the campaign. I've never called them Tartan Tories, or anything of that kind. I've always argued on the question of a separate Scottish state and having differences of political opinion.'

The 1962 West Lothian by-election was notable for the innovative nature of the SNP campaign. 'We introduced razzmatazz to Scottish electioneering,' smiled Wolfe. 'We didn't have music then, that came later – Jimmy Shand records. But we issued car stickers saying 'Vote for Wolfe.' And we had a series of advertisements in the local papers. The Labour Party didn't like that at all. They wanted to know where we were getting the money from. It was great fun. People said we were copying what went on in America, but none of us had been to America or knew anything about American politics. It just seemed the right thing to do.' Two days before polling, on Tuesday 12 June, the *Glasgow Herald* commented: 'It has been, by modern standards, a vigorous campaign, made so perhaps by the youth of the candidates. Certainly West Lothian in 1962 is, or ought to be, a young man's county. It is at the heart of the region which more obviously than any other part of Scotland is engaged in a minor industrial revolution.'

The day before polling, the Liberal candidate, David Bryce, born in Armadale in the heart of the constituency, was claiming he stood a good chance of victory. He forecast a 65 per cent poll and Dalyell thought it could be as high as 75 per cent. The constituency traditionally polled between 75 and 84 per cent in general elections. Those representing Ian Stewart, the Tory candidate offering himself to the West Lothian electors for the second time in less than three years, predicted that two or more candidates would lose their deposit. It would have been contrary to nature if the agent concerned included his own candidate in this gloomy prediction, but in the end that's what happened.

In a 71.1 per cent turnout, more than half the electors favoured the Labour candidate. Those attending the declaration in the County Buildings, Linlithgow heard the Returning Officer, Sheriff W. Ross McLean QC, announce 21,266 votes for Dalyell, against 9,750 for William Wolfe. Third in the poll, and clearly suffering for the perceived sins of the Macmillan government, was the Conservative candidate, Ian Stewart. An advocate by profession, well used to pursuing the burden of proof, he was presented with what appeared to be incontrovertible evidence of a significant shift in public opinion. Having convinced a substantial number of the same electorate that he was the man for them in 1959, Stewart now gained a mere 4,784 votes and lost his deposit along with David Bryce, the Liberal candidate, who polled 4,537 votes, and the Communist candidate, Gordon McLennan, who finished with 1,511 votes.

Dalyell could be satisfied with a result which saw him hold the seat with an increased majority although his share of the vote fell substantially, from the 60.3 per cent won by John Taylor in 1959 to 50.9 per cent in the by-election. The West Lothian result 'jolted the Tory Central Office as it had never been jolted before, made the front page in every leading newspaper in the country, and prompted a positive flood of leading articles and radio and TV comment'. As one local paper, the *West Lothian Courier* observed: 'West Lothian has never had such publicity before, not even with the coming of BMC to the county.'

Dalyell evidently believed the result showed 'the determination of people living in West Lothian to have a government who understood technological change. I expected the Tories to do badly,' he added. 'During the campaign I visited 2,700 houses, canvassing. It was clear to me that the Nationalists would come second.' However, Ian Stewart believed the Nationalists' euphoria would be short lived. Most of William Wolfe's votes came, he claimed, from him. And he fully expected the Conservatives to win them back 'at the next general election'.

Other participants in the drama thought differently. It was, as the *West Lothian Courier* announced, the worst defeat the Conservative Party had suffered in Scotland in 42 years. 'The drop in the Conservative share of the poll – 28.27 per cent – is the largest in any by-election this year,' the paper added. 'Of all the elections in West Lothian since 1918, this one has provided the lowest Conservative vote.' On the strength of the West Lothian result, the *West Lothian Courier* reported, Hugh Gaitskell, the Labour leader, had challenged the Prime Minister to go to the country. 'All of us, most of all the Tories, know what the result of that would be. They must put their house in order, and quickly. A new deal for Scotland is high on the list of priorities.' The *Glasgow Herald* suggested that the SNP vote was a measure of 'the widespread feeling that Scotland is not getting a square deal'. In fact, the newspaper claimed, 'Scotland has suffered no worse than England from the trade recession'. And, it maintained stubbornly, the fact that William Wolfe attracted nearly 10,000 votes in West Lothian added 'not a whit to the force of the nationalist argument, which is irrelevant to the economic realities of the 1960s'.

William Wolfe, however, believed there was more than raw emotion at work behind his result. 'We fought this election on hard economic facts, unemployment, immigration and the drain of money into England,' he claimed. 'We got more than half our votes from former Labour supporters, the rest from people who were previously anti-socialist voters. In a by-election in Glasgow last November, we finished third. This time we are second. Next time we'll win.'

Dalyell was quoted as saying after the election, 'I'm going to raise hell in London. They've got to realise down there that we don't want our communities broken up. We want work brought to us – and in good time.' The *West Lothian Courier* commented approvingly: 'Already he is chasing the ministers and the bureaucrats with all the fervour and enthusiasm with which his famous ancestor, General Tam Dalyell, once harried the Covenanters. His mission is no less urgent, and decidedly more popular as far as Scots are concerned.'

Dalyell, in addition to winning a seat at Westminster, enjoyed a rare treat: an unsolicited apology from the former Fife miner and undisputed boss of the Labour Party machine in Scotland, Will Marshall. 'Willie could be a pretty gruff character at times,' Dalyell recalled with a smile. 'And not one to apologise very often! But once the result was known, and with it the size of the SNP vote, he said to me, rather sweetly, "Tam, I'll always remember you were right, and I was wrong on this." If you want to know the truth, I think he rather liked me after that.'

Afterwards, there was a party at The Binns for everyone who had worked on the campaign. Dalyell also made a point of writing personally to thank all the volunteer helpers who'd helped send him to Westminster. All except one. 'She never spoke to me during the campaign and she didn't bother to add her name to the list of canvassers,' said Dalyell. 'And because she was working in Glasgow, she missed the celebration party. So we didn't actually meet until after the election.'

Kathleen said: 'I wanted to do something to help the Labour Party, which had been an important part of my life for as long as I could remember. Arthur Houston said I could go with him and a few others, including John Smith and Donald Dewar, to West Lothian and do some canvassing during the by-election. I knew a lot of people were saying Tam was an unusual choice for the Labour candidate in a predominantly mining constituency. I'd heard about The Binns, of course, and the story of General Tam and the Covenanters. But, apart from that I didn't know anything about Tam. We never met during the campaign, for the simple reason that I was always canvassing at a different part of the constituency from him, before going straight home to Glasgow. Anyway, I was there because I wanted to help the Labour Party. When we did meet and were introduced, it was in London, in March the following year. I was in the Central lobby of the House of Commons, for a meeting with my father's old friend Jimmy Hoy, when Tam appeared in the company of a large group of young people. Uncle Jimmy pointed him out and asked if I knew him. I said no, but I'd worked hard with a lot of other people to help get him elected. It later turned out that Tam had been asked to entertain a group of visiting German students and didn't mind being interrupted.'

Twenty-four years old, convent educated, and working in Glasgow as a history teacher at St Augustine's Secondary School in Milton, an uncompromising neighbourhood on the city's northern rim, Kathleen Wheatley's socialist credentials, inherited from her parents, were impeccable. Her father was Lord Wheatley, a Senator of the Court of Session and a future Lord Justice Clerk. Earlier in his career as a lawyer and politician, he had been Labour MP for East Edinburgh, as well as Solicitor-General and Lord Advocate in Attlee's first post-war administration. Kathleen's mother was Nancy Nichol, once an active member of the Labour Guild of Youth, who assisted her father, Sammy Nichol, with his duties as secretary and treasurer of the Shettleston Independent Labour Party. Nancy Nichol and her future husband met while attending an Independent Labour Party conference in Carlisle. John Wheatley was already a famous name in Glasgow's East End.

Lord Wheatley could trace his immediate family to Ireland and the village of Bonmahon in County Waterford. Half a century earlier his miner grandfather had emigrated to the west of Scotland, looking for work in the rapidly expanding Lanarkshire coalfield. According to Menzies Campbell, another lawyer and politician from Scotland, the future Labour minister and distinguished judge was steeped in 'a robust Christian socialism which is less popular now than it was when his uncle was a member of the first Labour government. Although his formal religion was Roman Catholic,' added Campbell, 'he had a strictness about him which seemed to owe as much to Calvinism as anything else.' Wheatley's uncle was MP for Shettleston and one of a large group of Labour MPs, famous in Labour legend as 'The Clydesiders', who arrived at Westminster from Scotland following the 1922 general election. Two years later, when Ramsay MacDonald formed the first Labour government, the highly respected and serious-minded John Wheatley was in the cabinet with responsibility for housing. His friend, James Maxton, believed he should have been leading it.

Nancy Nichol was of Border stock; Selkirk and Hawick. 'She was steeped in the literature and tales of the Scottish Borders,' commented Dalyell, 'and was proud to be related to James Hogg, the Ettrick Shepherd and radical poet.' As a young girl Nancy Nichol had been in George Square clutching her father's hand when the Red Flag was raised and a mass demonstration of workers was charged by mounted police. The following day, with the government in London apparently convinced that a full-scale revolution was about to begin on Clydeside, troops and tanks appeared on the streets of Glasgow. In an affectionate tribute, written following her death, Dalyell recorded: 'Her tough repartee was legendary. Imagine calling Emmanuel Shinwell "a right chancer" to his face – and living to tell him so every time they met!' According to Dalyell: 'There was no subject on which Nancy Wheatley did not have a decided and usually perceptive opinion.' Seated next to Dr Tom Carberry, former chairman of the IBA in Scotland, at a dinner in Edinburgh she inquired: 'Do you know my son-in-law?'

'Oh, aye,' said Carberry.

'He's a daft chiel!' said Lady Wheatley.

Five months after being introduced in the lobby of the House of Commons, with a long-serving Labour MP in the role of unsuspecting matchmaker, Tam Dalyell and Kathleen Wheatley announced their engagement. Dalyell broke the news at a meeting of his local constituency party on 11 August 1963. A reporter from the *West Lothian Courier* thought it necessary to invite Dalyell to comment on the couple's 'religious differences.' Dalyell told the paper: 'Kathleen will remain a catholic and I will stay a protestant. If we are blessed with any children, they will be brought up as catholics.' Kathleen revealed: 'My father is a catholic and my mother is a protestant. They have been happily married for more than 25 years. My mother intends to remain a protestant – she has her own convictions and we respect her all the more for it. What better example could we have to follow?'

Tam Dalyell and Kathleen Wheatley married on 26 December 1963. They have a son and a daughter. Ask about Dalyell, and those who know them will always mention Kathleen. 'She would have made a great MP in her own right, even a minister,' said one observer. 'She has the wit, the style and the passion to succeed in parliament.'

Kathleen Dalyell dismisses the idea of herself as an MP with a firm shake of the head. 'I decided long ago that only one of us could go down that particular road,' she said. 'It was my job to stay here and look after the children and The Binns, and help with the constituency.' Her decision not to pursue a formal political career also meant she could concentrate on other interests, serving on various heritage committees and as chairman of the Royal Commission on Historic and Ancient Monuments of Scotland. 'She is a very busy lady,' said another source. 'It's also fair to say that she has been a great asset to Tam, not least in the constituency. I don't think he does very much without talking it over with her first.'

SIX

HELPING HAROLD

Dalyell arrived at Westminster with all the usual ambitions of a newly-elected MP – to see his party win power, his leader as Prime Minister, and himself, in the quickest possible time, as an important member of the government. 'It isn't true I never wanted to be a minister,' said Dalyell. 'I always wanted to run a department and make things happen.'

According to Professor Alan Thompson, then MP for Dunfermline, he was regarded by many English members as 'an exotic and unusual addition to the Scottish contingent'. Herbert Morrison, a member of Churchill's war cabinet and a Labour Party legend, was among the first to welcome Dalyell to Westminster. Morrison didn't bother to conceal his belief that 'too many academic and public school candidates were being chosen for winnable Labour seats'. Years earlier, Morrison's leadership ambitions had been foiled by Clement Attlee, with the powerful support of Ernest Bevin, and then again in 1955, when Attlee resigned and Hugh Gaitskell defeated Morrison in the leadership contest which followed. It no doubt rankled with the largely self-taught Morrison that Attlee was a product of Haileybury and University College, Oxford; while Gaitskell attended Winchester and New College, Oxford. 'Contrary to popular belief,' reported the latest public school recruit to the ranks of the Parliamentary Labour Party, 'Morrison took a great interest in politics outside London. And it was obvious he was well aware of my tussle with the nationalists in West Lothian.'

Morrison didn't subscribe to the general Labour view, common at Westminster, that the SNP result in West Lothian was either a flash in the pan or a protest vote over wage differentials and unemployment. 'Laddie,' he told

Dalyell, 'you and your colleagues in Scotland may think you did a good job, causing Macmillan's candidate to lose his deposit. I think you may have great problems.' Morrison, from his seat in the House of Lords, believed it might prove necessary to introduce some measure of local government reform, to appease the feeling of discontent which was evident in Scotland. Dalyell's proposal that the Scottish Grand Committee meeting in Edinburgh could provide a positive counter to accusations of Westminster remoteness didn't appeal to the Labour veteran. Scottish MPs were entitled to be present at Westminster: to attend important party meetings and to participate in the regular business of the House of Commons. This included scrutinising the performance of departments such as the Treasury and the Board of Trade, which were 'no less vital to the people of Scotland than the Scottish Office.' Morrison, a renowned parliamentary 'fixer' who combined the roles of deputy Prime Minister, Lord President of the Council and Leader of the House of Commons in the reforming post-war Labour administration, also recognised that the fate of the Government could depend on the votes of Scottish MPs.

As Dalyell soon learned, vital to his role as an opposition MP and of paramount importance to the smooth running of the party machine, opposing the government meant voting with his colleagues as required by the whips. In the first few days, he was reported missing on eight separate occasions during the committee stage of the Finance Bill. 'Herbert Bowden, the chief whip, sent for me to ask where the hell I was,' recalled Dalyell. 'I explained I had a problem at home with my bees swarming. He was quite unsympathetic when I told him I had been forced to spend quite a lot of time scrambling about in bushes trying to locate them. It seemed that in my new life, trying to keep swarms of bees under control, and the chief whip happy, were mutually incompatible activities.'

Harold Macmillan was Prime Minister, and Hugh Gaitskell the Leader of the Opposition, when Dalyell arrived in the House of Commons. Both expected to win power at the next election. West Lothian offered an important guide to the mood of the electorate, at an important stage in the electoral cycle. But neither man had bothered to visit the constituency during the by-election campaign. Television coverage of politics was in its infancy and the importance of 'soundbites' to a leader's image on the wider political stage as yet undiscovered.

Hugh Gaitskell waited until Dalyell took his seat in the House of Commons before asking him to report on the significance of the result. 'I told him there was considerable resentment in many parts of Scotland because unemployment was higher there than in certain parts of England, particularly the London area and the Midlands,' reported Dalyell. He also advised Gaitskell: 'It is hard to exaggerate the role in politics of insult, real or alleged, in the rise of Scottish nationalist feeling. It is true that London has often been pretty gauche in small matters, and equally true that the Scots are a prickly people, who often take a sneaking enjoyment in professing outrage at some "insult" which has been perpetrated against them. We Scots are unsurpassed when it comes to making a mountain of invective out of a mole-hill of a slight, or an unintentional slight, upon us.'

It was the custom, Dalyell discovered, when he first took his seat in the House of Commons, for MPs to listen in silence while the Prime Minister answered questions. These were expected to relate 'to the special responsibilities or public actions of the Prime Minister. Anything else was dealt with by the minister responsible. As a matter of course, if appropriate,' explained Dalyell in his 1987 book *Misrule*, 'Harold Wilson, as Shadow Chancellor, might question Harold Macmillan on economic matters, George Brown might question him on defence matters, or Patrick Gordon Walker, if the substance of the question related to foreign affairs. If the Leader of the Opposition intervened at all, it was a newsworthy matter of weight.'

Writing at a time when Margaret Thatcher was still Prime Minister, and he had spent more than a quarter of a century viewing a dozen variations of the same flawed routine with several more to come in the course of a long parliamentary career, Dalyell complained: 'Inevitably, I suppose, if questions are geared to political point-scoring at its most naked, there will be cheering, snarling and counter-snarling, farmyard noises and blow-by-blow commentary from incontinent parliamentarians who develop verbal diarrhoea every Tuesday and Thursday at 3.15 p.m. The result of this is that it is virtually impossible to hear what the Prime Minister says and latch on to those answers that are clearly inadequate. From being what the textbooks have claimed is one of the glories of British democracy, Prime Minister's questions have deteriorated into farce as an exercise in monitoring a Prime Minister's actions.'

The period allocated to Prime Minister's questions was 'more related to the publicity requirements of the questioner than any serious scrutiny of the Prime Minister's actions,' Dalyell maintained. 'This creates the conditions for yah-boo politics and turns the House of Commons into what any reasonable person listening to the exchanges would call a bear garden.'

Harold Wilson, when he succeeded Hugh Gaitskell as Leader of the Opposition in 1963, chose his interventions with care, according to Dalyell. 'You could hear a pin drop,' he claimed. 'And this was infinitely more dangerous for vulnerable Prime Ministers than the contemporary hullabaloo.' However, he also blamed Wilson for 'starting the rot' which finished with the Prime Minister taking on all comers at the despatch box. 'Harold would insist on showing off how much he knew about every facet of government.'

The present custom of the Leader of the Opposition engaging in a weekly joust with the Prime Minister began with Neil Kinnock, claimed Dalyell. He thought Kinnock, from what he witnessed of his performance on the National Executive of the Labour Party, would have been capable of running a cabinet and government effectively. He also considered Kinnock to be 'highly principled, good at handling the Labour Party and often an excellent platform speaker and television personality'. But it was a mistake, in his view, for Kinnock, as Leader of the Opposition, to engage Mrs Thatcher 'in a joust in which she has formidable briefing, has the last word by right, and in which he is thus at a disadvantage'.

Dalyell's own reputation as a skilful framer of questions to the government front bench was established within weeks of arriving in the House of Commons. 'I can recollect Tam emerging from the Commons library with armfuls of Blue Books, White Papers and files, probably his research for a single parliamentary question,' Alan Thompson offered. 'No wonder ministers quickly became apprehensive of his supplementaries.'

George Younger, his friend of more than 60 years, watching initially from a seat in the Strangers' Gallery, thought 'he was one of those chaps who immediately swing into the business of being an MP, asking difficult, complicated, searching questions of the government, harrying ministers. For a new MP, I thought it was a pretty quick and impressive start.' David Steel, the man who succeeded where Dalyell failed by winning the Borders, Selkirk and Peebles constituency from the Tories, judged him 'a master of the art of parliamentary questioning'. The former leader of the Liberal Party, and first presiding officer in the devolved Scottish Parliament added: 'Other members in more than one parliament could take a leaf out of his book as to how to ask effective questions. Tam asks short sharp questions, often quite brilliantly. People on the receiving end cannot dodge giving him an answer.'

Tony Benn, first elected to the House of Commons in 1950, claimed: 'His factual questions are usually the most powerful. They are always carefully thought out, always relevant, and always backed up by his own inquiries and research. Think of them as the parliamentary equivalent of a smart bomb, always on target. That may be one reason why some people don't like him,' added Benn, 'they don't like a Member of Parliament performing that kind of function. They think an MP should be offering congratulations to the Foreign Secretary, or whoever. You know the sort of thing – "Could I trouble the

Prime Minister to remind us of his latest triumphs since last Wednesday?".
There are so many planted questions during Prime Minister's questions they
should rename it Gardener's Question Time, and that's really the death of
parliament. Tam, on the other hand, is absolutely persistent. And he does it
very respectfully. I think of him as someone who uses parliament brilliantly
for the purposes for which he was elected – to represent his constituency and
his own convictions.'

Thirty eight years after Dalyell was first elected to the House of Commons
he explained, in a letter to Dr Tony Wright, chairman of the Select
Committee on Public Administration, the principles he adopts when
submitting questions. Overwhelmingly, he claimed, his PQs 'relate to policy,
not statistics'. If he needed statistics he obtained them from the library, or
wrote to the minister. 'If I do want figures, I insert the word "conveniently
available". If there is ambiguity, I phone the private office of Tory as well as
Labour ministers, to clarify what I am on about.' Dalyell was appalled by the
number of MPs who put down parliamentary questions to obtain 'reams of
statistics, which I bet they never use to any effect'. Many MPs, he claimed,
also abused the system by simply putting down PQs to attract the attention
of their local newspapers. Dr Wright and his colleagues on the Select
Committee had been seeking to establish if questions were going
unanswered, or information was being withheld from MPs, on the grounds
of 'disproportionate cost'. Dalyell responded: 'In 38 years as an MP, I have
never had a question unanswered on terms of "disproportionate cost". How
come? I am a very inquisitive MP!'

The destruction of the Tory candidate in the West Lothian by-election,
resulting in the first lost Conservative deposit in Scotland since a similar
contest at Paisley on 12 February 1920, ensured the victor was received at
Westminster with ringing Labour cheers. It had been a miserable month for
the Tories – the humiliation suffered in West Lothian was only part of it. A
by-election at Middlesborough West had been won by the Labour candidate,
Jeremy Bray, with a majority of 2,270, against a Tory majority of 8,710 at the
previous election. In a much reduced poll, Bray actually attracted fewer votes
than his predecessor. Fortunately for him, the Tory vote simply collapsed.
West Derbyshire narrowly escaped going the same way, despite the presence
of a famous candidate, Aidan Crawley. Latterly a familiar face on BBC
television, he had been Minister for Air in the last Labour government,
before switching to the Tories in 1957. Given a chance to return to the
Commons he took it gratefully, despite a slump in the Tory vote, from 8,109
at the last election to 1,220 this time.

On 13 July 1962 – the 'Night of the Long Knives' – the famously unflappable Harold Macmillan, in a desperate attempt to revitalise his government, sacked six members of his cabinet. Told that the Prime Minister had rid himself of half his cabinet, the shadow chancellor Harold Wilson memorably quipped: 'Unfortunately, it was the wrong half!' Jeremy Thorpe, the Liberal leader, added to the fun with what Alan Clark called 'one of the century's wittiest political aphorisms'. Said Thorpe, 'Greater love hath no man than that he lay down his friends for his life.'

Among those dismissed was the Secretary of State for Scotland, the gentlemanly Jack Maclay. Dalyell met him in a Westminster corridor the following day. 'Well,' said Maclay cheerfully, 'you succeeded in getting me the order of the boot. But that's political life and you will learn,' he added. Dalyell was full of admiration for the dismissed minister. 'The political columnists of today would not have given him star rating as a Commons performer,' he wrote years later. 'But when it came to bringing the bacon home in terms of Treasury agreement, Maclay was a very formidable operator indeed.' Maclay had been instrumental in bringing steel to Ravenscraig, BMC to Bathgate and car manufacturing to Linwood. 'It was a tribute to Maclay's weight in the cabinet that he was able to persuade his colleagues, and leaders of industry, that it was necessary to do something about the Scottish unemployment problem of the day,' claimed Dalyell. 'And, whatever people say now, the fact is that high quality employment was given to many thousands of ex-miners and their families, who would not otherwise have had it. It seemed at the time that Maclay was doing the right thing for the industrial infrastructure,' Dalyell added.

In fact, weeks before the Prime Minister's image changed from Supermac the hero of Moscow, to Mac the Knife, the destroyer of colleagues and friends, the new young Labour MP for West Lothian had been left in no doubt that the BMC factory at Bathgate, the main employer in his constituency, faced an uncertain future. On a visit to the parent plant at Longbridge within a fortnight of Dalyell's election, one senior executive informed him bluntly: 'I want you always to remember it was the cabinet and not us who wanted to go to Bathgate. I hope that before you cease to be MP for West Lothian this doesn't end in tears. We think it will.' Nearly two decades after the Bathgate experiment collapsed and the factory that was once the largest machine shop in Europe under one roof closed forever, Dalyell observed: 'I was very angry with George Younger, when he was Secretary of State for Scotland, for saying he was doing everything possible to preserve Bathgate and then not doing so. I think, in retrospect, my anger might have been misplaced. Now I realise there were difficult commercial considerations. Of course, the whole concept was flawed.' He added: 'I used to be a great believer in direction of industry.

Now I believe if half the money that had been spent on attracting American industry had been given to indigenous industries, such as the old steel foundries of West Lothian, we would be infinitely better off today.'

Dalyell, as many people both inside and outside the constituency continued to remark, appeared out of place representing working-class West Lothian at Westminster. 'He has complained to me time and again that having an Eton accent is his biggest handicap,' his long-serving constituency chairman, Allister Mackie, revealed. 'I don't agree that it's a big handicap, but that's how he perceives it. He once told me he wanted to make sure his children weren't burdened with an Eton accent. So they went to a local school.'

Ken Waddell readily acknowledged Dalyell's problem. 'You would have thought the way he spoke, and his background, would have alienated him from the miners in Bo'ness,' said Waddell. 'Instead, it was the very opposite. He made himself one of the boys, he mingled with them. He and his wife Kathleen, for all the years I knew them, went to everything; dance competitions, bowling club dinners, Tam was always there. He was just so loyal and so attentive to everything in the area.' Allister Mackie smiled. 'Now and again, he'll come away with what he imagines to be a typically working class response, and say things I'd never dream of saying. A woman councillor was complaining to him once about something or other and he said, in that wonderful voice: "Heather, you don't have to get your knickers in a twist over this." The conversation stopped dead for a moment. Then everyone laughed, including the councillor. It was so inappropriate. But he thinks that's how working class people behave.'

Dalyell's ambition to progress in the Parliamentary Labour Party, and hopefully become a minister at some future date, received an important and unexpected boost barely six months after his arrival at Westminster. 'I was approached by Harold Wilson, then shadow chancellor, and asked if I would be willing to serve on the Public Accounts Committee of which he was chairman,' said Dalyell. 'These were the days before the introduction of Select Committees, and membership of the Public Accounts Committee was quite an honour for a young MP.' As Harold Wilson observed in *The Governance of Britain*, membership of the Public Accounts Committee traditionally carried great prestige. The members included senior MPs, ex-ministers and 'usually some of the most promising younger Members, with bright prospects of promotion', who had been 'selected by their whips for an apprenticeship there. Many brilliant ministerial careers began as a result of PAC service', added Wilson.

Established in 1861 by Gladstone as part of his reform of the country's financial institutions, the Public Accounts Committee spent four hours a week interviewing permanent secretaries in their capacity as accounting officers. It could, according to Wilson, invoke terror in even 'the toughest, most experienced permanent secretaries' called before it. One highly experienced permanent secretary, who had been a war hero in World War I, admitted to Wilson that 'the night before he appeared before the PAC each year he never slept a wink. Other accounting officers have told me the same,' wrote Wilson.

It was as a member of the Public Accounts Committee that Dalyell first made his name as a stubborn, inquisitive parliamentary freebooter with a nose for trouble. Sir Edmund Compton, then Controller and Auditor General, later the first parliamentary ombudsman, went out of his way, according to Dalyell, to educate him in 'asking the right questions' of very clever men and women. 'I have never known a man,' commented Dalyell, 'who could pose such difficult questions and yet give so little offence to those he was questioning.'

A contract for work on Livingston New Town helped establish Dalyell's early reputation for tenacity in the face of official intransigence. The contract had been awarded to a small firm based in Montrose. When the company 'got into difficulties' and subsequently went bankrupt, Dalyell was approached by a constituent who wanted to know why 'a small firm from north of the Tay had landed a huge contract south of the Forth'. Dalyell agreed to raise the matter in Parliament. 'The response from the Scottish Office was an attempt to fob me off,' he claimed. 'Douglas Houghton, who was now chairman of the Public Accounts Committee in succession to Harold Wilson, and Sir Edmund Compton, the Controller and Auditor General, agreed it would be appropriate for me to raise the matter as a member of the PAC.' The news, according to Dalyell, sent shock waves through the Scottish Office. 'Being asked a parliamentary question by a novice MP was routine and of little consequence,' he said. 'Being arraigned before the Public Accounts Committee, and before the Commons had spawned Select Committees, was quite another matter.' He added: 'In what was then rather a secluded backwater, the mandarins were not used to this kind of assault. Even when the report proved I was justified, a lot of senior persons (among them a group of somewhat aghast Scottish Labour MPs) were not best pleased. But it taught me a lesson – never be fobbed off with an inadequate answer.'

The novice MP disregarded by the mandarins in St Andrew's House was forming strong opinions about the purpose of parliament, and its relationship with the executive. Anyone who came to believe that 'when politicians mount their high horses in public, invoking this sacred principle or that, it is wise to sup with a long spoon' was bound to pose a threat to any establishment figure who maintained that no change was necessary in the way Britain was governed.

Dalyell has acknowledged he was 'irritatingly self-righteous' as a young MP: by his own admission, there was too much of the 'knight in shining armour' about his approach, which didn't help many of his causes. 'Ex-public schoolboys in their 30s are not very reflective about how others may perceive them when they know they are right, and that great men with huge responsibilities are wrong. More than most, the issue politician, embarked on a crusade, had better be careful about his manners and personal tact.' It was in the nature of the man that he worried about MPs in the governing party being dependent on Downing Street to further their careers. Dalyell found himself drawn to the American system, where 'a member of the House of Representatives or the US Senate depends for his preferment on the judgement of fellow congressmen and senators, and on Buggins and his turn, rather than on the patronage of the White House.'

Significantly, soon after becoming an MP he had been impressed with the response of Sir Eric Errington, the large and independent-minded Tory who represented Aldershot, when faced with an angry whip, furious at his failure to vote on some measure proposed by his own government. In Dalyell's remembered version of events, Sir Eric declared: 'Young man, be careful what you say! You and the Prime Minister can give me nothing that I want. So I'll use my own judgement, thank you.'

'Even as late as the 1960s and '70s,' commented Dalyell, 'there were a phalanx of trade union MPs on the Labour benches, and Tory 'knights of the shire' on the other side, who wanted nothing for themselves, and were content to fulfil the proper role of a backbench MP: to scrutinise.'

In an article written for *The Herald* 38 years after he was first elected to the House of Commons, Dalyell reflected: 'There is a real dilemma built into the heart of government in Britain. And in the last 20 years it has become ever more acute. How does the same body, Holyrood no less than the House of Commons, provide both the personnel to form the executive government of Scotland or the UK, and at the same time provide the personnel who are going, without fear or favour, to hold that selfsame executive to account?' Historically, Dalyell noted, this was probably unimportant since 'Gladstone and Disraeli had only a score of ministers at most, and Tories and Liberals came from the Shires to cast judgement on relatively simple issues. There was a crude and generalised accountability. If the consensus of the Commons did not like something, that something tended not to happen.'

Writing in *Misrule* two decades earlier, he likened the House of Commons to 'a flight of starlings. We move on from one perch to another. A chorus of opinion expresses itself on the issue of today and yesterday's issue is all but forgotten. For my part I'm an unashamed yesterday's issue politician, who thinks Parliament moves on far too fast and has unhealthily developed forgettery.' Dalyell himself believed firmly in the doctrine of ministerial responsibility. 'How else do we ensure that civil servants are protected from being made liable for carrying out their orders?' he demanded. 'How else do we ensure that ministers are accountable to Parliament for the acts of their departments?' The idea of politicians blaming civil servants in order to get out of a difficult corner was always anathema to Dalyell. 'There is something particularly unpleasant about attacking civil servants when they are only trying to be honest with the elected Parliament, but then harbouring them, with the impression that they are at fault, when the real mischief is the work of politicians for highly political purposes,' Dalyell maintained.

Two events in 1963, the first occuring barely seven months after Tam Dalyell was elected to the House of Commons for the first time, changed the future of British politics completely. Hugh Gaitskell, leader of the Labour Party, died suddenly on 18 January 1963. Ten months later Harold Macmillan, suffering from a prostate condition, resigned as Prime Minister. 'Macmillan was very nice to me,' said Dalyell. 'Once, during Prime Minister's questions, I asked him why the Finance Bill was so complicated. I thought it could be presented in simpler language, for the benefit of MPs and anyone else who wanted to read it. He took me aside in the corridor afterwards and said he would arrange a meeting with the Chief Parliamentary Draughtsman to explain why it was necessary to be absolutely precise about such things. And the very next morning, at nine o'clock, the Chief Parliamentary Draughtsman, Sir Noel Hutton QC, arrived with two suitcases full of tomes to see this green backbencher and try to make him understand why it was important to present bills in this fashion. I hadn't been taken apart so effectively, in the nicest possible way, since I was a first year undergraduate! It was really nice of Macmillan to take the trouble. A few days later when I saw him in the corridor, he asked me how I'd got on with Sir Noel. He knew damned well how I'd got on with Sir Noel! So I gave him a watery smile and mumbled something and he said, "Well, that will teach you a lesson." And indeed it did! I was a great admirer of Macmillan's skill in the House of Commons, even in his latter days,' added Dalyell.

A bruising battle for the Labour Party leadership was unavoidable following Gaitskell's death. Harold Wilson, George Brown and James Callaghan all offered themselves for election. Voting was restricted to members of the Parliamentary Labour Party. 'I sought advice from a number of people whose political judgement I valued, including my agent Jimmy Boyle and Charlie Sneddon, the Provost of Bo'ness,' said Dalyell. 'They all favoured Wilson. If you'd asked me who I thought was the best of the three candidates, I'd have said Callaghan. In a straight fight, Wilson against Callaghan, I am pretty certain Callaghan would have won. The trade union vote, which was very important, mainly supported Brown. I voted for Wilson, in preference to Brown, because I thought he stood a better chance of winning the next general election. Brown, on his day, could be superb. But I thought, maybe wrongly, that he was too volatile and would prove unelectable. Brown was furious with me. He thought I ought to have voted for him because he had been friendly to me, and visited our house in Scotland, and because I was seen to be on his wing of the party.'

Prior to the vote, the chief whip, Herbert Bowden, advised Dalyell as a newcomer to the Parliamentary Labour Party not to let himself be bullied by his senior Scottish colleagues into voting for their preferred candidate, George Brown. 'Willie Ross and Peggy Herbison both tried to bully me into voting for George Brown,' admitted Dalyell. 'They didn't trust Wilson. But I always liked Wilson, and I think he always liked me, although I know I exasperated him on occasion. But ever since he made me a member of the Public Accounts Committee, when he was chairman, he would chat to me very freely, even at the height of his premiership, on a number of subjects.'

The result of the first ballot of the election was announced at a meeting of the Parliamentary Labour Party on 7 February 1963: Wilson 115 votes, Brown 88 and Callaghan 41. Most commentators agreed that Callaghan's presence helped Wilson. Others concluded that if Callaghan had been the first choice right-wing candidate, instead of the erratic Brown, he could have won. 'But it was too late,' as historian Ben Pimlott noted, 'Callaghan was out of the contest, and Wilson only had to pick up eight of his votes to win.'

The final result was announced at a meeting of the PLP on 14 February 1963: Wilson 144 votes, Brown 103. Dalyell reckoned that only one member of the existing shadow cabinet voted for Wilson: 'A number of people turned the election for Wilson,' he claimed. 'I am pretty certain Herbert Bowden's personal vote went to George Brown. But as chief whip, he was determined there should be fair play. Without his determined neutrality, Harold Wilson might never have become leader of the Labour Party.'

With a general election due at the latest the following year, the new Labour leader embarked on a campaign to convince 'the educational and scientific establishments that Labour was fit for office'. In a rousing speech to the party conference in Scarborough on 1 October 1963, Wilson committed the next Labour government to redefining and restating socialism 'in terms of the scientific revolution'. As a democrat, said Wilson, he rejected 'the methods which communist countries are deploying in applying the results of scientific research to industrial life. But because we care deeply about the future of Britain, we must use all the resources of democratic planning, all the latent and underdeveloped energies and skills of our people, to ensure Britain's standing in the world.'

Wilson's 'white heat of technology' speech was part of a cleverly targeted campaign. This included a series of conferences entitled 'Two Way Traffic in Ideas' which Dalyell, assisted by his wife Kathleen, helped to arrange. 'With Richard Crossman in charge, we did a lot of the groundwork, organising 34 separate meetings, involving scientists and politicians, in different parts of the country,' Dalyell explained. Believing the chances of a Labour government were extremely high, 'the heavyweight scientific establishment, almost without exception, accepted an invitation to attend the first conference in the stuffy basement of the Bonnington Hotel. The famous names rippled through Whitehall and academia, and added to the credibility of the opposition.'

According to Dalyell, the prospect of a Labour government generated an excitement in opinion-forming circles, without which Wilson's words at Scarborough 'would have fallen on stonier, less receptive ground. And without this groundswell of enthusiasm,' claimed Dalyell, 'Wilson would probably not have got his knife-edge majority in 1964.'

SEVEN

EAST OF SUEZ

Throughout the spring and summer of 1963, Harold Wilson looked increasingly like a Prime Minister-in-waiting, with his performances in the House of Commons, forceful speeches outside and clever use of television. Every move he made was planned on the assumption that there would be an election sooner rather than later, with Harold Macmillan leading the Tories. Macmillan's resignation stunned everyone unconnected to the mysterious higher reaches of the Conservative Party. His eventual replacement by the supremely aristocratic Lord Home was no less surprising. The veteran political reporter James Margach claimed the premiership had been thrust upon Home. 'He cantered home in the most elegant style imaginable,' wrote Margach, 'by never trying.'

The unexpected difficulties besetting his opponents, and the convoluted business which surrounded the transmogrification of Lord Home, Secretary of State for Foreign Affairs with a seat in the House of Lords, into Sir Alec Douglas-Home, Prime Minister and Member of Parliament for Kinross and West Perthshire, delighted Harold Wilson. 'It was not that he underestimated Douglas-Home, still less despised him,' Philip Ziegler explained, 'but he saw immediately how the contrast between the two men could be exploited. Wilson would make his case predominantly on the basis of the future against the past.'

In fact, the gentlemanly Home with his grouse-moor image, redolent of privilege and class, proved a tougher opponent than many people expected. Dalyell, watching from the backbenches, thought: 'Alec Home was much underrated. In a sense, it's all very well to say he didn't understand economics. After all, he was the one who said he used matchsticks to do sums. But he also had the good sense to leave the whole economic policy to a man who understood economics very well: the late and brilliant Reginald Maudling.'

On 9 April 1964, the Prime Minister formally confirmed what most parliament watchers expected: the government would remain in office 'until the last months of its legal life'. Against all expectations, Labour's two-year lead in the opinion polls began to shrink. Philip Zeigler noted: 'In the summer of 1964 the Tories were clearly on the way back, and though Labour still started the campaign as favourites, nobody imagined that it was a sure thing.'

When the country finally went to the polls on Thursday, 15 October 1964, an increase in the number of people entitled to vote in West Lothian wasn't matched by the number of candidates on offer: they had been reduced from five to four, due to the non-appearance of the Liberals. Tam Dalyell's principal concern was the continued presence of the personable and dedicated SNP candidate, William Wolfe. Wolfe had been campaigning non-stop in the constituency ever since his good showing in the by-election. His performance then had been dismissed in some quarters 'as an aberration, a flash in the pan'. According to Wolfe, even sympathetic journalists visiting West Lothian – 'there were a few,' the SNP leader commented tartly – dismissed the SNP's forecast that he would obtain 15,000 votes against Dalyell. 'We arrived at this figure about a month before polling day,' said Wolfe. 'In the event we had 87 votes to spare.'

The main election issue was economic efficiency. Dalyell, as the Labour candidate in West Lothian, based his campaign on the policy document *Signpost for Scotland*. This promised a programme of vigorous government planning and direction of industry as the means of discouraging people from deserting Scotland for England, looking for work. 'Those were brave, optimistic days,' remarked Dalyell. 'We were about to emerge from 13 wasted years of Tory rule, as Harold Wilson kept reminding everyone. People could look forward to a better life, thanks to the "white heat" of the technological revolution.'

Dalyell's share of the vote dropped marginally. However, on an increased turnout, his principal opponent claimed more than 30 per cent of the vote, reducing the Labour majority from 11,516 at the by-election to 9,846 this time. Another 6,168 votes separated Wolfe from the Conservative candidate, R.A.G. Stuart, who this time had the consolation of keeping his deposit. There was no such small cheer for Mrs Irene Swan, the Communist candidate, who polled 610 votes and lost her deposit. Dalyell suggested that an election day headline, 'Vote for Scotland', had been answered by the result. 'Although I have profound differences with the Nationalist candidate as to the method of helping Scotland,' he said, 'West Lothian voters underline the need.'

Those who believed the Nationalist challenge wouldn't last were entitled to take some satisfaction from results elsewhere in Scotland. A total of 14 other candidates polled fewer than 50,000 votes between them. The *West Lothian Courier*, based in Bathgate, described the result locally as 'a personal tribute to Mr Wolfe, plus the effect of first-rate organisation'. It believed West Lothian could be considered a 'safe' Labour seat so long as the SNP faced two other candidates. 'If, however,' the same newspaper suggested, 'it resolved itself in the future to a straight fight between Dalyell and Wolfe, the result would be anybody's guess.'

Nationally, the result was closer than anyone expected. At one stage during the night, Harold Wilson was certain he'd lost. Despite the increase in the number of people entitled to vote, Labour attracted fewer votes than in 1959. Wilson owed his victory in no small measure to the Liberals, who added two million votes to their tally at the previous election. The new House of Commons would be Labour 317; Tories 304; Liberals 9.

Sir Alec Douglas-Home blamed the absence of Enoch Powell and Iain Macleod from his government team for the Tories' narrow defeat. 'Had these two pulled their weight,' Home suggested, 'I have no doubt at all that our short-head defeat would have been converted into a narrow victory, and a win at that time for the Conservative Party could well have smashed the socialists, for they could scarcely have survived four defeats in a row.'

There was never any likelihood of Dalyell gaining a place in the new administration, except on the lowest rung of the ladder, Parliamentary Private Secretary. His close friend Richard Crossman was widely expected to become Secretary of State for Science and Education. Crossman had been in charge when Dalyell helped arrange the 'Two Way Traffic in Ideas' conferences. He enjoyed close personal relations with the Prime Minister, and had helped to mastermind Harold Wilson's leadership election campaign against George Brown. However, instead of offering Crossman the expected portfolio covering Science and Education, Wilson made him Minister for Housing and Local Government, with Dalyell as his PPS.

The fact that he was a very junior MP didn't stop Dalyell confronting the Prime Minister personally over the issue. 'I asked him why Crossman hadn't been sent to science and education like everyone expected,' remembered Dalyell. 'He explained, with a majority of four, he didn't think there would be time to achieve anything of importance in science before he was forced to call another election – he thought there would be another election within months, rather than years. He also said he was in a way very sorry, as I might think that all the work of 18 months, which I and others had done to cement the Labour Party's relations with scientists, had been wasted. But he left me in no doubt that the paramount consideration for a Prime Minister was to notch up some achievements in the short term before going to the electorate. He believed housing was the sole area where this could be achieved.'

Dalyell, writing more than 25 years after his highly unorthodox approach to Wilson, couldn't resist a sideways swipe at the woman then occupying 10 Downing Street: 'Today it would stretch the imagination that an MP of less than three years' standing could ask the present Prime Minister why she appointed so-and-so to her cabinet.' Notwithstanding his well-documented antipathy towards Margaret Thatcher, and even taking account of what Dalyell himself described as his natural 'cheek', asking Harold Wilson to explain himself required nerve.

Tellingly, however, Dalyell also recounted the impact of a typically needless row involving the sharp-tongued Crossman and a delegation from the National Union of Teachers who wanted to discuss the working conditions of teachers in nursery schools. 'It was one of those occasions,' Dalyell reported, 'when Crossman was embarrassingly rude to those who were in no position to fight back, and where his friends present could only cringe with embarrassment.' Dalyell thought there had probably been an approach to Wilson on behalf of the NUT, pleading with him not to inflict such 'an awful bully' on them. Dalyell concluded: 'Wilson heeded their advice.' Dalyell disagreed with the view, widely held within the Westminster parliamentary village and throughout Whitehall, that the famously brusque and arrogant Crossman was a bully. With studied care Dalyell asserted: 'He was a thug and a basher, but not quite a bully.' In a biographical portrait of his old friend, published in 1989, Dalyell also affirmed: 'He would bash colleagues when they offered dogmatic opinions on issues that he thought they knew little about. The offence threshold of MPs is not high; and like a basher boy, he did not realise the power of his own punch.'

The two men had been friends for more than 20 years when Crossman died in 1974. For more than a decade, whenever he was in London attending parliamentary business, Dalyell lived as a rent-paying guest at 9 Vincent Square with Crossman, his wife Anne and their two children. Their arguments, carried on late into the night, had a lasting influence on Dalyell. Crossman was 'a parliamentary John the Baptist of devolution', much to Dalyell's dismay. 'One of the reasons I was so supremely confident about voting against my party over 100 times on three-line whips during the debates on devolution in 1978-79,' he claimed, 'was that a decade earlier, the whole issue had been hammered out on the anvil of argument with Crossman.' He believed their friendship lasted so long because 'we were both in our own rather different ways, and could afford to be, issue politicians'.

When Crossman died, Dalyell arranged his memorial service. Years later, following the posthumous publication of his old friend's hugely controversial *Diaries of a Cabinet Minister,* and the outraged response it attracted from some of his former colleagues, Dalyell agreed to write a biography of Crossman on the grounds that he believed 'the dead have rights and one of these rights is, where possible, the right of fair treatment by posterity and certainly by their friends. Those of us who remain have obligations to the dead. I was annoyed by derogatory, denigratory and, in my view, unjustified comment, coming close to genteel and sophisticated slur.'

Crossman, according to Dalyell, seldom if ever had any doubts about his place at the very epicentre of the British establishment. He had been born into it as the son of a judge who could trace his ancestry to William of Wykeham, the founder of Winchester College. Dalyell also maintained: 'Crossman tended to presume that all those he came across, through work or socially, liked nothing better than to have their intellectual sacred cows challenged, their arguments questioned, and their assumptions subjected to loud interrogation. His provocative talk could raise the hackles of his intellectual equals, and when combined with tactless teasing, could leave a residue of burning resentment.' Dalyell added: 'As a clarifier of other men's thought, Crossman was a unique, if relentless and uncomfortable, interrogator. Scrutiny for its own sake may sometimes have been carried to excess. Like a character from Shakespeare, he had an "experiencing nature".'

Crossman had been a star at school, where the other pupils he outshone included Hugh Gaitskell. Crossman never eradicated Gaitskell the schoolboy from his mind, Dalyell claimed. He was convinced that if Gaitskell had lived to become Prime Minister, there was little likelihood he would have found 'a worthwhile post, let alone a cabinet post' for his fellow Wykehamist. According to Dalyell, when Gaitskell died Crossman was 'neither callous nor vengeful' in his presence. He simply said, 'While there is death there is hope.'

Harold Wilson, according to Dalyell, took account of Richard Crossman's 'great energy and willpower' before handing him the housing portfolio, a key area in Labour's election winning strategy. Wilson's mischievous streak probably anticipated a titanic clash between the notoriously short-tempered

Crossman and his senior civil servant, the formidable Dame Evelyn Sharpe. Permanent Secretary in the Department of Housing since 1955, Dame Evelyn was respected and feared throughout Whitehall. On 31 March 1965 Crossman, perhaps wishing to demonstrate his strength or simply seeking new ways of obtaining information, hired Caxton Hall and invited everyone who worked for the ministry to a question and answer session. From his PPS he learned later that a large number of junior officials were 'immensely pleased that a minister had recognised that they might have views. Dame Evelyn's response to the Caxton Hall exercise was chilly to the point of being cryogenic,' commented Dalyell.

Crossman arrived at the Ministry of Housing and Local Government determined to rid the country of the worst excesses of the 1957 Rent Act, which permitted slum landlords to flourish, and brought the name of Peter Rachman to public attention. 'The Labour Party had created an enormous political hullabaloo about the situation,' Dalyell observed. 'Yet, horror of horrors, all the incoming minister found in the files of Labour Party headquarters at Transport House about the affair was one small series of notes by the shadow minister of housing, Michael Stewart.' Intent on seeing his proposed changes introduced with all possible speed, and new to the business of government, Crossman wanted to enlist the help of special advisers, recruited from outside the Ministry of Housing. Fiercely combative and proud of her department's abilities, Dame Evelyn resisted. Crossman insisted.

Dalyell, in the role he described as 'the minister's Sancho Panza', attended meetings in a listening capacity, and openly admired Dame Evelyn. But he was in no doubt that without outside assistance, no meaningful Rent Act would have reached the Statute Book in 1965. 'In those days,' he noted darkly, 'preferment in the civil service was virtually assured, provided a civil servant did not accumulate black marks through incautious advice. Caution was the recipe for a successful caree. It was Crossman's demonic energy that got a Rent Act on the statute book at all, and created a real counter-attack to the evils of Rachmanism.'

Crossman was less successful however in persuading the Treasury to release the funds he wanted to embark on a fresh house-building programme. 'He was aghast when I told him the country couldn't afford to build houses because of the vast amounts of money Denis Healey was spending on defence East of Suez,' remarked Dalyell. Both men believed that the government's determination to maintain a presence East of Suez was one policy the country could ill afford. But they also realised that the Prime Minister would throw his weight against them. As his official biographer, Philip Ziegler made clear,

Harold Wilson 'viewed any retreat from imperial responsibilities with regret and distaste'.

When the first Labour government in 13 years took charge of Whitehall spending priorities in October 1964, Britain was engaged in a near two-year-long 'confrontation' with Indonesia over Borneo. 'Confrontation' was a Whitehall euphemism, adopted in all official documents of the period, which concealed a long and vicious jungle war between the two sides. 'I wouldn't let the Royal Air Force drop a single bomb in Borneo,' said Denis Healey, Secretary of State for Defence for much of that time. 'The whole of the campaign was fought on the ground, using the SAS, SBS and Gurkhas. It was the most successful war we've fought and it's never had any publicity, because it was successful and there weren't many people killed. We suffered fewer casualties in Borneo than on the roads at home on a Bank Holiday weekend.'

Borneo, the third largest island in the world, covers more than 2,200 square miles. Prior to September 1963, when the Federation of Malaysia was created, the island contained three British dependencies: Brunei, Sarawak and North Borneo, later renamed Sabah. Three-quarters of the island belonged to Indonesia. The left-leaning President Sukarno of Indonesia hoped to create a new super-state by adding Malaya, Singapore, the Phillipines and the Borneo territories outside his control to his domain. Fighting flared in December 1962 with a rebellion in Brunei, a phenomenally rich oil state under British protection. A contingent of the Queen's Own Highlanders, 42 Royal Marine commandos and Gurkhas were despatched from Singapore to restore order.

By the time Harold Wilson arrived in Downing Street, there had been a significant shift in the status of the operation. Britain was no longer engaged in a colonial war. Instead, the fighting in Borneo was viewed by the Ministry of Defence as a counter-insurgency war, with UK special forces fighting alongside Australians, New Zealanders and Ghurkas in support of a fellow member of the Commonwealth: the fledgling Federation of Malaysia. 'It was,' said Denis Healey, 'a model of inter-service and inter-Allied cooperation in the face of guerilla action by hostile forces, which were always superior in numbers.'

In a report to the Defence and Overseas Policy Committee of the cabinet on 31 January 1967, six months after the war ended, Healey claimed operations throughout were under 'the strictest political and military control'. Healey also maintained the Borneo campaign 'was a unique example of what British forces can do outside Europe to maintain an international stability. Without this contribution to the Commonwealth effort, the whole of south-east Asia might have collapsed into disorder, bringing suffering to millions of human beings and perhaps inviting competitive intervention by other powers – with the consequent risk of general war.' Healey was convinced none of this would have been achieved if Commonwealth troops had not 'won and held the confidence of the local inhabitants, many of whom had lived until then with little or no contact with the 20th century. The "hearts and minds" campaign was as critical to Commonwealth success as containing the conflict, the continuing jungle patrols and the system of helicopter supplies,' Healey insisted.

The campaign was fought on two fronts, over 1,000 miles apart. Commonwealth naval and air forces patrolled more than 3,000 miles of coastline and the airspace above it. Whenever British troops strayed into enemy territory, they were under strict orders to leave no trace of their presence behind: 'No casualties who might be identified; no spent cartridge cases; no cigarette stubs; no identity discs, photographs or letters from home; not even the heel print of a standard British military boot,' wrote Tony Geraghty in *Who Dares Wins*, his account of the SAS in action.

Dalyell claimed: 'There was a lot of provocation by the British. I can't believe Healey kept what was happening from Wilson. But Wilson and Healey were probably very much in bi-lateral talks. Crossman didn't know – he guessed it, but it was kept from the cabinet. It was an OPD matter: Overseas Policy and Defence Committee, in other words. A lot of people were kept off that, including Richard Crossman and Tony Crossland.'

Unknown to anyone outside a small, tight-lipped group, the UK government was also involved in a desperate propaganda war to win 'the hearts and minds' of the people in the area and to prepare the ground for the overthrow of President Sukarno by his right-wing rival, General Suharto. Details of the operation were hidden from public scrutiny for more than 40 years. A report which appeared in the *Independent on Sunday* on 16 April 2000 credited Norman Reddaway, a Foreign Office agent based in Singapore, with masterminding the campaign. The paper claimed that Reddaway was 'behind stories that Sukarno and his tolerance of the Indonesia Communist Party (PKI) would lead to a communist dictatorship in Indonesia'.

Dalyell wanted to see for himself what was happening. 'I asked the chief whip, Ted Short, if I could go during the 1965 Easter recess. He told me to see Denis Healey, but Healey told me in no uncertain terms that he didn't have helicopters available to fly me around. I tried again at Whit Sunday when I saw Healey with Fred Mulley, the Army minister, and again I was told plainly that the Ministry of Defence wouldn't facilitate me. It wasn't until the summer that my luck changed. Ted Short was aware I had been present at every division, always voting for the government. This was during a period when the Tories were harassing the government with its tiny majority, and there were divisions at all times of the night. I was very fit and didn't miss a single vote. So the chief whip reckoned I was due some reward. And he put me down for an official visit, as part of a cross-party group going to Borneo and Singapore.' Denis Healey responded: 'My problem wasn't so much Tam as the PLP as a whole. The whole of the party was against our East of Suez position, very strongly led by people on the right, like Chris Mayhew. The PLP wanted us to walk straight out. But you can't let down people who have been depending on you. You have to negotiate your way out, so you don't get the Vietnam sort of tragedy. I wanted to get out, and in the end I did get out, and I got out without the tragedy caused by, say, the French when they left territories, or the Americans, indeed.'

Dalyell and his colleagues ended their tour of the war zone with a visit to Singapore and dinner with Lee Kuan Yew, Prime Minister of the infant state. 'We were treated to 16 courses,' said Dalyell, 'at the end of which I asked Lee Kuan Yew if we could have a serious political discussion. With his agreement, we went hammer and tongs about East of Suez.'

The academically brilliant Lee Kuan Yew, who gained a double first with distinction from Cambridge, argued forcefully against the immediate and complete withdrawal of British forces East of Suez favoured by Dalyell. Such a move 'would be disastrous for peace and stability and bad for British interest,' he warned. His preference was 'a gradual thinning-out, so that the vacuum could be filled by the US, supported by Australians, New Zealanders and the British, and a balance found between the regional forces'. It was his perception that the British people didn't want to surrender their world role. 'He also thought it would be harder, not easier, for a Labour government to be re-elected if my attitude prevailed,' reported Dalyell.

On his return home, Dalyell sought an urgent meeting with Harold Wilson. 'I told him we could be facing a British Vietnam in Sabah and Sarawak,' said Dalyell. Wilson listened very seriously and promised to make inquiries. But nothing happened. So then I made the mistake of going round his cabinet, looking for support. I spoke to Anthony Greenwood, Barbara Castle, all those people who'd sat very happily on platforms for the Movement for Colonial Freedom, and they wouldn't touch me. I went to Jim Callaghan and he told me straight that I was being a chump doing this. Dick Crossman supported me in private on my East of Suez stance, but after waiting 19 years for office, he wasn't about to resign.' Dalyell continued:

'Harold Wilson, who never liked personal confrontations, agreed to see me again. And again, he listened very patiently to what I had to say, before telling me it went against all the advice he was getting.'

Dalyell was going out the door when the Prime Minister asked: 'Tam, do you think you're a better democratic socialist than the most gifted alumnus of your university?' Unfortunately for Dalyell, the speed of his tongue outmatched that of his brain. 'Harold,' he snapped at the Prime Minister, 'this is it! You've been taken for a ride by that gifted, eloquent, brilliant Lee Kuan Yew!' Crossman was appalled when Dalyell told him what had happened. 'He didn't think MPs should talk to Prime Ministers like that,' recalled Dalyell with a shrug.

Two years later, Crossman told Premier Lee Kuan Yew, who was on a visit to Britain, that he was guilty of 'moral blackmail' over Britain's withdrawal from East of Suez. 'Our presence may be useful to you, but it isn't useful to us,' Crossman declared bluntly. 'We mustn't have a strategy beyond our economic strength.' Wilson had been told by Lee Kuan Yew: 'Singapore is the linchpin of south-east Asia. If your bases are out of Singapore, the Democratic Socialists are out also. We have no death wish.' According to his official biographer, Wilson believed firmly that 'Britain was still a world power, that the world was a better and safer place because of the British presence far beyond Europe, and that the British presence should therefore be maintained whenever it was humanly possible. To abandon a Commonwealth ally like Singapore might one day prove inevitable, but only as a last resort.'

Dalyell fretted anxiously – and needlessly, as events proved – whenever Harold Wilson visited Washington, in case the Prime Minister's usual good sense fell prey to President Johnson's blandishments on Vietnam. Johnson's powers of persuasion were legendary, first on Capitol Hill, where he was majority leader in the senate, later in the White House – and it was no secret he wanted a British presence in Vietnam to bolster the United States' image in south-east Asia. It was claimed he'd told Wilson, during a walk in the Rose Garden, that he would settle for a battalion of bagpipers, anything, so long as they were wearing British uniforms. Dalyell believed, in the special ambience of the White House, that the Prime Minister could have been tempted to oblige. Richard Crossman, his boss and landlord, believed Britain set too high a value on its special relationship with the US. Working closely with senior US military personnel in Algiers during the war convinced Crossman that there was no such thing. General Walter Bedell Smith, who served as Eisenhower's chief of staff, made it plain that 'in any crisis the interests of the US would come first'. The British, like everyone else, could settle for what was left.

In June 1965, with President Johnson's cautious approval, Harold Wilson persuaded other Commonwealth leaders, including Sir Robert Menzies of Australia and Kwame Nkrumah of Ghana, to join a Special Peace Mission to Vietnam: the idea didn't survive long. Wilson proposed visiting all the capital cities involved in the conflict. Phan Van Dong, the Prime Minister of Vietnam, left no one in any doubt that, no matter how distinguished or well-intentioned, there would be no welcome for the commission members in Hanoi. Soon after, it emerged that Harold Davies, an under-secretary in the Ministry of Pensions, had been sent to Hanoi as the Prime Minister's personal envoy to try and broker a deal with the North Vietnamese.

During one of their regular late night discussions at 9 Vincent Square Dalyell and Crossman quarrelled over the merits of Wilson's various initiatives. Dalyell argued that Harold Davies maintained close contact with the Asians and knew key Vietnamese personally, including Ho Chi-Minh. 'Crossman told me not to be a naive boy and to recognise stunts, even if they were dignified by being Prime Ministerial stunts, when I saw them,' noted a far-from-happy Dalyell.

The war in Borneo did not end until the late summer of 1966, five months after Harold Wilson led Labour to victory in a second general election. In his report to the Defence and Overseas Policy Committee on 31 January 1967, Denis Healey promised: 'Our aim will be that Britain should never again have to undertake operations on this scale outside Europe. The purpose of our diplomacy is to foster development which will enable the local people to live in peace, without the presence of external forces.'

President Sukarno responded to his failure in Borneo by declaring himself President of Indonesia for life. 'I was on a private visit to Indonesia, accompanied by my wife Kathleen and the late Colin Jackson,' revealed Dalyell. 'We asked for a meeting with the President and he suggested breakfast. This lasted from 8–11.30 a.m. because he insisted on showing the three of us round the Meredeka Palace, and all his art treasures. He didn't mind keeping his economics minister, the Sultan of Jog Jakarta, waiting in the wings, along with his generals. It showed who was in charge, as he thought.'

Sukarno's support for the Communist Party of Indonesia continued to worry the West. 'The PKI had been responsible for the biggest massacres since World War II anywhere in the world,' said Dalyell. 'Three-quarters of a million people were massacred on the islands of Lom Bok and Bali in 1966 and 1967. As a people they don't seem warlike, but they can be very cruel.'

The following year, Sukarno was ousted by General Suharto, whose murderous regime survived for another three decades. 'I'd met Suharto when he was a general,' said Dalyell. 'I vividly remember seeing this undergraduate type figure seated at his desk, with the pictures of six murdered colleagues on the wall behind him.'

Having noticeably failed to remain President for life, Sukarno died in 1970. 'We were the last white politicians to see him as President,' claimed Dalyell. 'And I must say, he charmed me at our meeting in the Meredeka Palace. I thought it was pretty remarkable that he'd united all these different islands. He is the father of the Indonesian state when it looked as if it would be different.'

Dalyell considers it was the war in Borneo, and his attitude to Britain's role East of Suez generally, which baptised him into the 'Awkward Squad' and shaped his political destiny as a frequent critic of his own government in the years ahead. Anyone who didn't know him, and he wasn't a national figure of any significance or influence outside his membership of the House of Commons at that time, would have been astonished to hear the Prime Minister of Singapore express his relief on BBC's *Panorama* programme that 'Britain wasn't governed by people like Tam Dalyell'. More than 30 years after the event, Dalyell continues to recall the moment with impish glee. 'My constituents couldn't believe what they were hearing!' he cried. 'They wanted to know, "What the hell has our Tam done?" But there it was. According to no less a person than Lee Kuan Yew, it would have been very serious for Singapore if people like me, and not better people like Harold Wilson, were running Britain. His remarks caused much ribaldry at the time. Lee Kuan Yew knew exactly what he was doing, of course. But there it was, as a matter of record. Britain was governed by better people than me. By Harold Wilson! The Prime Minister was greatly pleased.'

In fact, Lee Kuan Yew, the man recognised at home and abroad as the leading figure in the development of Singapore, accepted that Dalyell 'felt a duty to advance Britain's best national interest'. He also insisted: 'There was no personal animosity between us. We remained friends.'

Dalyell's relations with his own Prime Minister were on shakier ground following his Downing Street outburst. 'At first,' said Dalyell, 'talking to Dick Crossman about it, I thought Harold wasn't too upset about what had happened. In fact, it was my impression he took it rather well: that he didn't really mind letting me have my say. Later I decided it probably raised grave doubts in his mind as to whether he wanted me as a member of his government.'

EIGHT

SAVING ALDABRA

Harold Wilson had presented himself to the electorate in the 1964 general election as the future against the past. The same tactic could no longer be employed barely 17 months later, with Edward Heath leading the Tories. Wilson's response was to present himself as the man of experience, 'who inspires trust by his appearance as well as by his soothing words'.

In West Lothian, Tam Dalyell and his perennial SNP opponent, William Wolfe, appeared before the electors for the third time in less than four years. Wolfe was bitter about the nature of the Labour campaign: 'It did not much matter to Labour how they retained their solidarity: in elections there is only one winner and there are no prizes or garlands for the runners-up.' In his 1973 book *Scotland Lives* Wolfe complained: 'Until 1966 I had never experienced hysterical hatred of fellow Scots expressed against the party which stands for the virtues and morality of freedom. Political debate is one thing, but the dishonest rousing of emotions by feeding ignorance with lies about our patriotic and humanitarian hopes and wishes for our fellow citizens is quite another.' As the date of the 1966 general election approached, Wolfe continued to insist that: 'Scotland, in spite of her problems, gives considerable financial aid to England.' He also perceived 'the local Labour Party leadership were in a panic. We conducted three meetings a night for the duration. Tam had to do the same. It was a hectic campaign.'

Dalyell believed 'the SNP appeal is based on a conscious attempt to tap the wells of national feeling, which are somewhere inside most of us and to claim that it alone has the interests of the Scots people at heart.'

The SNP tried to blame 'faceless, bigoted Englishmen in Whitehall' for many of Scotland's grievances. In fact, as Dalyell constantly reminded his various audiences, some of the most sensitive areas of government in Scotland were the direct responsibility of the Secretary of State for Scotland, rather than the relevant ministry in London. These included education, health and housing: 'the real gut issues of politics'. Dalyell acknowledged 'it was an uncomfortable business, accepting one's own shortcomings'. However, he insisted, 'the truth of the matter is they are the direct responsibility of a fellow Scot, to whom very considerable powers have already been devolved'.

Wolfe later said: 'A lot of people thought we were going to win in 1966. In the event, the Labour vote remained pretty solid.'

On a 79.6 per cent turnout on 31 March 1966, Dalyell and Wolfe both continued to improve overall, at the expense of everyone else. Dalyell, with 26,662 votes, attracted 52.4 per cent of the electorate. Of the rest, 35.3 per cent favoured Wolfe with 17,955 votes. Dr D. L. MacKinnon, the Tory candidate, and the persistent Mrs Irene Swan, representing the Communists, forfeited their deposits, polling 5,726 and 567 respectively. Elsewhere, another 22 candidates representing the SNP helped Billy Wolfe push the total nationalist vote to 124,000 – a considerable improvement on the previous election. Wolfe was jubilant, noting: 'In four constituencies, SNP candidates won more than 20 per cent of the vote.'

Much of the credit for Labour's overall triumph went to Wilson personally. James Callaghan, in *Time and Chance*, acknowledged his 'tactical skill, his determination, his orchestration, and the confidence he conveyed to the electorate'. From a majority of four at the last election, Labour increased its hold over all other parties in the House of Commons to 97, providing an ironclad guarantee that its programme was assured.

However, in a party renowned for the ferocity of its internal feuding, differences of opinion and approach were bound to confront the Prime Minister before long. It didn't help that the 1966 intake of new Labour MPs included many bright, industrious and well-educated individuals who were set on making their mark at Westminster. Harold Wilson was clearly aware of the danger of not giving them an early opportunity to find their proper level. Barely a week after the election he asked the Leader of the House of Commons, Herbert Bowden, to seek ways of keeping his backbenchers 'active, busy and happy.' One idea was the introduction of more committees, in which 'members could air their views and perhaps practise their drafting skills on such issues as health, pensions or education'.

If this marked a significant commitment on Wilson's part to the idea of

Select Committees, it also matched the desire of many on his own side to exercise more control over the machinery of government. Following the 1966 general election, there was a clamour among the ambitious new intake of Labour MPs for parliamentary reform: essentially, they wanted greater control over the executive and a real measure of input into the business of government. Dalyell believed some ministers 'conveniently forgot' that Labour had been elected in 1964 and again in 1966, with a much enhanced mandate, because of a public desire for reform. Many ministers appeared 'to have lost contact with the parliamentary rank and file and were hardly ever in the Palace of Westminster except for votes. They were doing their boxes of departmental papers, participating in ministerial committees, were often outside London on official visits, and increasingly, with a few notable exceptions, divorced from Westminster life.'

In a late summer reshuffle, the Prime Minister moved Richard Crossman from Housing and Local Government to succeed Herbert Bowden as Leader of the House of Commons. Crossman's relations with the Prime Minister had been cooling in recent weeks, due to the latter's response to a crippling strike by the National Union of Seamen. Wilson blamed a 'tightly knit group of politically motivated men' for the dispute, before naming names within the privileged safety of the House of Commons. There was a strong feeling in some quarters of the PLP and within the cabinet that this 'smacked altogether too much of the techniques of the late Senator Joseph McCarthy'.

Dalyell noticed that the 'length and frequency of the early, sometimes interminable, morning telephone calls between 9 Vincent Square and 10 Downing Street declined'. According to Dalyell, prior to his appointment as Leader of the House his landlord showed 'no interest whatsoever' in parliamentary procedure. Now, he began to work wholeheartedly for the rights of backbench MPs to criticise the executive seriously. Before long, he proved himself 'a militant, passionate champion' of the rights and position of the House of Commons. Having 'languished for 19 years on the backbenches, Crossman understood the extent to which the whole of the parliamentary system is geared not to help backbenchers criticise ministers, but to help ministers overcome backbenchers'. Crossman, according to Dalyell, was uneasy that the executive in Britain saw themselves as being on a pedestal, and felt that they gave the impression of not wanting to be bothered with the legislature. He was unique among senior ministers in calling for Select Committees to scrutinise parliamentary departments fairly. Many of his colleagues expected the whips' office to ensure that Select Committees didn't become 'the tough inquisitors of their own Labour ministers which Crossman desired'.

Dalyell's close friend in the cabinet became even less popular with many of his colleagues when, supported by the Prime Minister, he championed the case for a Parliamentary Commissioner for Administration, popularly known as the ombudsman. It would be the ombudsman's job to protect the rights of individual citizens against central governmental maladministration. Some ministers believed that this innovation altered the entire constitution by jeapordising the doctrine of ministerial responsibility. Opponents of the idea were less than enamoured by the prospect of the ombudsman 'delving into secret files in their departments, discovering which civil servant was responsible for which mistake or controversial decision, and enjoying the capacity to get well behind the facade of ministerial responsibility to parliament, to see how decisions were really taken in a department'. Their objections were even more pronounced when the name of the favoured Downing Street candidate, Sir Edmund Compton, began to circulate in Whitehall.

Dalyell had been on friendly terms with Compton since his days on the Public Accounts Committee under Harold Wilson. When he was first appointed to the committee, Wilson told him: 'Just follow the lines of what Edmund Compton advises and learn from him. He is one of the shrewdest, cleverest and nicest men in Whitehall.' Dalyell noted that Compton's former colleagues in the Treasury were in 'awe of his capacity for work and for detail'. As the first ombudsman, Sir Edmund Compton embarked on a dangerous journey through uncharted parliamentary waters. MPs who visited him 'on a rather exploratory basis' found Compton's interpretation of the remit covering his new role narrower than they might have wished. However, as his admirer, the inquiring Tam Dalyell, readily acknowledged: 'By fastidiously sticking to his terms of reference, Sir Edmund Compton ensured the office of ombudsman developed an authority which might not have been the case in less careful hands.'

The introduction of Select Committees was approved by a narrow vote of the cabinet on 17 November 1966. If the decision had been delayed until later, they might never have been introduced. At best, according to Dalyell, nothing would have been heard of them for another two decades. He claimed that Labour was 'beset with problems in 1967 and 1968, and therefore the cabinet would not have countenanced any reform which added to their burdens. By 1969, it was the fag-end of the parliament, and there was no steam left for embarking on reform. When Labour lost in 1970, the idea of introducing Select Committees stood little chance of finding favour with Ted Heath. Between 1974 and 1979

Labour lived a 'precarious existence' under Wilson and then Callaghan. In addition, 'the composition of the Parliamentary Labour Party was by then far less radical and reform-conscious than a decade earlier'. Any forum whose prime purpose was making the executive accountable to backbenchers from both sides of the House of Commons was unlikely to appeal to the ferociously strong-willed Margaret Thatcher.

Against this general argument, however, Dalyell is convinced that Select Committees would have developed in time, even with a Prime Minister who was 'very cool about it. There was a crying need for a system which produced a closer examination of particular problems than parliamentary questions or a debate on the floor of the House allowed,' he explained. 'Also, as you had more and more full-time MPs, it was necessary to find something to keep them busy and profitably occupied. When I was first elected to parliament, the House of Commons was a very different place from what it is now. On the governmental side there were lawyers who came in from the courts in the early evening, followed by businessmen with companies to run, who arrived in time for the vote. Equally, on the Labour side, there were those who were deeply involved in their trade unions. I call them pensioners, although that's less than fair – people who had been active senior trade union officials, who had been rewarded with a bit of time in parliament, and who weren't really going to exert themselves on committees. Certainly, there wasn't the thrust and demand for position and action that we have now, with so many young full-time politicians about the place.'

The introduction of Select Committees pleased Dalyell and his friends, although he recognised Select Committees of the House of Commons would 'never aspire to the power or status of US congressional committees. Crucially,' Dalyell explained, 'they don't have the power of veto over cash. An American committee can actually stop government money from being used. British committees can only talk, examine and write reports, which the executive may not deign even to have discussed on the floor of parliament, let alone acted upon.'

Dalyell was less enthusiastic when Crossman turned his attention to reforming the House of Lords: 'Once you start rationalising the House of Lords and eliminating its anachronisms, by definition you create a rival to the House of Commons,' he warned. Reforming the Lords had been at the forefront of Labour thinking for generations, continuing to the present day under the non-traditionalist Tony Blair. Crossman envisaged a two-tier Upper House, in which only appointed life peers would be entitled to vote. After 1969 membership would be by appointment only: hereditary peers would be allowed to continue for the period of their own lifetimes, without voting rights. The government of the day would be expected to assume a small majority of about 10 per cent of the combined strength of the opposition parties. In addition, the powers of the House of Lords to delay legislation would be seriously curtailed. 'I and others,' Dalyell wrote later, 'repeatedly told Crossman that his dream of being the man who reformed the House of Lords would never materialise and would end in tears.' Later, the changes powered through parliament by Tony Blair failed to impress Dalyell. 'They don't offer any improvement on the proposals put forward by Richard Crossman more than 30 years ago,' he claimed. 'And now they think they've got electoral credibility. I'm an absolute dinosaur on this. I would have left the Lords virtually untouched.'

Despite his opposition to the idea, Dalyell learned a lesson from the parliamentary prevarication which bedevilled his friend Richard Crossman's attempts to reform the House of Lords: without cooperation on timetabling, it is impossible to force controversial constitutional change through the House of Commons. Just how much he took this discovery to heart showed a decade later, when he spent 47 days on his feet in the House of Commons opposing devolution.

His appointment to the new Select Committee on Science and Technology gave an important boost to Dalyell's career. A quarter of a century earlier the committee chairman, Arthur Palmer, had been one of a small group of engineers working at Battersea Power Station, credited by Sir Christopher Hinton, former chairman of the Central Electricity Generating Board, with 'keeping London's lights, heating and cooking going during the Blitz and the doodlebugs'. During the next four years, while the second Wilson government remained in office, the work of the Select Committee on Science and Technology included a study of the UK nuclear reactor programme, problems of the UK coastline, the future of carbon fibres and the Natural Environment Research Council and a visit to the highly secret chemical research establishment at Porton Down. 'Arthur Palmer had the happy knack of choosing subjects that were topical before most politicians deemed them to be important,' commented Dalyell. 'He was the antithesis of a ya-boo politician, and his deepest loyalty was to British industry and science.' When the work of the Select Committee on Science and Technology was brought to a halt by Mrs Thatcher following her election in 1979, Palmer told Dalyell in a voice ringing with despair: 'How on earth could a girl who boasts that she was a pupil of Dorothy Hodgkin ever do that?'

Dalyell's interest in scientific matters had been encouraged by Hugh Gaitskell. 'I'd put down a number of questions on science institutions soon after I arrived in the House of Commons,' Dalyell explained. 'Gaitskell sent me a note saying well done, the party needs people to take an interest in this area.' The lost Labour leader never lived long enough to see how closely Dalyell followed his advice. Prior to 1967 – and what Denis Healey grudgingly described as 'a brilliant campaign of parliamentary questions from the assiduous Tam Dalyell' – few people anywhere in the world had heard of Aldabra, an uninhabited coral atoll located in the Indian Ocean north of Madagascar.

On Friday 25 February 1967, the *New York Times* revealed: 'The Royal Society, Britain's equivalent of America's National Academy of Science, has asked the Ministry of Defence to spare the Indian Ocean island of Aldabra, home of an almost extinct species of giant tortoise and such rare birds as the pink-footed booby and the flightless rail.' The report explained that the British and American governments had been studying the 60-square-mile atoll for possible use as a joint communications centre, complete with a 9,000 foot landing strip. 'The Royal Society contends that these projects would upset the balance of nature and doom creatures that have survived so long only because of the absence of man and the animals most closely associated with him, such as goats, dogs, cats and rats.'

'We wanted the base for strategic purposes,' Denis Healey explained. 'It had been decided that our future operations East of Suez would utilise the Royal Air Force. Now, of course, you can fly direct to Singapore and beyond. But then our long distance flying capability didn't stretch to the Far East.'

There were two main flying routes from Britain to Singapore. One went by way of Cyprus, Bahrain and Gan. The other was west-bound, across America and US-controlled staging posts in the Pacific. The west-bound route required an additional 14 hours travelling time, and defence planners complained of congestion on the route. An important element in its favour, however, was the absence of 'political inhibitions to military overflights of the kind frequently encountered in the Near and Middle East'. In a letter to *The Times*, dated 14 August 1967, Marshal of the Royal Air Force Sir Dermot Boyle tried to explain high-ranking military thinking in an era of 'increasing reliance on United-Kingdom-based forces and rapid deployment to areas overseas where our help may be needed'. Wrote Boyle: 'To be certain of meeting our obligations quickly and economically, we must be able to reach a variety of possible destinations, in circumstances which cannot be foreseen. For this, we need the flexibility which can be provided only by staging posts under our direct control, which will be immediately available whatever the political circumstances of the time. Aldabra is well located for such a purpose. Equally, it would form a useful focal point from which the RAF could discharge its future responsibilities for protecting shipping and land-based aircraft.'

Aldabra had been targeted by the Ministry of Defence as the proposed site of a possible new staging post in the Indian Ocean as early as 1962. A decision by the Labour government to cancel two new aircraft carriers, and shift responsibility for providing air cover for the Royal Navy in the Indian Ocean to the RAF simply accelerated the need for this perceived requirement. Aldabra was part of the British Indian Ocean Territories, a new colony created in 1965, which also included Farquhar, Desroches and the Chagos Archipelago. Colonial Secretary Anthony Greenwood explained the purpose of the new colony in simple terms: 'It is intended that the islands will be available for the construction of defence facilities by the British and United States governments.'

It was hoped, as Charles Douglas-Home reported in *The Times* when the controversy over Aldabra was at its height, to evacuate the local population as soon as construction of the bases was complete. That way the government could 'adhere to the Prime Minister's oft-repeated statement that Britain will no longer build or occupy defence bases against the wishes of the local population. In contrast to most other defence policy decisions,' Douglas-Home noted pointedly, 'the bases will remain and the locals themselves will be removed.'

Scientists considered Aldabra unique in the world because of the richness of its fauna and flora, and an ecological system almost entirely unaffected by man. According to the Royal Society: 'All the ecologically similar islands to Aldabra in the south-west Indian Ocean have been ruined by guano digging during the last 50 years.'

The atoll was a Portuguese discovery which first appeared on a map of the known world in 1509. In 1814, it was added to the British colony of Mauritius. Sixty years later an attempt to establish a mangrove-cutting operation on the atoll collapsed after a number of leading scientists, including Charles Darwin, voiced their concern. Giant tortoises weighing 500 pounds, which could grow to a length of four feet and live for 200 years, were among the creatures on Aldabra that the world's scientific community wished to protect. One leading zoologist, Professor George Hutchinson of Yale University, told the *New York Times* he believed 'an understanding of the factors affecting survival of a long-lived species like the giant land tortoise could elucidate such mysteries of evolution as the disappearance of the dinosaurs, themselves long-lived reptiles'. Aldabra was one of the few places in the world where reptiles dominated the terrestrial fauna. According to Professor Hutchinson, 'the study of island life as a means of unravelling the mysteries of evolution is a science bristling with new excitements and sophistication'.

Ornithologists were equally dismayed by the prospect of a military presence on Aldabra endangering rare and exotic bird life such as the red-tailed tropic bird, the pink-footed booby, the Aldabran drongo and the flightless white-throated rail. As one expert explained: 'The species of rail found on Aldabra cannot fly at all and has survived because the island has remained isolated.'

Aldabra was also home to a vast colony of frigate birds from all over the Indian Ocean. Frigate birds could soar to a height of 3,000 feet and, assembled in large numbers, presented an obvious danger to aircraft. As Charles Douglas-Home reported in *The Times* on 16 August 1967: 'One of the hardest problems may turn out to be bird interference with aircraft flights, caused mainly by the frigate bird, millions of which nest at Aldabra in the dense vegetation on the island. Any serious attempt to reduce their numbers to reasonable proportions would have to be repeated every year for at least three years because most of them only return to nest at Aldabra once every three years.' Sir Dermot Boyle was confident that the problem could be overcome. He also assumed the RAF 'would not wish to proceed' with a staging post at Aldabra unless it was safe to fly. Tam Dalyell hoped the RAF, in seeking an answer to the high-flying frigate birds, wouldn't follow the example set by the US Air Force at Midway Island. There, he alleged, with aircraft lost and pilots killed, they 'tried to eliminate the albatross population of the Central Pacific'.

When it was suggested a base on Aldabra would be an aid to science, making it easier for scientists to visit the island, the Royal Society responded damningly: 'Future scientific study of Aldabra depends on its remaining undisturbed. The disturbance during construction will be so great that meaningful work in many areas will be no longer possible. By the time the RAF station is operational, the ecology will have been damaged irreversibly.'

Dalyell had been alerted to the crisis on Aldabra by his friend Sir Ashley Miles, biological secretary of the Royal Society. 'I was appalled when he told me what was going on there and how the pink-footed booby, the flightless rail and the giant tortoises were all in danger.' Aldabra was a campaign made in heaven for Dalyell, with his high level contacts, dogged determination and growing mastery of the House of Commons, involving as it did science, the environment, government posturing East of Suez and MoD secrecy, surrounding what appeared to be an ill-conceived and under-costed plan.

His serious work began with an adjournment debate in the House of Commons on 25 October 1969, with Dalyell going out of his way to sound placatory. The object of his speech, he explained, wasn't to 'castigate the government, but rather to pose some very awkward and difficult questions, before such time as the government get themselves into a position of adopting any kind of a public posture. In all I shall advocate, there is no question of the government losing face, because the decisions are not yet taken.' Aldabra was a multi-dimensional question, Dalyell continued, affecting the Department of Education and Science, the Ministry of Defence, the Foreign Office and the Treasury. He wondered if £20 million, which had been mentioned as the cost of the enterprise, was a realistic figure. 'I would even go so far, after discussions, as saying that if the various schemes that are planned were carried out, the cost might well amount to £100 million,' Dalyell declared.

It had been stated that the main purpose of the base was to ferry troops to Singapore or Australia in times of trouble. Dalyell thought it was 'absurd' to think Australia would be attacked by any power in Asia other than China – in which case, he argued, 'America would inevitably be involved and British power would be only marginal. It seems to me that the basis on which, from a military and defence point of view, this staging post is required is extremely and deeply misguided.'

Replying for the government, the RAF minister, Merlyn Rees, assured Dalyell that: 'If the project were to go forward, the scientific bodies concerned would be fully and continuously consulted on the way in which it would be carried out.' He also insisted: 'A decision has not yet been reached about whether or not to go to Aldabra.'

The next important phase in Dalyell's campaign was a bombardment of written questions to the ministers concerned. Dalyell's close friend on the Tory benches, John Biffen, thought he 'over-egged his case. Aldabra had no political significance whatsoever,' added Biffen. 'There were no votes in Aldabra. But he pursued it relentlessly.' On 6 November 1967, he learned from Robert Mellish, Minister of Public Building and Works, that an aerial survey of the island had been followed by a visit in 1962, 'supplemented by further visits in 1966 and 1967 by senior ministry officials, with experience of airfield and marine engineering'. The same day, several questions to the Secretary of State for Defence included reference to the activities of a member of the Ministry of Agriculture Infestation Control Division Laboratory, Mr Ernest Wright, who had been to Aldabra and prepared a report 'showing how thousands of frigate birds can be destroyed to avoid bird-strike'. Dalyell wanted to know if this report would be published. Denis Healey responded: 'I will consider whether it will be appropriate in due course to publish an assessment of the problem.'

In his speech to the House of Commons on 25 October 1967, Dalyell announced that he would be discussing the whole question of Aldabra with the Director of the United States Marine Science Programme over lunch in London the following day. It was also his intention, he said, to send a copy of the reply to a question on the implications for India of a new British base in the Indian Ocean to Mrs Gandhi, 'with whom I had an interview in Delhi last year,' he added.

Dalyell made no mention of the fact that he also believed he was on a fast track to the ear of the President of the United States, Lyndon Johnson. 'On a visit to Washington I stayed at the home of Bill Carey, science director of the Bureau of the Budget,' Dalyell explained, 'and he introduced me to the President's science adviser, Don Hornig. I also met Glenn Seaborg, chairman of the Atomic Energy Commission, and a Nobel prizewinner as the man who discovered plutonium. Others on my list were Senator John McClellan from Arkansas, chairman of the Senate Appropriations Committee, and Hubert Humphrey, the Vice-President. I sent copies of my questions on Aldabra, together with the answers, to each and every one of them. Then, purely by chance, I heard that Dillon Ripley, secretary of the Smithsonian, was passing through London and staying at the Connaught. I went to see him and told him what I knew about Aldabra. And he agreed to exercise his right, as secretary of the Smithsonian, to go direct to the President.'

On 10 November, asked if there had been any communication between himself and President Johnson on the subject of Aldabra, the Prime Minister replied: 'None.' Three days later, Fred Mulley, Minister of State in the Foreign Office, informed Dalyell: 'Consultations with the United States government are continuing, but no decision has yet been taken to construct an airfield. All the information at present available to us and the United States government indicates that only Aldabra is suitable.' The same day, seeking to obtain an indication of the cost of building an airfield on Aldabra, Dalyell learned: 'It is not customary to publish estimates of the cost of defence projects before a decision has been made, and before contractual arrangements have been completed.'

Two days later, Hansard showed the Secretary of State for Defence, Denis Healey, facing a barrage of questions from all sides of the House of Commons. Eight other MPs, in addition to Dalyell, submitted written questions on the subject of the proposed staging post on Aldabra. Among them Andrew Faulds wanted to know if, in view of the fact that temperatures on the atoll reached 110 degrees fahrenheit, there would be money available to cover the cost of air conditioning. Healey replied wearily: 'If it were decided to build an airfield at Aldabra, building specifications would naturally take the local climate into account.'

A week later, Dalyell turned his attention to the need to ensure the safety and comfort of the giant tortoises if and when an airfield was built on Aldabra. In particular he wanted to know if provision had been made for a safety wall round the landing strip and artificial watering holes for the natural fauna. Denis Healey's answer indicated there would be a statement by the Prime Minister on Aldabra later the same day.

A devaluation of the pound had been announced the previous Sunday. The attendant enforced savings included a government pledge to reduce defence spending by £240 million. In his statement, the Prime Minister indicated that the contribution made by the navy, army and air force were 'relevant particularly in the sense that they involve a release of productive resources – including research and development resources – for transfer from military to civil use.' When he went on to say that it had been decided not to proceed with the Aldabra project, Hansard records a simple interruption. Dalyell beamed: 'That was people shouting "Well done, Tam!"'

More than 30 years later, Denis Healey insisted that the decision to abandon the Aldabra project wasn't a result of the devaluation or the defence cuts announced in November 1967. 'It was probably useful to Harold Wilson to say it at that time, to show we were trying to reduce our expenditure,' said Healey. 'In fact, it wasn't costing us anything then. And I had already decided it did not make military sense.' In his 1989 book *The Time of My Life*, Healey admitted: 'Since it was inhabited only by giant tortoises, frigate birds and the great booby, we expected no political difficulties. We reckoned without the environmental lobby which won its first great victory against us, aided by a brilliant campaign of parliamentary questions from the assiduous Tam Dalyell.' Years later, Healey confessed: 'The Aldabra thing was a nuisance. We should have given it up earlier in my opinion. Obviously somebody in the Ministry of Defence didn't want to and I gave in to them. But we had no real interest in it. I suspect being nagged to go meant we held on to it a little longer.'

Harold Wilson commented wryly on the matter some months after the project was abandoned: 'You certainly went to the right people in Washington to scupper our proposal,' he told Dalyell. Dalyell's enlisting the help of the secretary of the Smithsonian, with direct access to the President of the United States, impressed Tony Benn. It showed, observed Benn, 'a depth of research, both constitutionally and scientifically, which really puts him in a class of his own in the House of Commons'.

Denis Healey argued differently. 'Having access to the President doesn't mean he takes any notice,' he grumbled. 'I was never under any pressure from the Americans to leave Aldabra. I am sure there was great public interest and I can imagine the various environmental lobbies worked hard on the likes of the *New York Times*. Once I was at dinner in London with Anthony Lewis of the *New York Times* and his family. His children lobbied me on the subject – they were greatly worried about what might happen to the giant tortoises and the booby birds, just like Tam. So, when we finally decided to get out, I wrote them a letter saying they were the ones who persuaded me. They were delighted.'

Those who suffered from Dalyell's relentless attention to detail over Aldabra included the affable Bob Mellish, Minister of Public Buildings and Works. In the course of his campaign, Dalyell had been told by the ministry that 'in-filling for the runway would be mined on the atoll itself. Apart from the appalling damage to the mangrove and other vegetation,' commented Dalyell, 'this seemed to me not to add up. I happened to know about the nature of coral limestone. It is hard and brittle on the extreme surface. A few inches underneath it is soft and chunky and utterly unsuitable for in-filling, let alone as a basis for carrying heavy long-distance transport planes on a runway.' Asked on 27 May 1968 if anything had been learned about the difficulties of forward estimating techniques when trying to assess expenditure, Mellish retorted ruefully: 'One thing we have learned is not to try to build bases in places like Aldabra.'

Fifteen years after the UK government decided not to use the atoll for military purposes, Aldabra was adopted as a UNESCO World Heritage site, administered from Mahe, the capital of the Seychelles. Naturalist Sir David Attenborough can be counted among those who are 'hugely grateful to Tam Dalyell for championing its defence'. It would have been a disaster, observed the world-famous broadcaster, to blight the atoll for the sake of a few years military use.

Dalyell takes considerable pride in his achievement. 'As a campaigning politician, I'd say Aldabra was a great success,' he declared. 'Parliamentary questions wouldn't have dissuaded Harold Wilson from going ahead with the Aldabra staging post. But a question from LBJ, prompted by Glenn Seaborg and Dillon Ripley, was altogether another matter.'

NINE

PORTON DOWN

Ministerial nervousness, civil service intransigence, and the usual expressions of gloom which attended any attempt to improve the workings of the House of Commons surfaced quickly, following the cabinet's decision to add Select Committees to the established Westminster machinery. The process began with two committees, covering Agriculture (classified as a 'department' committee) and Science and Technology, which operated as a 'subject' committee. Dalyell was one of 14 MPs appointed to the first Select Committee on Science and Technology, confirming his current good standing with the whips.

A high profile start, attracting wide public attention, was required to establish the committee's credentials. Dalyell suggested inviting the Prime Minister to explain his views on nuclear power. 'The hornet's nest that descended on my unsuspecting head was unbelievable,' he recalled. 'The government chief whip in a tizzy and that great libertarian Richard Crossman, telling me in lurid language that I was acting above my station in life! In fact, in retrospect, I am more than ever convinced it was a good idea. Why shouldn't Prime Ministers appear before Select Committees of the House?'

Britain's civil nuclear power programme had been in existence for 12 years and, according to one knowledgeable observer, 'a public inquiry was overdue'. There was widespread agreement that the committee performed well in its new role, and in the face of witnesses who were 'articulate, arrogant and supremely confident'. Another reporter suggested that while 'witnesses were appallingly good mannered, they rarely said what they meant'. At one stage, the committee appeared to establish that 'the country had paid several million pounds too much for the Hinckley B station'.

Among its recommendations, the Select Committee proposed a special study to establish whether a body similar to the US Joint Congressional Committee on Atomic Energy could operate successfully within the British system of government. The new body would require 'an adequate, expert staff' and would be expected to deal with 'all aspects of energy policy'. Stonewalled by the Ministry of Power, the committee refused to shift from its conviction that 'closer scrutiny by parliament of all matters relating to energy policy' was badly needed. At least one observer thought it 'difficult to imagine any British government permitting the creation of such a formidable power centre'.

There was a hint of things to come for the whole Select Committee process when the government responded to the committee's findings with a marked show of indifference. One appraisal of the committee's efforts, written by Dr Roger Williams of Manchester University, noted: 'There is no doubt that the members of the committee hurried to finish their report because of the effect they believed it might have on the industry, and because they understood that the Minister of Technology was keen to have it at the earliest possible date. Their disappointment, expressed in a Commons debate, that nothing of importance had been decided or agreed after six months was thus entirely natural.'

Just as natural, for Dalyell at least (given the high level of scrutiny he liked to apply to matters involving the Ministry of Defence), was his increasing awareness that not much was known about the government's germ warfare centre at Porton Down, Wiltshire, or its main ancillary station at Nancekuke in Cornwall.

Porton Down was a dark, worrisome secret at the heart of the military establishment. It dated from the First World War and the days of trench warfare, when Germany first employed gas against the Algerian Division of the French Army at Ypres, followed a week later by a gas attack on British lines. The British commander, Sir John French, expressed clearly his desire for the War Office to take immediate steps 'to supply similar means of most effective kind for use by our troops'.

An urgent search for a suitable area to conduct highly secret and dangerous experiments began. In January 1916, seven months after the first German gas attack on British lines, the War Office settled on an area in Wiltshire as the best place to locate what was then called The War Department Experimental Ground, Porton. The new establishment had been ordered to 'develop a retaliatory chemical capability' to the German gas. Its first experiments, using hydrogen sulphide, were conducted on 26 May 1916, when 'gas from 120 cylinders was released to drift downwind over a system of trenches containing rats in cages and men of the mine rescue team, protected by self-contained breathing apparatus'. Under a new commander, Lieutenant Colonel A.W. Crossley, Professor of Organic Chemistry at King's College, Cambridge, 'activity continued all day and most of the night in support of chemical warfare activity by the Special Brigade RE on the western front in France and in the anti-gas protection of British and Imperial troops'.

Acquired under the Defence of the Realm Act, the 2886 acre site at Porton Down more than doubled in size over the next two years. When the war ended in 1918, the facilities at Porton Down included 'a vast hutted camp' of laboratories, workshops, foundries, offices and 'all the facilities necessary' for experimental work and field trials. While the world awaited 'decisions by the League of Nations on disarmament and on the legitimacy of chemical warfare,' the cabinet agreed to let research work continue at Porton Down. However, in a history of the germ warfare centre, written for the Royal United Services Institute 75 years after scientists first began their deadly work in the Wiltshire downs, G.B. Carter, a former head of the Technical Intelligence and Information Section at Porton, maintained: 'When war began in 1939, the UK was equipped with little beyond the chemical concepts of the Great War.'

During the war, according to Carter, 'considerable developments in chemical weapon design, involving vast numbers of trials at Porton, were finalised'. But it was the discovery, following the German defeat, of enemy stockpiles containing 'an entirely novel nerve agent' and its development which was to 'change the face of chemical warfare and chemical defence for the next 30 years'. Those who argued that atomic weapons made chemical warfare obsolete in the immediate postwar years failed to bring experimental retaliatory work to an end at Porton. A new generation of 'quick-acting lethal organophosphorus-based agents' presented a new challenge. G.B. Carter explained official thinking at the time: 'The UK needed to acquire a retaliatory capability based on nerve agents, as well as an optimum means of defence against these particularly unpleasant agents which posed significant problems, particularly in detection and in prophylaxis and therapy.' The fact that a number of nations who were potentially hostile to Britain possessed nerve agents was probably, as Carter argued, a 'significant factor' influencing such decisions.

By the late 1950s, official thinking turned against Porton Down. Public opinion on both sides of the Atlantic was almost entirely negative on the subject of chemical and biological warfare: in future, it was decided, all experiments conducted at the Chemical Defence Experimental Establishment would be 'solely defensive in orientation'.

The existence of the establishment was a matter of scant knowledge to the public at large. Dalyell and several other MPs believed this should change. They wanted to know how staff at the Chemical Defence Experimental Establishment spent their days. Nobody had told them, for example, about the four service volunteers who between 1965 and 1967 were given the incapacitating drug BZ. It took almost another 30 years for this information to emerge, in a letter from the chief executive at Porton Down to Ken Livingstone MP dated 16 March 1995, which stated: 'The purpose of the studies was to assess the effects of a potential agent which might affect the volunteers' behaviour. The conclusion of the evaluation of BZ was that it could affect the behaviour of service personnel, and as such presented a hazard which should not be ignored in considering the potential hazards to which UK forces might be exposed.'

Similarly, on 17 March 1998, the House of Commons learned from Chris Mullin MP of an experiment at Porton Down in which a service volunteer, recruited on the basis that he was assisting with a research project on the common cold, was 'put inside a sort of gas chamber and ordered to stand in front of a stream of gas so acrid that he could bear it for less than a minute'. His constituent also told Mullin that other gas tests 'left him nauseous, dizzy and weak at the knees'.

On 18 January 2000 the MP for Falmouth and Camborne, Candy Atherton, claimed that more than 20 tonnes of the nerve agent GB sarin had been produced at Nancekuke: 'Rather a large amount, one might think, for research purposes alone.' The Minister for the Armed Forces, John Spellar, insisted: 'Various nerve agents were produced, but only on a laboratory bench scale.' However, he also explained that in addition to the small-scale production of chemicals and agents, Nancekuke was concerned with 'riot control agents, chemicals for detectors, drugs for development as counter-measures, training stimulants and charcoal cloth for NBC – nuclear, biological and chemical – protective suits'.

Detailed information about work in progress at Nancekuke, the country's main chemical weapons research and development facility, was almost totally unobtainable during its operational years. Located near Portreath on the Cornwall coast, Nancekuke was known formally as the Process and Research Division of the Chemical Experimental Establishment, Porton Down. Opened in 1951, a pilot plant was built with a 'capability of producing up to one ton of nerve agent a week'. As the House of Commons learned on 18 January 2000, 'plans were also laid for a large-scale production plant. However, those never came to fruition because the UK decided to abandon its offensive chemical warfare capability in 1956.'

According to a report based on a confidential House of Commons document which appeared in *The Observer* on 26 May 1968, CS gas manufactured at Nancekuke was transported by road to a Surrey factory, where the canisters were made and filled. The report also revealed that CS gas manufactured at Nancekuke was supplied to certain foreign and Commonwealth countries: CS gas had been used by the US Army in Vietnam and by the French authorities against the Paris insurgents. However, as *The Observer* also noted, the UK government 'consistently denied' supplying America or France with CS gas.

On 19 June 1968, Dalyell pressed the Secretary of State for Defence to disclose the names of 60 countries whose police forces purchased CS nerve gas made at Nancekuke directly from Britain the previous year. The reply he received was a model of prevarication: 'No CS gas was sold direct to police forces abroad during 1967. Quantities of CS gas were, however, sold to a British firm which makes riot control devices and exports them to a number of countries overseas, under export licences issued by the Board of Trade. It is not the practice to disclose information about export licences.'

Dalyell had been one of six members of the Select Committee on Science and Technology, headed by Arthur Palmer, who travelled to Wiltshire on Monday 6 May 1968 to question the men in charge at Porton Down. G.N. Gadsby, Director of the Chemical Defence Experimental Establishment, assured his visitors that it was his intention to answer their questions 'as fully and frankly as I possibly can, subject to instructions I have received on security'. Asked by Arthur Palmer if there was 'very much difference' between research for defence and research for attack, Dr C.E. Gordon Smith, Director of the Microbiological Resesarch Establishment, replied: 'The difference lies mainly in the field of development. You either develop the necessary weapon or you do not. We do not. We know how this might be done but we do not produce the equipment in this country to do it.' Pressed by Dalyell on the subject of battlefield dispersal, Gadsby explained it was one thing knowing how to produce a chemical agent in a laboratory; producing it in sufficient quantities to fill a delivery system was quite another. 'This is not really a question of using larger test tubes,' he remarked, 'it involves the whole complex business of chemical engineering.'

When questioned about the need for stockpiling, his colleague, Dr Gordon Smith, expressed the view that if someone proposed 'attacking the whole of China then considerable stockpiling would be required. If, on the other hand,' he added, 'you were considering an attack on a military objective such as an airbase or a vessel at sea – both of which are highly susceptible objects – then you could make enough and just use it more or less straight away.'

Gadsby suggested that Porton Down differed from other military research and development centres in the UK, 'in so far as you have no chemical corps, or its equivalent, in the services. You have no body of professional users who spend their lives giving attention to the operational aspects of this particular form of warfare. Therefore, it falls upon the establishment to do assessment work and to formulate and put operational ideas to the service staff, so that perhaps we are consulted on the operational aspects more than might be the case in other fields.' Dr Smith acknowledged it was possible to assign a direct medical or public health interest to much of the work undertaken at the Microbiological Research Centre. 'You may therefore regard a high proportion of what we do as of civil interest,' said Dr Smith, 'but we are doing it for military reasons.' Both men denied that there was any research in progress at Porton Down aimed at discovering new offensive weapons. They were only concerned 'with looking at biologically active chemicals that might constitute a potential chemical warfare threat'.

However, Dalyell's interest in Porton Down didn't end with his day out in the Wiltshire countryside. On 13 May 1968, a week after his visit to the germ warfare centre, he asked the Secretary of State for Defence if he would be publishing details of any agreements covering chemical and biological warfare which existed between Britain, Canada, Australia and the United States. He was told that there were no special agreements between these countries covering chemical or biological warfare. Nine days later, on 22 May 1968, he sought to discover the extent of Porton Down's involvement with the World Health Organisation. Answer: The Microbiological Research Establishment was engaged in three projects, including tests on human and monkey serum for evidence of infection. The Chemical Defence Experimental Establishment was not 'currently engaged in any work for the World Health Organisation'. Dalyell also asked if the Secretary of State for Defence would be publishing details of 'the commercial agreement between the Microbiological Research Establishment, Porton, and the Wellcome Foundation, in relation to the development of pharmaceuticals'. Answer: 'It is not our normal practice to publish commercial agreements of this kind.'

Laying down an endless barrage of parliamentary questions was a tactic guaranteed to irritate a number of people on Dalyell's own front bench, especially with his stance over operations East of Suez and the retreat from

Aldabra fresh in everyone's mind. 'He would raise an issue and nag away at it forever, whether or not he had any support,' Denis Healey complained. 'Sometimes he had support, sometimes very little.' It also weighed heavily with Healey that 'all our potential enemies' had biological and chemical weapons; although, as Secretary of State for Defence, he didn't believe anybody would 'use that kind of weapon against a country with nuclear weapons because they would be frightened of nuclear retaliation. They've only once been used,' Healey added, 'and that was by the Americans in Vietnam, with tragic consequences for the people. And it didn't win the war for them.'

Dalyell's childhood friend George Younger, now an MP and a future Secretary of State for Defence in one of Mrs Thatcher's cabinets, was an amused and interested spectator of the divisions in Labour's ranks over Porton. 'Tam was always very much a House of Commons man,' said Younger. 'He's the kind of chap who is naturally inclined to look for the flaw in anything that's happening and go for it.'

'Going for it' over Porton Down was a key event in Dalyell's parliamentary career. A telephone call from Laurence Marks of *The Observer* helped seal his fate. Marks explained he was preparing an article on government research departments and their links with the universities, and the two men arranged to meet at the House of Commons. 'I didn't know him at all,' Dalyell explained. 'I hadn't even spoken to him on the telephone before. So we sat on the terrace and he told me about the article he was proposing to write. He wanted to see me because I had been asking a lot of questions about Porton Down and Nancekuke in the House of Commons. It was clear from what he told me that he had been able to put together a lot of information on the subject of the universities and the research establishments, including names. I told him about the Select Committee visit to Porton Down. I also handed him a copy of our report, thinking it was in the public domain. All I asked him to do was check with the secretary of the D Notices Committee to make sure none of it was subject to a security veto. Otherwise, I said, he was free to use anything he wanted.'

A few days later, on 26 May 1968, *The Observer* carried a prominent front page story, headlined 'BIOLOGICAL WARFARE: DONS NAMED'. By-lined Laurence Marks and Joanna Slaughter, the report claimed that universities and research institutions 'which are carrying out work for the Ministry of Defence's chemical and biological establishment at Porton Down in Wiltshire will be named for the first time in a report to be published this week'.

What followed was a detailed account of the visit to Porton Down by

members of the Select Committee on Science and Technology three weeks
earlier. Those named among the famous institutions allegedly involved with
Porton Down included King's College, London; Middlesex Hospital Medical
School; Queen's University, Belfast; Manchester University; St. Andrews;
Edinburgh; Oxford; and Wales. It was particularly embarrassing that these
disclosures coincided with student protests against university involvement
with the government's germ warfare programme. *The Observer* report
acknowledged that some of the work involved might 'contribute to the cure
of disease or the enhancement of life', but it clearly troubled the writers
concerned that 'without this kind of direct cooperation, chemical and
biological warfare would be impossible'.

Marks and Slaughter claimed that evidence provided to the Select
Committee on Science and Technology by Mr G.N. Gadsby and Dr C.C.
Gordon Smith, although guarded, provided 'the most coherent official
account to date of Porton Down's activities. It disclosed for the first time that
the Chemical Establishment costs just over £1.6 million a year and employs
70 scientists and engineers, and about 120 experimental officers. The
Microbiological Establishment costs about £900,000 a year and employs 48
scientists and 76 experimental officers.' According to the report, scientists
'with conscientious objections to any kind of military chemical and biological
programme avoid [these establishments]. Not all of those who accept seem to
have a very clear idea of Porton's activities – which is scarcely surprising in
view of the secrecy surrounding the institution. The fact is that the money is
welcome.' It also maintained: 'It is the ministry's secrecy which has
heightened Porton's sinister reputation, which the campaigners are hoping
to break down. Mr Dalyell, who has been battering away with parliamentary
questions for months, will ask Mr Healey on Wednesday whether he will
follow the US Army's example and officially reveal the subjects of university
contracts.' The report disclosed that a new group against germ warfare would
be campaigning to have Porton Down de-classified. Tam Dalyell was among
those who wanted the germ warfare establishment transferred from the
Ministry of Defence to the Ministry of Health. There was a belief that 'greater
candour' would assist rational public discussion of a subject 'clouded by
emotion'. Scientists and politicians might also benefit from it. As Marks and
Slaughter noted: 'Nobody has forgotten Clement Attlee's admission that
when he agreed to the dropping of the first atom bomb, he knew nothing of
its genetic effects.'

The day following the appearance of *The Observer* report, Arthur Palmer
informed the Speaker, Dr Horace King, that it appeared a breach of
parliamentary privilege had been committed. 'So far,' Palmer explained, 'this

evidence has not been reported to the House and for the moment is entirely confidential to members of the Select Committee.' Speaker King promised to consider the matter 'in the light of the precedents' and provide a ruling the very next day. In the debate which followed his decision that the Select Committee chairman's complaint did raise a matter of privilege, the left-wing Labour MP Emrys Hughes appealed for 'more information from the Leader of the House, before we submit to the Committee of Privileges something which may be regarded as an attack on the liberties of the press'.

Hughes, the son-in-law of Keir Hardie and a former editor of *Forward*, saw little wrong with *The Observer* report. A well known pacifist, Hughes believed: 'We are entitled to the fullest possible information about bacteriological warfare and this article discloses nothing which would be of any use to a foreign power.' Most of the information contained in *The Observer* report had been published in American technical journals, Hughes claimed, including a quarterly magazine published by the US Defence Department which he had seen 'displayed in Peking'. Added Hughes: 'I insist that the question of whether we are preparing, by biological warfare, to wipe out this country and the whole human race is a matter for public discussion.'

It worried another Labour MP, David Winnick, that they were dealing with a resolution of the House of Commons first passed in 1837. 'I believe that in a free society the press has a duty to probe, to investigate all our workings, and should not necessarily be asked to limit itself to official reports,' said Winnick. 'What we seem to be saying is that a Select Committee took evidence which was later published in *The Observer*, but because it was not officially published by the Select Committee the press had no right to publish that information. I disagree.'

When the vote was taken, another 12 MPs agreed with Hughes and Winnick: 398 of their parliamentary colleagues wanted the drama continued on another stage. They included the Prime Minister, Harold Wilson, and the Leader of the Opposition, Edward Heath. Mingling with the rest, like a man voting for his own execution, was the MP for West Lothian, Tam Dalyell.

Throughout the period the committee gathered evidence against him, Dalyell continued to show his head above the parliamentary parapet and made no attempt to keep quiet on a subject which threatened his parliamentary career. Between 28 May 1968, when the Porton Down affair was formally referred to the Committee of Privileges, and 24 July 1968, when MPs gathered to decide his fate, he continued to bombard the Ministry of Defence with questions about Porton Down. An announcement of open days for MPs at the germ warfare centre was an important victory for openness over secrecy in government. Similarly, the amount of information released by the MoD on 29 May 1968, the day after the Committee of Privileges was authorised to begin its examination of the Porton Down affair, surprised many people. Dalyell wanted to know if the Secretary of State for Defence would provide details 'of the research sponsored in British universities and institutions by his department, relating to chemical and biological warfare'. Written answers take time to prepare: the question clearly pre-dated *The Observer* report on Porton Down. In its response, the Ministry of Defence covered much of the same ground; prompting questions, not least in Fleet Street, about the need for an inquiry.

Dalyell, who had asked to be called, appeared before the Committee of Privileges on 19 June 1968. He assured the committee that he had received no 'consideration' from the newspaper for the loan of the minutes. 'I did not even do it for reasons of publicity,' he said. He believed instead that a serious article on the subject could assist his campaign to have Porton Down transferred from the Ministry of Defence to the Ministry of Health – but it needed to be accurate. 'I think, rightly or wrongly, that one way in which a backbencher can be effective is to wage this sort of campaign so that ministers have at least to give their minds to the subject,' Dalyell suggested.

Officials at Porton Down had been given an assurance that there would be an opportunity for them to read a copy of the Select Committee report before publication, and request sidelining. Dalyell's action prevented this. He admitted to the Committee of Privileges that this was 'maybe arrogant' on his part, but he thought the request for sidelining was fatuous. 'Here,' he said, 'I am gravely at fault, I must admit.' Pressed by the Attorney General, Elwyn Jones, on this, Dalyell admitted he hadn't been thinking clearly. 'But in my consciousness,' he continued, 'I had really registered that the sidelining was, shall we say, of no consequence and anything that was in these minutes could be found in the scientific literature. As I say, this might be a very arrogant assumption on my part.' Asked by Duncan Sandys if he used confidential information obtained as a member of the Select Committee to frame questions in parliament, Dalyell insisted he was scrupulous about waiting until the relevant material had been published. 'But in substance,' he said, 'I am quite openly using knowledge that I have gained in the committee in order to frame parliamentary questions.'

Sandys was perhaps one member of the committee who might have been expected to sympathise with Dalyell's predicament. Thirty years earlier, he had been the central figure in one of the most controversial privilege complaints ever to come before parliament. Sandys had been able to ascertain that with war looming, the country suffered from a serious shortage of anti-aircraft guns. He informed the Secretary of State for War, Leslie Hore-

Belisha, that he proposed raising the matter in parliament. Reaction was swift. Sandys was summoned to a meeting with the Attorney General, Sir Donald Somervell, and told he risked contravening the Official Secrets Act – unless he divulged the source of his information, he could face a period of imprisonment. Sandys complained to the Speaker that he believed his rights as an MP had been infringed. An inquiry by the Committee of Privileges was ordered, but before it could meet, the War Office sprang another surprise: Sandys, an officer in the Territorial Army, was ordered to appear in uniform before a Military Court of Inquiry, which had been swiftly established to investigate the case of the missing weaponry. Again, he appealed to the Speaker.

Many people viewed the Sandys case as a straight challenge to the powers of the House of Commons over the executive. Chuter Ede, a future Labour Home Secretary, reminded the government front bench that 'at present the Ministers of this State cannot do what the Ministers of the State of Germany can do'. He also reminded everyone present that under the Protestation of 1621 when 'speaking, reasoning or declaring of any matter or matters touching the parliament or parliament business', MPs were free from 'all impeachment, imprisonment or molestation, other than by censure of the House itself'.

In its report, dated 30 June 1938, the Committee of Privileges which included the Prime Minister, Neville Chamberlain, the Labour leader, Clement Attlee, the leader of the Liberals, Sir Archibald Sinclair, and a number of prominent backbenchers, including Winston Churchill, noted the absence of 'any complete code to be found in a statute or elsewhere' covering parliamentary privilege. 'It is largely a matter of laws and customs and we have not been able to find any precise precedents for the circumstances of the present case,' the report added. Nevertheless, it did 'find that, taking all the circumstances of the case into consideration, a breach of privileges of the House was, in fact, committed. We do not, however, recommend that any further action should now be taken.'

Summoned before the Committee of Privileges 30 years later, Laurence Marks said he understood the purpose of Select Committees was to obtain information and 'get it into the public domain'. His editor, David Astor, argued that if a newspaper obtained information honestly, from a source it believed was acting honourably, and the material was of public interest, it had to find a reason not to publish. 'We did not see a reason not to publish the report having been given it,' said Astor. The Committee of Privileges decided both men were guilty of contempt of the House of Commons. Technically the offence carried the threat of a prison sentence, although the powers of MPs to imprison hadn't been used since 1870. On the recommendation of the Committee of Privileges, no further action was taken against the two journalists.

On the day the House of Commons met to decide his fate, there was support for Dalyell from *The Guardian*. 'Who would deny that the identity of the universities doing research work for Porton Down ought to be known?' the newspaper demanded, as MPs gathered to debate the Committee of Privileges' report. It was in little doubt that the Science and Technology Committee would have omitted most of the information from its report that officials at the germ warfare centre asked to be excluded. 'And the reasons for exclusion,' *The Guardian* suggested, 'would not have been security, but to avoid political controversy.'

TEN

BREACH OF PRIVILEGE

The rarity of the occasion heightened the drama when the House of Commons assembled on 24 July 1968 to consider the report of the Committee of Privileges into the Porton Down affair. It had been more than 20 years since the last breach of privilege case. If those MPs who chose to vote accepted the committee's findings, it would be left to the Speaker to 'reprimand Mr Tam Dalyell for his breach of privilege and his gross contempt for the House'. Among those who disliked Dalyell, there was a general feeling that his behaviour was simply the product of 'arrogance, born of Eton'. Invited by the Speaker to make a statement, far from looking and sounding arrogant, however, Dalyell appeared genuinely contrite.

When the question of privilege was first raised, said Dalyell, he had informed the Leader of the House that he was 'deeply involved'. Following the Speaker's ruling, he asked to appear before the Committee of Privileges. In an appeal to his parliamentary colleagues lasting barely a minute, Dalyell emphasised: 'I received a full and fair hearing and it would be quite improper for me to try to add or subtract from what I said in answer to the committee's questions or to attempt an explanation on any point. In particular, I deeply regret any injury which I have done to the cause of scrutiny and inquiry in the House of Commons.'

Following his statement, Dalyell was asked by the Speaker to withdraw and Fred Peart, the Leader of the House, informed those present that officials of the Ministry of Defence interviewed by the Select Committee on Science and Technology at Porton Down on 6 May 1968 had been given assurances that, subject to the discretion of the Select Committee, 'they would have an opportunity to sideline passages in their oral evidence', prior to publication of the committee's report. An unexpurgated version of the report had been issued to members of the committee, bearing 'an inscription to the effect that it was a confidential report for the special information of members of the Select Committee'. It was this 'confidential proof' which Dalyell handed to Laurence Marks of *The Observer*, 'on the understanding that subject to its being checked against D notices, he was at liberty to use it as source material for a report which he was preparing'.

Dalyell volunteered his role in the affair and did not seek 'at any stage either to conceal or to share with anyone else his responsibility for it'. The Committee of Privileges wanted him 'reprimanded by Mr Speaker for a breach of privilege and a serious contempt of the House'. As the Leader of the House explained, parliamentary privilege provided MPs with 'the minimum degree of protection, without which they could not effectively carry out their duties in the House of Commons'. Select Committees were at the experimental stage and depended largely for their success 'on the existence of mutual trust and confidence between their members and those who would appear as witnesses before them'.

Dalyell was now at the mercy of his fellow MPs. The outspoken Willie Hamilton believed Dalyell's action to be a grievous error of judgment, born of 'a curious mixture of innocence, ignorance and arrogance'. There was a deep suspicion, Hamilton suggested, that 'a good deal of sinister activity' was being conducted at Porton Down. Dalyell had been trying to throw the light of publicity on it. 'Perhaps,' said Hamilton, 'he was trying to do it in a mistaken fashion, perhaps in a fashion that is unforgivable to some people, but at any rate the government have conceded the case to some extent by having open days at Porton. That is not enough, but at least they have conceded that light should be thrown on what had previously been dark places.'

Michael Foot told MPs that what a psychologist might call a 'hate-hate relationship' existed between Fleet Street and Westminster. Very often the public interest, as conceived in Fleet Street, was different from the public interest as conceived in the House of Commons. In his opinion, the House of Commons 'should not be so arrogant as to think that it is always right and Fleet Street is always wrong'. Foot had spent about half his working life in Fleet Street, the other half as a Member of Parliament. It would be going very far, he warned, 'if the House were to insist that Fleet Street should never make inquiries or seek to publish matters' prior to obtaining a report from a Select Committee of the House of Commons. The future Labour leader believed this was particularly true 'on matters of this nature, where there may be attempts by the government to suppress information which should be published in the public interest'. Dalyell's actions had been prompted, Foot suggested, by 'his legitimate and worthy passion to try to get at the truth of this matter'. If, as a result of this affair, people learned more about Porton and 'we discover eventually whether or not this country is manufacturing offensive weapons of this nature, then,' said Foot, 'the debate will be associated in history with much more than any question of privilege'.

Ian Gilmour, thought it was 'plainly wrong' for Dalyell to give a copy of the report to *The Observer*. However, he questioned whether or not it was 'wrong' of the newspaper to publish it. Said Gilmour: 'If a newspaper gets a document in good faith from a Member of Parliament, it is entitled to print it because it is the paper's duty to print the news and not to suppress it.'

Emrys Hughes praised Dalyell as 'a good, young, energetic Member of Parliament with courage. He is obviously not out for a job,' continued Hughes. 'He is never likely to become Prime Minister. He is never likely to become a member of the cabinet. This incident will be against him all his life.' Eric Heffer also defended Dalyell against charges of arrogance. 'I think he is a man with great certainty, but that is not the same thing as being arrogant. He is a man with deep convictions, and when he thinks he is right he says something.' Among those seated on the benches opposite, Sir Spencer Summers, Conservative MP for Aylesbury, was disposed to treat him gently. Dalyell, he suggested kindly, was 'certainly not a knave but most certainly a fool. Mad, if you like, but not bad.'

The debate lasted the best part of four hours. On a vote, the members present divided 244 in favour of the motion to reprimand the MP for West Lothian, 52 against. Harold Wilson, Edward Heath and the little known Margaret Thatcher voted with the ayes. Those against included the future Liberal leader David Steel. Among those who didn't vote, James Callaghan told Dalyell he 'disapproved of blood rituals. Tony Benn hid in the lavatory.' In his diary entry for 24 July 1968, Benn confirmed: 'I went into the lobby because I understood it was a three-line whip. But I just couldn't face voting with all those Tories against Tam. So I saw the chief whip and said "I can't", and he said "don't bother". So I went into the lavatory and I didn't vote.'

Following the vote, the Speaker entered wearing 'the sort of hat an eighteenth century soldier would have worn: very large and very black, it rested on top of his wig'. Dalyell, who had been absent throughout the debate, was summoned to reappear. MPs were ordered to stand clear of the bar to await his entrance, accompanied by the Sergeant at Arms. Tense and uncertain, Dalyell went to his accustomed seat in the third row below the gangway. Called upon by name he stood and faced the chair. Speaker King, 'covered' by his large black hat, remained seated. The verdict of his fellow MPs was conveyed to Dalyell, followed by the ordained reprimand that he had been found 'guilty of a breach of privilege and of a gross contempt of the House'. These proceedings were dismissed as a 'medieval pantomime' by one MP in the course of the day's debate. However, according to John Biffen, who was present, what went on was 'no joke. I am sure it was a very unpleasant experience for Tam.'

According to the *Glasgow Herald* reporter seated in the press gallery overlooking the chamber, the Speaker's words were followed by 'an awkward silence'. Dalyell sat down slowly, as the other MPs shuffled in their seats and waited for the day's business to continue. The silence was broken by the Leader of the House, Fred Peart, who moved that 'the reprimand be entered on the journals of the House'. As the *Glasgow Herald* reported: 'Dr King said he would see that this was done. Mr Dalyell remained in his seat while the House moved on to the next business. MPs who passed him on their way out clapped him on the shoulder and exchanged words of sympathy with him.'

Dalyell admitted: 'It was quite unnerving, what happened. Speaker King, in his black hat, clearly revelled in the proceedings. Harold Wilson was furious and wanted me sacked as PPS to Dick Crossman. Dick refused. He gave me an almighty rocket in private. But he told the Prime Minister to calm down. He thought the House of Commons made a meal of the whole thing. It was very good of Crossman, standing up to the Prime Minister on my behalf.'

Dalyell also felt 'a lot of people were a bit nauseated by the whole process, and were exceedingly uncomfortable about the substance of the issue I'd raised; namely, chemical and biological weapons. Outside parliament, people were asking how the House of Commons could berate me on questions of parliamentary procedure and etiquette, rather than considering the substance of the issue. Remember, I hadn't transgressed the Official Secrets Act, or done anything legally wrong. At the time I thought everyone else enjoyed the spectacle. I suppose it was a bit like seeing one of the village locals put in the stocks. But after what happened to me, it was decided no MP should go through this sort of procedure again.' The Clerk of the House of Commons, W.R. McKay, confirmed that Dalyell was the last MP to be formally reprimanded by the Speaker in this way. 'It is not that the rules on privilege have been relaxed,' Mr McKay explained, 'but that different methods of punishment have been preferred.'

An expurgated version of the Select Committee report appeared on 8 July 1968, heavily marked to show where the committee's original inclusions had been sidelined in response to requests from the Ministry of Defence. A number of MPs supported Dalyell in wanting executive responsibility for

Porton Down switched from the Ministry of Defence to the Ministry of Health, or the Medical Research Council. Shortly before the 1968 summer recess Harold Wilson told the House of Commons: 'I have answered a great number of questions on this. I have said that the matter is continuously under review. I do not rule out a decision to change at the appropriate time, but no such decision has been taken yet.' Asked if it would be possible to arrange for a minister to appear before the Select Committee on Science and Technology ahead of any change, the Prime Minister stressed: 'I would not want the House to get the idea that any change was imminent. I just said that we keep the matter under review and there could be a change one day.'

Into the new century, Porton Down continues its work as an adjunct of the Ministry of Defence, its reputation for 'secrecy and mystery' apparently intact. As the MP for Falmouth and Camborne, Candy Atherton, told the House of Commons on 18 January 2000: 'I have felt as though I have been involved in a cloak-and-dagger operation since I started raising concerns about Nancekuke. Several figures in the county have implied that I am taking a risk in asking these questions. I find that rather fanciful, but respected individuals in the area have suggested I take care.'

Twenty years after the last truck left Nancekuke bound for Porton Down, the Ministry of Defence admitted to the *Independent on Sunday* that 'decontaminated manufacturing equipment had been dumped down mineshafts on the 1,000 acre site'. According to the newspaper, findings by an independent firm of environmental consultants 'point to a series of "hitherto unmarked" dumps at Nancekuke which will need to be investigated, raising fears that traces of deadly sarin nerve gas may also be present'.

Tony Benn believed Dalyell was 'very courageous over Porton Down. The breach of privilege motion was really an early example of a freedom of information issue coming up in the guise of an individual case. I had such a huge respect for Tam,' added Benn. 'I can't imagine ever voting against him.'

Still, the recriminations which followed Dalyell's appearance before the Speaker were deep and lasting. Four months after he was reprimanded for breach of privilege, Dalyell was dropped from the Select Committee on Science and Technology. He didn't bother to conceal his disappointment. 'It is true I am vexed about it,' he told reporters, 'because I had done so much detailed work over a 15-month period on the inquiry into defence research establishments. But since there was pressure to have me dropped, there was little I could do about it.'

Dalyell blamed the Ministry of Defence for stirring up trouble against him. 'They disliked the way I kept asking awkward questions about the Borneo War, East of Suez costs, Aldabra, the Anglo-French Variable Geometry aircraft, the future of the Argyll and Sutherland Highlanders and much else,' he claimed. 'The moment I put a foot wrong, by talking too freely to Laurence Marks, my career was derailed.' Told that Dalyell believed the Select Committee report was in the public domain when he passed a copy to Laurence Marks, the former Secretary of State for Defence, Denis Healey, retorted: 'You don't give a journalist a paper if you think it's in the public domain. You tell him where to get it.'

His departure from the Select Committee on Science and Technology was a serious blow to Dalyell's ambitions. He'd accepted the role mainly to please his friend Richard Crossman. 'I knew how hard he'd worked to convince the cabinet there was a need for Select Committees,' Dalyell explained. 'When it became clear he wanted me to serve on the first Select Committee on Science and Technology, it seemed an obvious thing to do.' His own preference would have been to continue as a member of the Public Accounts Committee. 'I made a great mistake, and it's one of my absolute regrets about my public life, not doing so,' he said. 'It's the one committee that really matters. They had the whole mechanism of the National Audit Office to support them. I was very young when I was first put on the PAC. If I'd stayed for years, my life would have been very different. That kind of experience would have meant I was in a good position to become a Treasury minister.'

Anyone who believed that the Prime Minister shouldn't be above appearing before a Select Committee of the House of Commons clearly didn't lack belief in the supremacy of parliament over the executive. Dalyell ranked high among those MPs who entertained high hopes for the new procedure. But he also learned an important truth about the Westminster 'village'. 'If you have an enthusiasm for a subject, you'd better not be on the Select Committee,' maintained Dalyell, 'because if you campaign on it, you are always thought to be the leak.'

He also detects a fundamental flaw in the present system, which gives control over the membership of Select Committees to the whips. 'Chairmen of Select Committees might want to become ministers, or members of the House of Lords,' said Dalyell. 'Younger people are also looking for promotion. If any of them create any kind of meaningful fuss, putting the work of the Select Committee before the Party, they are not going to succeed. Then, of course, there are what we might call the middle people, particularly with the Tories, to whom a knighthood is important. Do you think they are going to be given a knighthood in preference to someone else if they are made members of a Select Committee and then start making trouble for the executive, if it's a Tory executive?' Dalyell believes that 'a lot of Select Committee reports have been absolutely anodine'. It also troubles him that a Select Committee 'might take infinite trouble preparing a report and no good use is made of it. Take as an example the case of the Select Committee on Transport. Gwyneth Dunwoody, who is a very good chairperson, did a long, detailed report on air traffic control. What notice has John Prescott taken of it? Zilch!' said Dalyell. 'If I had been on the Transport Select Committee and spent six months working extremely hard, interviewing all the air traffic controllers, and then found it was just brushed aside, I wouldn't be very happy.'

In fact, Dalyell hasn't served on another Select Committee since his enforced departure from the first Select Committee on Science and Technology more than 30 years ago, preferring to make his contribution to the work of the House of Commons in standing committees. 'I have been on a good many standing committees, and made a real contribution to them,' he claimed. He also insists his relations with the whips have always been 'rather good personally. I never felt I was being frozen out, as a result of what happened over Porton Down and the Speaker's reprimand. If they are looking for someone to go on a jaunt, I'm pretty sure my name won't be the first that springs to mind, but I've never had an angry word with any of them.'

He doesn't doubt that the Porton Down affair and the Speaker's reprimand affected his career, however. 'I'm sure a lot of people thought I was a bit of a loose cannon. And they were right, of course. I was a very dangerous loose cannon on issues which were extremely sensitive to the government. I wasn't interested in lightweight publicity stuff, the kind of thing that made the papers but didn't embarrass anyone. The trouble I created went to the very heart of some of the most sensitive areas of government policy, especially defence. Willie Ross wasn't alone in thinking young MPs shouldn't meddle. He took the view my behaviour over Porton Down and the future of the Argyll and Sutherland Highlanders, which happened about the same time, justified his attitude towards me.'

ELEVEN

HARRYING THE ARGYLLS

It's unusual for a backbench MP to figure prominently in two major front page stories in a single day. Those who believe there is no such thing as bad publicity might welcome the prospect. Wiser heads might reason that to feature in one story could be good news and career enhancing, but a double dose of interest from the daily scriveners? Pass!

On 25 July 1968 the front page of his country's biggest selling broadsheet, the *Glasgow Herald*, made sombre reading for the MP for West Lothian. The main splash extended across more than six columns and proclaimed, 'ARGYLLS AND COLONEL MITCHELL CLEARED'. A subheading explained that Denis Healey, the Secretary of State for Defence, found there had been 'No lack of discipline in Aden.' Immediately below this, another headline, barely less prominent, reported, 'REPRIMAND FOR DALYELL OVER PORTON DOWN'. In its introduction to the main story, the paper stated: 'The Argyll and Sutherland Highlanders are cleared of the charges of lack of discipline in Aden made in the House of Commons by Mr Tam Dalyell, Labour MP for West Lothian.'

It was the culmination of a frantic few months, involving the survival of one of the country's most distinguished regiments and the future career of a soldier who was assuming almost mythic status in his homeland: Lieutenant-Colonel Colin Mitchell, known to one and all as 'Mad Mitch' following his exploits in Aden. A government proposal to disband the regiment as part of army reorganisation was fiercely contested. A high profile campaign to 'Save the Argylls' set as its target a million signatures. Several newspapers, most notably the *Daily Express* in its great days as a campaigning broadsheet, rushed to its aid. The campaign's supporters included George Younger, a future Secretary of

State for Scotland and Secretary of State for Defence, and the flamboyant Colonel-of-the-Regiment, Major-General Freddy Graham. A popular figure in Scotland, Graham was well known for his unusual moustache, black on one side, white on the other. He suggested calling the campaign 'Save the Badger' after the badger's head which adorned the regimental sporran: the slogan 'Save the Argylls' stuck and prospered. Tam Dalyell, caught in the midst of a fiercely contested war of words, commented later: 'I had anticipated a sharp controversy in the Commons, perhaps some reference in the press, but I didn't expect a major Scottish, let alone British, controversy.'

More than 30 years later, an unrepentant Dalyell recalled: 'It all started in a very odd way. Nothing was planned. George Younger had been making a speech in the House of Commons, saying how important it was to save the Argylls because of what they achieved in Crater. I interrupted him to say that what happened in Crater wasn't so wonderful, and it certainly didn't provide justification for saving the Argylls. Other regiments had won battle honours and were equally entitled to survive.' Also, on a visit to Egypt, with a group of Lloyd's underwriters seeking the release of ships still stranded in the Suez canal from the war with Britain and France, Dalyell had been told that Mitchell's behaviour left a 'terrible impression' of Britain in the Arab world. He told the House of Commons: 'If one asks in the Arab world, one finds that our activities in Aden are mostly counter-productive. This is the view, not only of politicians of the left, but of a great many British businessmen.'

Aden, on the south-western tip of the Arabian peninsula, had been an important trading centre since biblical times. Legend claimed it was the burial place of the murderous Cain. There had been a British garrison stationed in Aden since the early part of the 19th century. Its barren rocks, as well as inspiring a famous bagpipe tune, played a significant part in the growth of the British empire East of Suez. It was crucial as a coal station in the early days of steam navigation. A Crown colony since 1937, it had been granted independence 30 years later when it became the capital of the People's Republic of South Yemen. The last few months of British rule were among the worst in colonial history.

On 20 June 1967, terrorist action in the old commercial quarter known as Crater left a dozen men of the 1st Battalion Royal Northumberland Fusiliers and the 1st Battalion of the Argyll and Sutherland Highlanders dead in the street. Crater was a labyrinth of mean streets, set inside an extinct volcano – dark, hot, dirty and very dangerous. Ambush was easy. Snipers and grenade throwers presented a constant threat. An off-duty party of sergeants from the Royal Air Force and the British Army had been murdered while fishing near the harbour a few days previously.

When the 1st Battalion of the Argyll and Sutherland Highlanders arrived to begin the last tour of duty by British soldiers in the colony before independence, the prevailing military philosophy maintained that 'the best way to keep the peace in Crater was to keep out of Crater'. The man in command of the newly arrived Argylls, Lieutenant-Colonel Colin Mitchell, believed this was 'a policy of appeasement. Appeasement always fails.'

Colin Mitchell had been an army man since the age of 17, when he enlisted in the General Service Corps straight from school. Commissioned into the Argyll and Sutherland Highlanders during the penultimate year of the war, he was wounded in the Battle for Monte Cassino. 'Peacetime' service in Palestine, where he was wounded in the campaign to control the Jewish Irgunzwai Leumi, the war in Korea, the emergency in Cyprus and the Borneo confrontation, brought him to Aden. As a soldier, he was credited with 'a most perceptive military mind in dealing with insurgency'.

Mitchell's belief in himself and his methods, and the capacity of his men to restore order in Crater, was absolute. 'I had no time,' he admitted later, 'for senior officers who had failed to spend the years since 1945 in pursuit of active service.' His commitment to the name and values of the Argyll and Sutherland Highlanders was even less in question. No Argyll would ever be abandoned in Aden, he promised. His officers had been well briefed: 'If you have no ammunition you are to go in with the bayonet. It is better the whole battalion dies in Crater to rescue one jock than that any one of us comes out alive.' To his men, and large sections of the British public, especially the newspapers, the brave and colourful Mitchell was a hero. There were some who thought he exemplified the old values of the British empire. He particularly enjoyed repeating one story: 'The first Briton to arrive in Aden hanged the mayor of Crater from the mast of his ship.'

Tam Dalyell could be counted among those of his countrymen who instinctively disapproved of 'Mad Mitch' and his strutting ways. 'It really got to me,' he told one reporter, 'especially that stuff about the first Briton who ever landed in Aden and what he did to the mayor.'

Crater had been abandoned by the governing authorities following the events of 20 June 1968. 'The enemy was understandably jubilant,' Mitchell noted later, in *Having been a Soldier*, his frank, riveting, and at times bitter account of his military career. 'All the prisoners in the jail were released, to add their weight to the terrorists. In the eyes of the Argylls, this was a disgrace.' Mitchell pressed for permission to stage an assault on Crater. Higher authority feared this would result in heavy casualties. If large numbers of Arab civilians were killed 'the South Arabian Army might mutiny and British troops outside Crater itself could have a major battle on their hands'. Mitchell persisted and was authorised to prepare a plan, to move forward in stages. On 3 July 1968, the assault on Crater began. In addition to the 1st Battalion Argyll and Sutherland Highlanders, the UK mixed force included men from 'A' Squadron, the Queen's Dragoon Guards in armoured cars; a troop of 60th Squadron Royal Engineers; a helicopter from 47th Light Regiment Royal Artillery; a rear link wireless set from 15th Signal Regiment Royal Corps of Signals; and additional transport from 60th Squadron Royal Corps of Transport, all under Mitchell's command. As they prepared to move forward, he ordered Pipe Major Kenneth Robson to play the Regimental Charge. In his 1969 autobiography, Mitchell explained: 'It is the most thrilling sound in the world to go into action with the pipes playing: it stirs the blood, reminds one of the great heritage of Scotland and the Regiment. Best of all, it frightens the enemy to death!'

Two days after the bagpipe sound of 'Monymusk' penetrated the night sky, and the high peaks around Aden began to echo to the noise of gunfire, Mitchell and his force commanded the whole of Crater. His next task was to hold it, in a political climate he clearly loathed. He began by imposing what he called 'Argyll Law' – any man who appeared in the streets of Crater carrying a weapon, Mitchell warned, would be shot dead. Ordered to 'throttle back in the interests of a political settlement', Mitchell risked a charge of insubordination, or at least disloyalty, by bringing the matter to the attention of his troops through 'a special order on the widest distribution for the whole battalion to read'. This acknowledged that the methods adopted by the Argylls to 'dominate and pacify' Crater had resulted in 'a flood of complaints from local nationals and the federal government authorities'. They had been accused of stealing, brutality, wilful damage and arrogance. This was the smear campaign he'd warned them to expect. Mitchell informed his men it was bound to come whatever they did, and some of it was bound to stick. 'Life,' he wrote, 'will become more dangerous now that we are prohibited from dominating the situation in our own way. In the Argylls, we thrive on danger, so let us be even more alert – with fingers on the trigger for the good kill of terrorists which may soon present itself.'

Between the beginning of September and the middle of October, there was a long period of relative calm in the colony, without a single terrorist incident, which appeared to confirm the merits of Mitchell's tactics. Then, as independence neared, bitter fighting flared between the various Arab factions. There were two main protagonists: the Front for the Liberation of South Yemen (FLOSY) and the National Liberation Front (NFL). Mitchell and his men, in their distinctive red-and-white-diced glengarries, did what they could to hold the line, in Crater at least. Mitchell believed he was witnessing 'perhaps the most cynical part of the collapse of British policies in Aden' following the collapse of the federal government. There were now two factions 'openly fighting it out, in an area for which we were still officially responsible'. Mitchell refused to take sides. 'We are impartial,' he insisted. 'We shall shoot anyone who practices terrorism – that is what being impartial means, in Crater.'

Finally, it was time for the 1st Battalion of the Argyll and Sutherland Highlanders and their opinionated CO to return home – to a barrage of praise and criticism and war of a different kind. This time, the main battles would be fought in the newspapers, on television and in the corridors of Whitehall, as well as the House of Commons.

Dalyell's very public clash with his childhood friend, George Younger, occurred on 15 July 1968, during a debate on a Tory motion deploring the government's latest defence proposals, which included disbanding the Argylls. In his usual quiet way Younger, himself a former Argyll, argued stoutly: 'When one looks back, surely one of the things which shines out in the minds of ordinary people as having been successful and having been well done has been the conduct of the Argyll and Sutherland Highlanders, particularly in Aden.' Yet, he complained, this was the regiment the government wished to disband and abolish. 'Can they be surprised that the people of Scotland are raging mad about it?' Younger demanded. Younger addressed the threatened demise of the Argylls with all the passion of a former officer for his regiment. Dalyell contrived to find a place in the argument for his famous ancestor, General 'Black Tam' Dalyell. 'From all we know,' he informed fellow MPs, 'he was a realist who founded a troop of cavalry with a clear and definite operational objective: to restrain the activities of a group of seventeenth century Scottish religious bigots. I would have thought he would have been appalled at keeping regiments for which there are no operational requirements. I would have thought he who founded the Scots Greys would have been the first to have moved the closing order on them.'

To a growing murmur of interest from the surrounding green benches, Dalyell warned that he was 'prepared to use the privilege given to members of the House of Commons, to say in the House of Commons, things that might not be said outside for fear of the courts. I would like to ask some pretty loaded questions,' Dalyell declared. Among them, he wanted to know if it was true that Colonel Mitchell disobeyed administrative and operational orders in Aden and if so, why he wasn't relieved of his command. 'I have to be very blunt about it,' Dalyell continued. 'Is it or is it not true that the Argylls in Aden, far from being the superbly disciplined force they were claimed to be by the British press, in fact suffered from a lack of discipline? Is not that the actual truth of what happened?' Younger, who served with Mitchell in Korea as a subaltern on national service, accused Dalyell of making a 'quite scandalous allegation'.

The following day, Dalyell was attacked from all sides for his views. The *Glasgow Herald* dismissed his contribution to the debate as 'contemptible', and his attack on Mitchell as 'outrageous and grossly improper'. It found his motives 'obscure' and complained that his speech had 'no bearing whatever on the matter in hand – the fate of a regiment whose history goes back to 1698'. One writer observed: 'He admits his irritation at the "Mad Mitch" image of rough, tough subjection of troublesome natives added gall to his words. The majority of people here may have approved, but Tam didn't.'

With the campaign to save the Argylls filling acres of newspaper space, Denis Healey cleared Mitchell of disobeying administrative and operational orders in Aden. In a written answer he also assured the Commons that although the Argylls were tough and spirited in performing their duties in Crater, 'they were extremely well-led and well-disciplined'. Dalyell was present for part of the debate which followed. Unusually, however, considering his earlier high profile, he didn't participate in it. According to one report, 'he had decided to speak only if any critical reference to him was made from the opposition benches. None came. The Conservatives, bearing in mind Wednesday's vindication of the Argylls by the Defence Ministry and also Mr Dalyell's harrowing ordeal in being reprimanded by the speaker for a breach of privilege on the same day, evidently decided that enough was enough.' Talking to reporters afterwards, Dalyell refused to apologise for his actions over Mitchell and the Argylls. But he was 'positively glad' to accept the findings of the inquiry that 'the Argylls were a well-disciplined and well-led unit'.

George Younger suspected that Dalyell had been 'just raring to have a go' at the Argylls, having fallen out with the regiment during an official visit to Singapore. 'It centred on some issue about how the jocks were being treated there,' the former Secretary of State for Defence explained. 'Tam went out, with the agreement of the regiment, to see for himself. It had been arranged he would be met officially at RAF Changi, where his plane landed. But when the welcoming party went to meet him, they couldn't find him. Tam had somehow managed to get off the plane on his own, without anyone seeing him, hired a taxi, and gone straight to the barracks. He was found eventually in the sergeants' mess creating mayhem, asking all sorts of questions. And, of course, the jocks were responding to this enormously well. But it caused a terrific amount of trouble and outrage. Everybody, including the High

Commissioner in Singapore, the General Officer Commanding and the Regimental Sergeant Major, was furious with Tam. For a time, the whole visit was in jeopardy. It was an example, I believe, of the enthusiasm of the stout backbench champion of the poor, as it were, making a counter-productive move, making it more difficult to achieve what he wanted to achieve. But I also believe that visit coloured his view of the Argylls. And that's why he had a go at Colin Mitchell and all of us over the Save the Argylls campaign.'

A century before the Argyll and Sutherland Highlanders found themselves the focus of so much campaigning zeal, public petitions numbered around 30,000 a year. As the *Glasgow Herald* explained: 'The procedure is a relic of parliamentary history. The original purpose of the public petition was to voice the grievances of those who were denied representation in parliament.' The petition to Save the Argylls was signed by more than a million people. Twenty-two boxes containing the signatures were despatched to the office of the Committee on Public Petitions and a copy of the committee's report went to the Ministry of Defence. No further action was expected, however. The boxes containing the petition forms were 'locked away for all time' in the Victoria Tower at Westminster. Apart from showing it had been able to secure a considerable degree of public support and sympathy for the plight of an honoured and well-loved institution, the campaign failed in its main aim: to persuade the government to spare the regiment.

In his autobiography, Colin Mitchell savaged the decision. Bile was heaped on the 'faceless committee men' of the Ministry of Defence and on government ministers who with 'dreary finality' defended their action by 'sheltering behind the decision of the Army Board – another committee,' Mitchell complained, 'with the distinction of having no Scottish representation on it whatsoever'. He had been understandably furious when his enemies in the MoD blocked his appearance before the inquiry into the charges levelled against him and the regiment by Dalyell. 'This was an impossible situation for me,' Mitchell observed, 'as I was still a serving officer and the attack was launched under parliamentary privilege.'

Passed over for promotion, and offered no special honour in recognition of his work in Aden, Mitchell abandoned his army career in 1968. His autobiography appeared the following year. In it Mitchell expressed some powerful opinions and a jaundiced view of life in the modern army, which appeared to him to be 'going haywire, jumping around to suit every politician who had a rush of blood about "reorganisation" and introducing new badges for no good reason'.

For the benefit of any of its readers who might think the campaign to Save the Argylls was all a waste of time and newsprint, the *Glasgow Herald* maintained its only purpose was 'to make a demonstration'. If this was true, then it succeeded. A change of government, wishing to make an impact in Scotland, did the rest. In 1970, the new Tory administration under Edward Heath announced a reprieve. Among those cheering from the government benches was the recently elected MP for West Aberdeenshire, Colin Mitchell. 'Despite our differences over the Argylls, we became good friends during the short period he spent in the House of Commons,' said Dalyell. 'Colin said it was the row with me that made him such a good prospect as a Conservative candidate. So in a sense I helped make him an MP.'

As an MP, Mitchell won swift promotion, serving briefly as PPS to the Secretary of State for Scotland, Gordon Campbell, despite voting alongside Labour and against the government over Europe. Then, in a move as surprising as his decision to become an MP, the man who spent a good part of his military career condemning politicians announced he was quitting politics at the next election. 'Colin hated the House of Commons,' said Dalyell, 'but he also regretted leaving it. Shortly before he died in 1996 he told me, in hindsight, that he believed the "Mad Mitch" image ruined his prospects of a serious senior military career. He also believed it was the reason he was never taken seriously as a politician. And that was something he craved.'

ABOVE: His schooling followed the traditional route for children of the prosperous and socially ambitious Scottish aristocracy – the low road to England. Dalyell (back row, fourth from right) attended Harecroft Hall, an exclusive preparatory school 'for the sons of gentlefolk' near Seascale on the Northumbrian coast.

LEFT: Dalyell's parents, both expert linguists, travelled widely in India and the Middle East, 'doing what they could for the Empire'.

ABOVE: Dalyell (far left) at Eton, where he was 'superbly well taught' and developed a passion for football.

RIGHT: Denied a commission in the Royal Scots Greys, the regiment founded by a famous ancestor, Dalyell was 'deeply affected' by his period of national service which he spent as an ordinary trooper, manning tanks.

Dalyell on his way to Westminster for the first time. His winning the nomination in a mining constituency surprised many people.

RIGHT: One reporter commented: 'He talks seriously but dresses so unstylishly he was married in a sports jacket and kilt.'

BELOW: Knowing 'people in high places' is part of Dalyell's stock in trade as a campaigning MP. Here, on a visit to Washington with his wife Kathleen, he is greeted by the Vice-President of the United States, Hubert Humphrey (far left).

ABOVE: Dalyell has a deep affection for 'old' Labour. On a visit to a conference he meets the man who introduced national service to Britain, former Labour stalwart Emmanuel Shinwell.

BELOW: A succession of Labour leaders, starting with Hugh Gaitskell, encouraged Dalyell's interest in science. Michael Foot believed his ability to bridge the gap between politicians and scientists like the Nobel prizewinning Scottish pharmacologist Sir James Whyte Black (left) would have made him a good Minister of Science.

ABOVE: Leading from the front! Dalyell, who has been an MP for nearly 40 years, enjoys an enviable reputation for hard work in his Linlithgow constituency. Here he helps celebrate the opening of a cycle path.

BELOW: The Binns, built alongside twin hillocks overlooking the Forth and Fife, has been home to the Dalyell family for nearly 400 years.

DAME MAGDALEN DALYELL
1673 ~ 1752

Magdalen Monteith, granddaughter of 'Black Tam' Dalyell,
emigrated to America in 1728. Her descendants included
the 33rd President of the United States, Harry S. Trueman.

General 'Black Tam' Dalyell vowed never to cut his hair or shave his beard until the monarchy was restored in Britain following the execution of Charles I. One of the few people ever to escape from the Tower of London, he earned lasting notoriety as the scourge of the Covenanters. Legend claims he played cards with the devil.

TWELVE

A NATURAL PROLETARIAN

These were bad days for Labour. The pound was weak, relations with Washington were strained. The cabinet was divided over arms sales to South Africa. Harold Wilson and his Foreign Secretary, George Brown, had been unable to convince General de Gaulle that Britain would be a worthy member of the EEC. The Prime Minister was convinced that some of his colleagues were plotting against him. A former Governor of the Bank of England, Lord Cromer, claimed Harold Wilson was unfit to lead the nation and should resign. The government's mid-term approval ratings were the worst since the war. Ben Pimlott, a Wilson biographer, has written: 'In the tea room, in Hampstead dining rooms, and in rumour-filled newspaper offices, innumerable scenarios for the Prime Minister's forced departure were painted in vivid colours.'

The most bizarre challenge to Wilson's leadership – which Dalyell and 76 other backbench MPs from his own side conspicuously failed to condemn – came from an unexpected source, the country's largest selling daily newspaper: the *Daily Mirror*. The newspaper was traditionally a staunch Labour ally, but on 10 May 1968, alongside news of Labour's poor showing in the municipal elections, and on the same day as Gallup Poll findings which rated Wilson the most unpopular Prime Minister for a generation, the chairman of Mirror Group, Cecil King, published a signed leader in which he specifically urged Labour MPs to get rid of him. King's attack appeared under a bold, black, unforgiving headline: 'ENOUGH IS ENOUGH'. His long-term lieutenant, Hugh Cudlipp, commented later: 'It was now accepted, or assumed, especially by Cecil, that he occupied some undefined, unelected but absolute position of authority and responsibility in the country, indeed in the western world, which few people challenged. The media rolled over on its back and gave time on the air, or space in rival newspapers to propagate his views, because they were sincere, uninhibited, different and provocative.'

King, who had been at the helm of the *Mirror* for 17 years, had been saying privately since early in the year that 'Wilson would be out of Downing Street probably within three months'. He foresaw a crisis in which the government 'would disintegrate, there would be bloodshed in the streets, the armed forces would be involved'. His answer to this bleak scenario was an emergency government headed by Lord Mountbatten, former Supreme Allied Commander in South-East Asia during World War II, last Viceroy of India, and an uncle to the Queen.

According to Cudlipp, a secret meeting took place during the afternoon of Wednesday 8 May 1968 at Mountbatten's London residence, 2 Kinnerton Street. Those present in addition to King and Cudlipp were Mountbatten and his close friend Sir Solly Zuckerman, chief scientific adviser to the government. According to Cudlipp's version of events, 'King did the talking and I sat back in my chair to observe the reactions, detecting an increasing concern on the part of the two listeners.' Zuckerman left the meeting the moment King finished speaking, saying 'This is rank treachery', and telling his friend Lord Mountbatten he should have nothing to do with it. Unsurprisingly, Mountbatten agreed.

Three weeks later, the board of Mirror Group turned on King and sacked him. In an interview with ITN, the deposed chairman said he thought his dismissal had been the result of a counter-attack by Labour supporters on the board, who were anxious to turn the paper back to 'a warmer attitude to the Labour Party' than had been apparent lately.

It would have been no less bizarre than the subject under discussion at 2 Kinnerton Street if word of the gathering hadn't reached Downing Street within the hour. Wilson added the proceedings to his 'dossier of horrors'. An attempt to enlist the support of the PLP, with a motion condemning the *Mirror*, caused further gloom in Downing Street. Seventy-seven MPs, many of them well known names, including several former ministers, refused to sign.

'There were two reasons I didn't sign,' Dalyell explained. 'For a start, I am very reluctant to sign motions condemning newspapers, even at the request of the Prime Minister. I really do believe in the freedom of the press. I am also extremely non-litigious. People have said to me I should sue over this, that or the other. But I don't want to spend my life in court, suing newspapers. I am rather a believer in the rough and the smooth, swings and roundabouts. The second thing was I had been asked to lunch by Cecil King. He asked MPs to lunch two by two. I have forgotten the exact year. But I remember two of us went into this enormous penthouse he had in the *Mirror* building, me and Dick Marsh. After about three minutes, King decided I was of no interest to him in the slightest, and that Dick Marsh was of enormous interest to him,' Dalyell laughed merrily. 'I have never felt like such a gooseberry! No, I didn't take to him. In fact, I think he was arguably the most vainglorious person I have ever met. But I wasn't going to condemn him. Besides,' added Dalyell, 'the *Daily Mirror* was the only friend we had in Fleet Street, even if it wasn't treating the Prime Minister in a very kindly fashion. But I can also imagine how not signing earned us all a black mark with Harold Wilson.'

Even the final, long-heralded departure of George Brown from the cabinet did little to ease the pressure on Wilson. As Philip Zeigler explained: 'Brown was allowed to go without a murmur because his instability and turbulence had finally been too much for his colleagues, but the fact his resignation caused no revolt did not mean that Wilson could count on continued acquiescence in his leadership.'

Trouble was looming over the government's policy on prices and incomes and – for Labour – the highly emotional issue of trade union reform, including the threat of legal sanctions against strikers. Powerful figures in the Labour movement such as Jack Jones, of the Transport and General Workers Union, were adamant in their opposition to any statutory penalties 'on workpeople or trade unions, in connection either with industrial disputes or with the compulsory registration by trade unions of their rules'.

Dalyell believed the cabinet was wrong not to separate prices and incomes policy from the whole question of trade union reform. Instead, he complained, everything was 'thrown into the melting pot when Mrs Castle produced her White Paper, *In Place of Strife*.' The determination of the Prime Minister, without the total support of his cabinet, to see the proposed Industrial Relations Bill, complete with penal clauses and the threat of fines for any trade unionist who fell foul of its various provisions, become law presented a fierce test of loyalty within the Parliamentary Labour Party.

The whole issue of discipline within the PLP had been festering since the 1966 election, when Harold Wilson returned to Downing Street with a vastly increased majority. Right-wing MPs, who had been loyally voting with the government, complained bitterly when Dalyell and other East of Suez rebels went unpunished by the whips. Wilson did nothing to improve relations with his wider colleagues when he appeared to suggest at a meeting of the PLP that his listeners were dogs and he was the licence holder, able to revoke their freedom to inflict damage after a single bite. One leading left-winger, Sydney

Silverman, reacted bitterly, accusing the Prime Minister of being 'too sure he is right, too contemptuous of other people's feelings'. According to Silverman, the government's proposed statutory incomes policy represented 'an abandonment of a clear socialist principle in favour of something very like a Fascist principle'.

On discipline within the PLP, Dalyell believed 'the issue was whether or not members elected to the House of Commons had the right to challenge their own government and abstain conscientiously – provided that conscience could reasonably be shown to be individual, not collective, and not organised by a faction'. Dalyell was firmly of the opinion that whenever the cabinet proposed measures which were deeply controversial and additional to the manifesto on which Labour was elected, the party's own MPs had 'every actual and moral right to challenge the government'.

In Dalyell's world, 'small ministerial inexactitudes are part of larger ministerial inexactitudes, small inconsistencies tend to be part of larger inconsistencies, and eventually small Prime Ministerial lies tend to be part of larger Prime Ministerial lies'.

His campaign to stop work on the proposed Anglo-French Variable Geometry aircraft, the swing wing, began while watching television over Christmas. 'I heard Denis Healey claim the Anglo-French Variable Geometry aircraft was the most advanced strike aircraft in the world. In fact, it was still on the drawing board, years from completion. The F111, on the other hand, was already winging its way over Edwards Air Force Base in the United States. So it was preposterous for Denis to say any such thing.'

Ever since Labour arrived in office in 1964, there had been uncertainty over the identity of the next generation of nuclear-capable strike aircraft to go on service with the RAF. The UK-developed TSR2, unlike the AFVG, was already test flying when it was scrapped as part of an earlier cost-cutting exercise. Supporters of the TSR2 claimed it was a first-class aeroplane, which could be expected to recoup a large part of its costs in foreign sales. Three completed planes, plus all the jigs and tools used in their construction, were destroyed as part of the government's directive. 'I understand there were serious doubts within the Ministry of Defence over the capabilities of the TSR2,' Dalyell explained. 'My information at the time suggested it might not prove as safe a construction as some people wanted us to believe.'

Plans to purchase the American-built F111 were later abandoned in favour of a joint project with France – the Anglo-French Variable Geometry aircraft.

Dalyell claimed: 'A battery of parliamentary questions exposed the AFVG for what it was, an expensive nonsense which would have been out of date as soon as it was off the production line. Also, one wanted to know in exactly what circumstances the AFVG would be used. If they were meant to be used in our defence, against what enemy? If there was going to be a war involving the Russians various other things would need to be taken into account. It was never very clear precisely what the AFVG was meant to be doing. Getting the agreement scrutinised a year or two before it would have been cancelled anyway saved many millions of pounds of taxpayers' money.'

There was also strong evidence that General de Gaulle wished to see the project cancelled on political grounds. The idea of an 'auld alliance' between Scotland and France, dating from the Middle Ages, couldn't have worked more effectively if it actually existed outside the imagination of many of Dalyell's countrymen. But the net result was bad news for the RAF and the British aircraft industry. 'It might have been worth taking a risk with the TSR2 for the long-term benefit of not just the British aircraft industry, but of European industry as well,' Dalyell admitted. 'People were giving a lot of thought to the development of the European Technological Community, and where to put scarce resources so that the ETC would thrive as best it could. Military aircraft development wasn't necessarily the proper place for this kind of effort. When the TSR2 was scrapped, many of us hoped the resources used in its construction would be made available to the civil aviation industry. Simply cancelling the TSR2 and going for the F111 was a mistake, as far as our industrial capacity was concerned. It gave a huge boost to the Americans.'

It didn't appear to worry Dalyell that he was creating what one cabinet minister, Anthony Greenwood, called 'a trail of mayhem' for the Labour government. There were those who suspected the familiar sight of the MP for West Lothian badgering his own front bench with written and oral questions over a wide range of defence and foreign policy matters was a front for his friend Richard Crossman. It was an open secret around the bars and tearooms of Westminster that Crossman desperately wanted to be put in charge of the Foreign Office or the Ministry of Defence. He believed, with uncluttered certainty, in his ability to outperform any of the people Harold Wilson entrusted with either role. Dalyell admits his career might have suffered from too close an association with the ill-liked Crossman, although as Crossman cheerfully observed: 'I have to hand it to you, Tam. Your capacity to annoy your colleagues surpasses even my own.'

Among those of his senior colleagues Dalyell seriously upset could be numbered the mightily irascible Willie Ross, MP for Kilmarnock and

Secretary of State for Scotland in every administration Harold Wilson formed. Wilson's first government was barely four months old when Dalyell, acting as PPS to the Minister of Housing and Local Government, arranged for his political master to visit Cumbernauld. Willie Ross was famously and bitterly opposed to devolution, and was for years a constant critic of the idea that Scotland required some measure of control over its own affairs, outside the Westminster parliament. But he also entertained a high opinion of his own importance, as Scotland's man in the UK cabinet.

Dalyell willingly conceded that Ross 'worked exceedingly hard' at the business of the House of Commons. But Ross was also extremely jealous of his own powers as Secretary of State for Scotland. Any suggestion that another senior minister proposed intruding on his patch was rarely, if ever, welcome. The fact that Dalyell approached the Scottish Office with a request for a car to ferry a man with no ministerial responsibility north of the border, simply added to his annoyance. Dalyell learned from the Prime Minister that Ross complained in cabinet about Richard Crossman's proposed 'Royal progress' through Scotland. 'Wilson appeared to enjoy telling me this,' said Dalyell. 'There was a distinct twinkle in his eye. But he also told me to be tactful in my dealings with the Secretary of State for Scotland.'

Ross possessed a famous growl and glare, as well as a mighty voice which earned him the nickname 'old basso profundo' from Harold Wilson. Angry, he could be a fearsome sight. 'I think he took a dislike to me right from the start,' admitted Dalyell. 'Then I stepped on his toes by arranging to take Richard Crossman to Cumbernauld. Later, when I said he should try and find a job for Willie Marshall, the long-serving secretary of the Labour Party in Scotland, he told me to mind my own bloody business.' Dalyell believed, with increasing certainty, that the Secretary of State for Scotland was the main obstacle between himself and a ministerial career. 'Wilson told Richard Crossman that one reason he couldn't promote me was because I had problems with my colleagues in Scotland,' said Dalyell. 'My only problem was with Willie Ross. John Mackintosh suffered in the same way.'

Dalyell considered John P. Mackintosh the most brilliant and stimulating university lecturer to be elected to the House of Commons since Richard Crossman took his seat more than 20 years earlier. Mackintosh was the author of *The British Cabinet*, a seminal work which revealed the growth and importance of secret cabinet committees and the increasing power of the Prime Minister, and caused a sensation in political and academic circles when it was first published in 1962. MP for Berwick and East Lothian from 1964 to 1970 and again in 1974, Mackintosh died of cancer four years later, not yet 50. His close friends included Roy Jenkins, David Owen, Bill Rodgers and Shirley Williams, etched in political memory as the Gang of Four, who deserted the Labour Party during a particularly gloomy period of internal feuding to form the Social Democrats. 'He was a man of enormous seriousness of purpose and demonic energy,' observed Dalyell. 'I am convinced if he hadn't died he would have persuaded Roy Jenkins and the others to stay in the Labour Party and fight for what they wanted, from the inside. He was also extremely blunt in his dealings with Willie Ross.'

During the summer of 1966, Dalyell's place as PPS to Richard Crossman had been taken by the MP for East Newcastle, Geoffrey Rhodes. 'Being a PPS meant I was technically a member of the government,' Dalyell explained. 'Rather than compromise my attitude over what was happening East of Suez, I decided to resign. But it wasn't long before we realised that Dick and Geoffrey were incompatible. I was back doing the job de facto after a fortnight. There was an official gap, but unofficially I continued to assist Crossman.' Crossman confirmed in his published *Diaries* that Rhodes didn't suit him. On 14 September 1967, Dalyell was persuaded to return officially. Crossman noted: 'The change will be very important to me, since a good PPS makes an astonishing difference, even to a minister without Portfolio.'

Dalyell endorsed his friend's view of the importance of what he called the 'Sancho Panzas' of the parliamentary system. They were the 'eyes and ears' of their masters in the bars and tearooms of Westminster and at meetings of the PLP. Among those Dalyell admired was his fellow Scots MP, Gregor MacKenzie, who served as PPS to James Callaghan during the period Dalyell worked for Richard Crossman. A few weeks after Dalyell renewed his formal working relationship with the volatile Crossman, the normally cautious Callaghan, then Home Secretary, spoke off-the-record to a large group of younger MPs at a meeting in St Stephen's Tavern. 'During the course of his talk,' Dalyell reported, 'he suggested to us that the Labour Party's sacred policy of banning the supply of arms to South Africa might have to be revised or even given up altogether. There was a furious row afterwards. Callaghan complained bitterly that within ten minutes of his private speech, the protesters among us younger MPs were lobbying the chief whip. A motion reaffirming the commitment to a total arms embargo was signed by 136 Labour MPs and presented to a meeting of the PLP. Mackenzie put Callaghan's side of the argument to the PLP, suggesting that he was trying to educate us in the need for unpopular policies. Had it not been for Mackenzie's efforts I believe that Callaghan would have been deeply hurt by this incident.'

A key element of the role of the PPS was telling the minister they were meant to assist 'that which he did not want to hear. It isn't altogether easy for a young MP to tell a formidable government and party heavyweight where he is wrong,' remarked Dalyell. His own relationship with Crossman had been sorely tested during the summer of 1967 when he was 'terribly abusive' after Dalyell expressed grave doubts about the government's prices and incomes policy. 'I nearly packed my bags and left Vincent Square,' confessed Dalyell. Peace was restored after Crossman explained at length how, in his view, 'the prices and incomes issue was between the Socialists in the Labour Party, supporting Mrs Barbara Castle, and the do-nothing muddlers-through, led by James Callaghan and Ray Gunter, who were the proletarians in the Labour Party'. Crossman suggested with wicked candour: 'As an old Etonian, Tam, I accept you are a natural proletarian in such matters.'

Instead of proceeding with *In Place of Strife*, which threatened strikers with legal sanctions, Dalyell believed the government would have been wiser to accept the findings of the Royal Commission on Trade Unions and Employers Associations under Lord Donovan. *The Economist* represented a large body of opinion which believed otherwise. It slammed Donovan as 'the high water mark of the particular sort of British indecisiveness which has done the most to damage the country in this third quarter of the 20th century'.

Following a three-year investigation of British industry, Donovan rejected the idea that collective agreements should be legally enforceable, or that trade unionists could be threatened with the possibility of criminal proceedings. Among its findings, the commission proposed the voluntary reform of collective wage bargaining, with settlements agreed on a factory-wide basis, instead of on the basis of different unions negotiating separately. 'Trade union reform,' *The Economist* commented acidly, 'will need to await the arrival of the next Tory government.'

Publication of the Donovan Commission report in June 1968 occurred during a painful period of industrial unrest, inflamed by the sharp rise in the cost of living which followed the November 1967 devaluation and the government's determination to keep a tight grip on wage demands. During the first eight months of 1968, a total of 3.5 million days were lost because of strike action in comparison to less than three million a year during the previous five years. Historian Ben Pimlott noted tellingly: 'Wilson had come to power in 1964 as the party leader who could get on with the unions. He did not want to be dismissed from office as the Prime Minister who was impotent in the face of them.'

On 5 April 1968, Barbara Castle replaced Ray Gunter at the Ministry of Labour, renamed the Department of Employment and Productivity. Incomes policy would be an important part of Mrs Castle's responsibilities at her new address. In addition, with the full support of the Prime Minister, she was determined to press ahead with plans for trade union reform. As David Butler and Michael Pinto-Duschinsky observed in their appraisal of the period preceding the 1970 general election: 'It is an indication of the deep effects on the Labour Party of two and a half years of almost non-stop crisis, and of the keen desire to get the balance of payments right by any means, that a Labour government was prepared to reintroduce penal sanctions against trade unionists in general for the first time in a century – and to do so with hardly a thought about the ideological implications of its actions.' Dalyell numbered among those who blamed Barbara Castle for the worst of the difficulties raised by the Government's furiously controversial reform document, *In Place of Strife.* 'Dealing with George Woodcock and Vic Feather at the TUC was pretty difficult,' he conceded. 'But she was absolutely put off course by the Girling strike and the idea that a few people could hold the whole of British industry by the throat.'

The strike at Girling, a small brake manufacturing company in Cheshire, centred on a demarcation dispute involving 22 workers, which threatened to engulf a large part of the motor industry. Supporters of the proposed legislation argued it was the type of action which 'underlined the need for legislation to provide a compulsory conciliation pause'.

At least one leading trade unionist, Jack Jones of the Transport and General Workers Union, decided that Donovan's findings 'were more favourable to my way of thinking than anything I dared hope'. He also believed: 'The reforms proposed by the Donovan Commission can make an immediate contribution to industrial peace, higher productivity, and higher living standards in the engineering industry, if employers will give the lead.' Dalyell maintained: 'If Barbara Castle had been content to legislate down the lines of the Donovan Report, things would have been different. It was a mistake to move Ray Gunter from the Ministry of Labour. The government was in trouble because Gunter wasn't around to carry out the reforms.' It was a fallacy, the TUC insisted, to imagine that the imposition of sanctions would solve industrial disputes. Jack Jones complained: 'Wilson and Castle were basically academics and it was difficult to persuade them to see things from a shop floor angle.'

Prime Minister and Secretary of State battled on into the following year in a doomed attempt to force *In Place of Strife* onto the Statute Book. Wilson and Castle 'believed this was a crucial moment in the party's relations with the trade unions. If we were to allow them to refuse to change any of their procedures in the national interest,' wrote Castle, 'the government was effectively their prisoner.'

Right from the beginning, it was evident that the cabinet was seriously divided over the issue. James Callaghan voted with the unions at a meeting of the Labour Party's national executive. 'George Brown was outraged by Jim's disloyalty and told him so,' wrote Castle. In the end, the weight of opinion was forcefully opposed to the legislation. Harold Wilson and Barbara Castle 'developed a contempt for our vacillating colleagues'. But they were almost totally isolated. 'Harold could easily have extricated himself, but he had entered into the spirit of the battle enthusiastically,' Castle recorded. 'I got the impression that the idea of resigning over an issue like this positively appealed to him.'

Most commentators agreed that the end result, a 'solemn and binding undertaking' from the TUC to intervene directly in industrial disputes in an effort to reach a solution, was a meaningless face saver. 'To say,' remarked Dalyell, 'that the atmosphere between the government and the trade unions became sour over *In Place of Strife* would be an understatement. It became rancid. And the internal wounds paved the way for defeat in 1970.'

A catastrophic run of seven by-election defeats between 21 September 1967 and 28 March 1968 provided dismal reading for Labour strategists looking ahead to the next general election. Six of the seven seats, fought in England, were won by Conservative candidates and included two gains, with the Liberals coming second on one occasion. But though seriously unwelcome in themselves – a similar performance at the next general election, as one analyst noted, would bring 'a disaster of 1931 proportions' – results at Cambridge, Walthamstow West, West Derbyshire, Meriden, Acton and Dudley in the course of that dreadful six-month period for Labour could be dismissed as 'business as usual' – with the two main parties winning and losing seats at Westminster.

Not so the result of the by-election at Hamilton, in Lanarkshire, on 2 November 1967, won by Mrs Winifred Ewing, representing the Scottish National Party. On her way to victory at Hamilton, the formidable, volatile Mrs Ewing, a solicitor in Glasgow before switching to full-time politics, secured 46 per cent of the vote and overturned a Labour majority of 16,000. 'Her election went off like an electoral atom bomb in the Labour establishment,' Dalyell recorded. 'To say that Party leaders in Scotland were shell-shocked for weeks is an understatement.'

Populist, passionate, clever with the media, and a good platform performer who never ceased to extol the virtues of independence, her victory at Hamilton made Winnie Ewing a political star in Scotland. But her victory, in the sense that it demonstrated a rising popular tide in favour of a Scottish Parliament, never mind full-scale independence, failed to impress Dalyell. 'People vote for a particular party for all sorts of dubious reasons which may have next to nothing to do with that party's politics,' he argued lugubriously.

In fact, Mrs Ewing wasn't the first member of her party to win a seat at Westminster. Shortly before World War II ended, Dr Robert MacIntyre won a by-election at Motherwell. His success was due almost entirely to the absence of the Conservatives, bound by a wartime agreement between the main parties not to contest vacant seats. MacIntyre began his Westminster career with a protest against the Speaker's insistence that he required sponsors. Six weeks later, Attlee informed Churchill, in a note from Blackpool, that Labour would be leaving the coalition. Normal political hostilities were immediately resumed. Faced with a full-scale challenge, MacIntyre's brief career as an MP ended at the general election.

Twenty years later, nearby Hamilton was the second safest seat in Scotland. For more than 20 years it had been represented at Westminster by Tom Fraser, a former miner. Fraser served as a junior minister at the Scottish Office in Attlee's postwar administration. He also spent a brief period as Minister of Transport in Harold Wilson's first cabinet. Chairmanship of the North of Scotland Hydro-Electric Board was judged a suitable reward for a lifetime's service to the Labour Party, and duly dispensed by the Secretary of State for Scotland, Willie Ross. Even in his worst nightmare, it is unlikely that the tough and abrasive Ross foresaw the consequences of his kindly act. 'Ten days before polling, I told Ross and Harold Wilson that the SNP would win Hamilton,' said Dalyell. 'Neither of them could believe it. Harold Wilson was incredulous and said I must be mistaken.'

Willie Ross, perhaps even more so than the Prime Minister, could have been indulging in wishful thinking when he dismissed Dalyell's warning of an electoral calamity awaiting Labour at Hamilton. For years, he had been damning in his condemnation of the SNP's attempts to gain a political foothold in Scotland, insisting to his London colleagues that nothing would come of their exertions. On the rare occasions he bothered to acknowledge their existence, his reviled opponents were usually branded the 'Scottish Narks Party' or the 'Tartan Tories', in the course of a ferociously calculated litany of abuse guaranteed to raise a cheer at Labour rallies throughout Scotland.

According to Dalyell: 'The government was divided over how Mrs Ewing's victory at Hamilton should be interpreted. A number of ministers, with Willie Ross among them, thought the government should treat the SNP successes at Hamilton and in local elections as a passing phenomenon, unrepresentative of the real views of the people of Scotland. Others believed deeper feelings were at work in both Scotland and Wales. They wanted the government to try and find out what these feelings were, and how they could most reasonably be satisfied – if only for cosmetic and political reasons.'

Dalyell's friend, Richard Crossman, thought the whole thing should be looked at not merely in terms of 'appeasing the Scottish and the Welsh nationalists, but as sensible, regional devolution.' In one late evening conversation at 9 Vincent Square, Crossman revealed he had been bombarding the Prime Minister with memos and minutes over a period of weeks. 'Crossman judged the Prime Minister was approaching the problem with considerable caution, and holding his options open,' remarked Dalyell.

Years later, when the need to contain the SNP caused a panic in Labour ranks inside and outside Scotland, an impatient Dalyell didn't hesitate to complain about the haste with which his colleagues addressed this new-found priority. In the immediate aftermath of the 1966 general election, for example, no minister in a position to do so made 'even a token gesture' in the direction of the SNP. Similarly, in the wake of Mrs Ewing's by-election victory at Hamilton, 'a large and distinguished company of ministers and most Members of Parliament' agreed with Willie Ross that the SNP's electoral advance was 'nothing more than a flash in the pan and was best dealt with in dismissive and scornful terms.'

A Royal Commission on the Constitution hardly merited that description. Nevertheless a good many Whitehall doubters suspected they had been treated to a classic fudge, crudely orchestrated by the Prime Minister, Harold Wilson, and his Home Secretary, James Callaghan, for short-term political gain. Dalyell disagreed. He maintained: 'Nationalism was something new on the political scene: politicians had to ascertain whether it was a flash in the pan or a long-term issue, and how the grievances which gave rise to it could best be met. Setting up a commission did, of course, have the additional benefit of putting the problem on ice: but to have acted precipitately without trying to find out what should be done for Scotland and Wales would have been extremely foolish.' The appointment of a Royal Commission on the Constitution suited his purpose. But this consideration didn't prevent Dalyell from offering a nod to his conscience. One couldn't help feeling, he mused, that 'neither the Prime Minister or the Home Secretary showed much interest in their brainchild once it had been established.'

There were now no fewer than three Royal Commissions at work on the governance of Britain: one on the constitution, headed by Lord Crowther, a former editor of The Economist; one on local government in England and Wales under Lord Redcliffe-Maud, a senior civil servant and former ambassador, and one on local government in Scotland under a Scottish judge, Lord Wheatley. Both men offered to suspend their deliberations to give Lord Crowther, with his wider remit, time to report. But their offer was refused – a sign to some people, including Dalyell, that the Wilson government wasn't serious about the subject of devolution. Harold Wilson and James Callaghan, he decided, weren't interested 'in meddling with the constitution, finding it boring and irrelevant to the real problems facing the government.'

THIRTEEN

DALINTOBER STREET

Labour expected to win the 1970 general election. They didn't. Opinion polls showed Harold Wilson on track to become the first Prime Minister to win three elections in a row since Lord Liverpool a century and a half earlier. Instead, the man framed in front of the famous black door smiling for the cameras on the morning of Friday 19 June 1970 was the Conservative leader, Edward Heath. A year earlier, a Tory victory would have been less surprising. Then the Labour Party, after years of internal wrangling over major policy issues such as prices and incomes, the role of the trade unions, defence and Europe, had been trailing hopelessly in the polls. 'Between 1964 and 1966, when the government survived on a tiny majority, Wilson was excellent,' said Dalyell. 'Then he won a tremendous victory, with a large majority, and things fell apart. Having won comfortably in 1966, the government went to sleep for three months. To be fair,' added Dalyell, 'people were absolutely exhausted. Never discount the physical exhaustion of those times. Harassed constantly by the Opposition . . . on our feet until three and four in the morning for 17 months – that's what happens when you have a majority of five.'

By the summer of 1966, the balance of payments appeared to be spinning out of control and the pound was faring badly in the world currency markets. Harold Wilson claimed the government had been blown off course by the seven-week-long seamen's strike. Dalyell dates his decline from 20 July 1966, when he told the House of Commons that the country was living beyond its means. As a result, said the Prime Minister, the government was 'calling for a six-month standstill on wages, salaries and other types of income, followed by a further six months of severe restraint, and for a similar standstill on prices'. Purchase tax, income tax, investments, dividends, hire purchase, telephone charges, foreign aid and holidays abroad were all covered in a wide-ranging emergency package, aimed at raising money and reducing personal spending. 'The problems with which I have been dealing are problems that have beset Britain's economy virtually since the end of the war,' said Wilson. 'The unsung achievements of keen executives and of hard-working, responsible trade unionists, of inventive scientists and creative designers, are all too often overshadowed by attitudes of selfishness and indifference, of indolence and indiscipline on both sides of industry.' Dalyell commented: 'That speech, and the emergency measures which accompanied it, almost finished him. The emergency measures were meant to stave off devaluation. They failed. Devaluation happened anyway, the following year.'

Between his July 1966 statement and the next election, Harold Wilson lived in fear of a *putsch*. His continued occupancy of Downing Street owed much to the fact that none of the main contenders was prepared to risk a leadership challenge for fear of losing, either to Wilson himself or to a leading rival. Richard Crossman, a close Wilson watcher, detected a change in his old friend's attitude towards the Labour Party and the trade unions. He told Dalyell that Wilson was 'in danger of becoming a Lloyd George figure, detached from the party, feeling not much loyalty or affection for the organisation. For Crossman there was nothing left of Wilson as a leader or a leftist,' Dalyell added. 'He was simply a figure posturing there in the middle, with no strategy, except to stay as Prime Minister for as long as possible.' James Callaghan, who had strong personal interest in the succession, took a different view. In his biography *Time and Chance*, he wrote glowingly of Wilson: 'When we were in difficulties, his sagacity and sang-froid were beyond doubt, as was his kindliness to his colleagues.'

Far from complaining about Wilson hanging on in Downing Street for as long as possible, to suit Richard Crossman's jaundiced view of the Prime Minister's performance, Dalyell hoped Wilson would delay the election until October 1970 or even March the following year, to permit 'all-but-finished measures' in the Department of Health and Social Security, where he was serving as PPS to Crossman, to become law. Dalyell told party workers he was 'honoured to go forward as the unanimous choice of the Labour Cooperative and Trade Union Movement in West Lothian'. His misgivings about the government's performance on several fronts were quietly forgotten as he urged them to help ensure the return of a Labour government. In private, he believed Harold Wilson had 'improved a bit' since 1968. Publicly, he gushed about the Labour government still gathering steam 'under that astonishingly resilient and resourceful man, the Prime Minister'. Indeed, he claimed, since the beginning of 1968 'we have become probably the most effective reforming government of the century'. Attlee's administration, according to Dalyell, started at a terrific pace in 1945 and achieved wonders in its first three years before beginning to run out of steam. Although it hadn't yet succeeded in achieving a place in the economic sunshine, the present administration had been successful in 'heaving' Britain out of the economic rain into more stable weather. According to Dalyell, it would be a dreadful pity if we 'allowed men of less vision to control our nation's affairs'.

He emphasised that he didn't intend to suggest Labour deserved gratitude, having borne 'the heat and burden of the day': there was no place for gratitude in politics. 'It is rather that Harold Wilson and his team, having fought to achieve the basic prosperity, and correct the balance of payments crisis, have a clear idea of the kind of Britain we ought to be building,' Dalyell explained. 'It makes sense to give us the chance. It makes sense to allow us to continue working on our unfinished business.'

To the SNP, Dalyell himself represented 'unfinished business'. For the fourth time in eight years their chosen candidate in West Lothian was William Wolfe, now the undisputed leader of the SNP. It was difficult to assess his chances, or those of his party, with any accuracy. In the municipal elections which followed Winnie Ewing's talismanic victory at Hamilton in November 1967, the SNP made substantial gains; winning a majority of the vote nationwide.

This highly creditable, and, for some, worrying performance, which included capturing 35.9 per cent of the vote in Glasgow, suggested the nationalists were about to emerge as a major political force in Scotland. However, they fared badly in the next municipal elections, held in May 1970, when, according to William Wolfe, the Labour Party 'made an unprecedented effort in canvassing and in election preparations. To them, of course, it was an integral part of their campaign for the general election, which they knew would almost certainly be within a few weeks of the local elections.'

Similarly, given the chance to shine in two by-elections held within months of the 1970 general election in rock-solid Labour seats, the results had been disappointing. In the Gorbals, because of the death of the much-loved Alice Cullen, they finished second with 25 per cent of the vote. But in Ayrshire South, where they appealed to barely 20 per cent of the electorate, following the death of the fiercely left-wing Emrys Hughes, they were pushed into third place by the Tories. Wolfe commented: 'The depressed mining villages of South Ayrshire, with a bleak and hopeless outlook, made a better battleground for the traditional class war than for the radical reforms of a party seeking what seemed to be such a distant thing as a parliament for Scotland.'

For the first time in its history, the SNP would be fielding candidates in all but six of Scotland's 71 parliamentary constituencies. Wolfe continued to believe the SNP's underlying support was a good deal stronger than its voting record suggested. In the Gorbals, a 'scientific and neutral survey of the electorate' conducted ahead of the poll showed nearly 70 per cent in favour of self-government – almost three times as many as the number of constituents who actually voted SNP on the day. Commenting on the Gorbals result, Wolfe mused: 'In that constituency, there were hundreds of people living in conditions worse than animals. We claimed some of their votes, but perhaps those with generations of hopelessness behind them regarded us as too new, too inexperienced, and possibly too bright and shiny to have any real concern for them.'

On two of the most important issues of the West Lothian campaign – independence for Scotland and Britain's entry into Europe – Dalyell and his SNP opponent differed fiercely. Dalyell was an ardent pro-marketeer; totally supportive of Harold Wilson's attempts to persuade General de Gaulle to withdraw his veto over British entry. To Wolfe, the political philosophy of the pro-marketeers was 'insidious to those who are steeped in the democratic tradition'. He likened them to the 'doctrinaire centralists' who occupied the Kremlin. Shortly before the election, he warned a meeting in Paisley: 'The distinct shape of political centralism which is now clearly over the horizon is an iceberg and we have seen only the tip of its dangerous and destructive might.'

Candidates from two other parties sought the approval of the West Lothian electorate. The Tories were represented by a rising new star, the Earl of Ancram, later, as his political career blossomed, plain Michael, while the Communists, apparently indifferent to their bleak history of lost deposits in the constituency, offered Chris Bett. The result was easily predictable: West Lothian appeared satisfied with the performance of its unlikely MP. In a 76.7 per cent poll, Dalyell attracted 52.9 per cent of the vote, slightly more than last time, compared to Wolfe who saw his support tumble to 28.2 per cent. Ancram pushed the Tory vote to five figures and saved his deposit. Chris Bett, polling even less than the previous Communist candidate, didn't.

The SNP's erratic performance overall kept the analysts busy for months. Their biggest disappointment was the loss of Hamilton. 'Winifred Ewing,' wrote Wolfe, 'had been an exceptionally active and conscientious MP.' Her place as the nationalists' lone standard-bearer at Westminster would be taken by the deeply decent Donald Stewart, the Provost of Stornoway, who'd succeeded in wresting the Western Isles from Malcolm MacMillan after a 35-year tenure. 'One out, one in, not much to worry about there!' was the general response from those in London who believed the nationalist threat had been much exaggerated. The danger, if it ever existed, had been well and truly demolished. As Dalyell noted: 'Whatever the reasons for the SNP's poor showing in the 1970 general election, its effect on the Labour Party was to push the problem to one side like a bad dream.'

During this period, Dalyell was 'absolutely immersed' in constituency problems, paying particular attention to the troubled BMC factory at Bathgate where strikes and other forms of industrial action were commonplace. 'It was thought the Scots were good engineers, which they are,' said Dalyell, 'but not that kind of assembly line engineering.' He cites the 'awful story' of the convener of the joint shop stewards' committee at Longbridge, on a visit to Scotland asking the local shop stewards why the men on the assembly line were going slow. 'He assumed they were in dispute with the management about something or other,' said Dalyell, chuckling grimly. 'In fact, it was their normal working pace!'

He hadn't forgotten BMC were in West Lothian as a direct result of government pressure, against the wishes of higher management. It might not take much in the way of provocation for them to decide it was time to leave. 'There was a period when I thought Bathgate was going to survive,' said Dalyell. 'They had a very good manager, Jack Smart, an engineer. But he retired and after he left, it became a sort of rough and ready management. I was the sole MP for the area. Two of the main unions, the Amalgamated Union of Engineering Workers and the National Union of Vehicle Builders, thought I could help. However, some officials didn't like the idea. They didn't think it was the job of an MP to be involved so closely in their affairs.'

Two events of largely unimagined importance occurred during the Heath years: Britain joined the European Economic Community and oil was discovered in the North Sea. The fall-out from what happened as a result continues to the present day. Dalyell, an ardent pro-marketeer, voted with the government on Europe, alongside such prominent Labour rebels as the future Gang of Four, Roy Jenkins, Shirley Williams, David Owen and Bill Rodgers. 'Along with Bob Sheldon, I am the only remaining Labour MP who voted against the three-line whip in order to go in, and that may be one of my good decisions,' said Dalyell. 'I thought not joining [Europe] would have been a mistake and still do.'

He was a good deal less happy about the political implications which accompanied the discovery of oil in the North Sea, particularly the threat to the unity of Britain posed by the growing importance of the SNP. Dalyell had been a member of the committee stage of the 1963 Continental Shelf Bill when 'the best informed geological opinion of the time tended to discount the possibility of there being substantial quantities of oil in the North Sea, and suggested that finds would be limited to natural gas. Within a decade, all that changed.'

By the mid-1970s, the SNP was campaigning on the potent slogan 'It's Scotland's Oil.' In his 1977 book *Devolution – the End of Britain?* Dalyell observed: 'What few people realised was that winning oil from the inhospitable waters of the North Sea was a far greater technological feat than had at first been supposed – and one that would cost five times as much as originally estimated.'

The Royal Commission on the Constitution, headed by Lord Crowther, was expected to report in 1971. It was already behind schedule when Crowther died of a heart attack at London Airport on 8 February 1972. His place at the head of the Commission was taken by a Scottish judge, Lord Kilbrandon. The report of the Kilbrandon Commission appeared on 31 October 1973. It wanted the essential political and economic unity of the UK preserved, but there was also a recommendation that powers should be transferred from London to a regional assembly, 'to determine policy on a selected range of subjects, to enact legislation to give effect to that policy, and to provide administrative machinery for its execution'.

That this idea didn't find favour with the Labour Party may be judged from the frigid tone of a policy document issued a few weeks earlier. In it, the Scottish Council of the Labour Party rejected the idea of a single authority with executive and legislative powers, covering the whole of Scotland, coming between newly elected councillors and officials and the Scottish Office. The document maintained: 'We are still of the opinion that an assembly, other than a committee of the UK Parliament, would be a mere talking shop and would not attract the right calibre of members.' Labour's governing body in Scotland also declared: 'We are convinced that the Scottish people do not wish total separation. Britain's democracy has been well served by a gradual evolutionary development of its constitutional processes. The alternatives are ineffective change with a window-dressing assembly, or constitutional upheaval with its attendant political and economic chaos. We are convinced that the gradual but continued extension of administrative and legislative devolution within the UK Parliament is in the best interests of the Scottish people.'

A week after the Kilbrandon Commission report appeared, Labour suffered a cataclysmic loss when Margo MacDonald won Govan for the SNP. The previous Labour majority in this heartland seat was 16,000. Her winning margin was 571. As Dalyell himself readily acknowledged, it was 'a landmark, even a watershed'. He also believed: 'Without question, the shattering by-election result helped to determine Wilson's response to the Kilbrandon proposals, and marked the beginning of the Prime Minister's conversion to devolution.'

Three months later Edward Heath, locked in what seemed a hopeless struggle to the death with the National Union of Mineworkers and caught in the mire of a State of Emergency, went to the country on the desperate slogan 'Who Governs Britain?' – and lost! Harold Wilson was back in Downing Street, without an overall majority and at the mercy of the Liberals.

Dalyell won again in West Lothian. In normal circumstances, 6,422 votes represented a respectable margin. Here it was a warning. William Wolfe's personal disappointment was profound. Dalyell's departure had been widely predicted. 'It never occurred to the SNP that they would take Perth and Clackmannan and not West Lothian,' said Dalyell. William Wolfe, a popular figure, expected to win in a constituency he coveted, and didn't. Margo MacDonald, equally robust, failed to hold Govan. Still, the SNP enjoyed its greatest electoral triumph to date, winning seven seats: Aberdeenshire East, Argyll, Banff, Clackmannan, Dundee East, Moray and Nairn and the Western Isles. The result caused palpitations in the ranks of the other parties. 'The Heath government, with its three-day working week and all its industrial troubles, was unpopular,' Dalyell explained. 'The Labour government was deemed not to have been a success last time. There was very much a spirit of the time: give the nationalists a shot, it will be quite a good thing for Scotland! I don't think people were serious about wanting a nationalist government.'

The narrowness of Wilson's victory, and the absence of an overall Labour majority, ensured there would be another election within the year. Dalyell reflected gloomily on 'the fluke chance of a near tie' in the House of Commons. Normally, he wrote, a party which 'has either won or lost at the polls has time in which to settle down and formulate its policies, after a lot of argument at conferences, and a reasonable amount of mature reflection among the leaders of the party. But the situation in 1974 was not normal, and there was little time to spare. The closeness of the February and October polls meant that many decisions which would normally have been taken in a deliberative manner were hasty and rushed.'

It was what he perceived as the absence of thought on the part of leading members of the cabinet which concentrated Dalyell's mind on the problems of devolution. Harold Wilson's first priority on his return to Downing Street had been to seek an immediate settlement with the NUM, and bring an end to the State of Emergency. Days later, the government announced its programme for what everyone expected would be a curtailed parliament. The Queen's Speech promised discussions in Scotland and Wales on the Report of the Kilbrandon Commission, leading to 'proposals for consideration'.

Writing in 1977, Dalyell observed: 'If ever there was a case in recent British political history of chickens coming home to roost, the Kilbrandon Committee was it. What had started half a decade earlier in the minds of James Callaghan and Harold Wilson as a temporising and expedient device to counter the SNP and Plaid Cymru had now matured into a controversial set of proposals, which their incoming government was going to have to do something about.'

The Nationalists wanted to know why the government needed to engage in further talk. On 12 March 1974, during the debate which followed the Queen's Speech, Winifred Ewing, back in the House of Commons after a four year absence, interrupted the Prime Minister to ask: 'Could we not now have proposals instead of discussions?' Harold Wilson responded: 'We on this side believe in full consultation and discussion. We are not an authoritarian party. Of course we shall publish a White Paper followed by a Bill.' Dalyell wrote later: 'This was news indeed. Since the general election result, there had been no formal discussion within the Labour Party as to the right course to adopt in view of the SNP's success.'

The promised discussion document appeared on 3 June 1974 under the title 'Devolution Within the UK: Some Alternatives for Discussion'. Dalyell believed it bore 'all the marks of being ill thought out and designed simply for the purposes of an imminent general election'. The Secretary of State for Scotland, Willie Ross, explained: 'What we are doing at present is consulting and asking people to let us know their views. At this stage, we have an open mind. No possibilities are excluded, apart from separatism and federalism.' Donald Stewart, on behalf of the SNP, claimed: 'The Labour government does not understand the mood of Scotland, which is quite clearly for a directly elected Scottish parliament with legislative and economic powers.'

Press reaction was muted. *The Scotsman* thought the document did nothing to dispel doubts about the extent of Labour's conversion to 'meaningful and useful devolution' for Scotland and Wales. The view from North Bridge suggested there was plenty of evidence of popular demand for political devolution, in Scotland at least. It scented danger in the large number of questions raised about each of the Kilbrandon Commission's proposals, 'questions which will appeal to students of constitutional law rather than to the public at large, most of whom will be bored or bamboozled, if they pay any attention at all'. Devising a practical scheme to satisfy most of the present demand was 'a job for experts, for politicians, for governments'.

Polls suggested that two-thirds of the electorate in Scotland wanted more self-government, with a clear majority in favour of a Scottish parliament. Professor John P. Mackintosh, who had been an MP and would be again, believed: 'Much of the dissatisfaction is due to disappointment over the economic failures of successive governments, and to the hope that Scotland could opt out of these persistent and debilitating difficulties.'

With an election looming, it didn't help Labour's chances that the formal position of the party in Scotland, last expressed in their response to the Kilbrandon Commission four years earlier, was hostile. It was also a tad embarrassing that Scotland's man in the cabinet, Willie Ross, had been a long-term opponent of any form of Home Rule. Common sense, as well as political expediency, demanded a re-think.

A letter from Transport House to the chairman of the Scottish Council of the Labour Party argued the case for devolution. A meeting was scheduled for Saturday, 22 June 1974. It didn't appear to matter to whoever kept the diary that Scotland were due to play Yugoslavia in Frankfurt in the World Cup Finals, with the match live on television. With the Scots in serious danger of qualifying for the next stage of the competition, for the first time in World Cup history, the date assumed a rare significance. Out of 29 members of the council entitled to vote, only 11 attended the meeting in Keir Hardie House. A statement issued later captured the prevailing mood: Labour was in business 'to change the economic and social basis of society'. A majority of those present didn't believe 'constitutional tinkering' would help the Labour Party to achieve its socialist objectives. The new regional and district authorities should be given time to prove themselves as satisfying the needs and aspirations of the Scottish people.

By the narrowest possible margin, the meeting decided to reject 'all the proposals in the government's consultative document as being irrelevant to the real needs of the people of Scotland'. *The Scotsman* declared itself 'baffled' by the decision. 'Socialist ideology matters more to them than giving the Scottish people power to deal with their own affairs,' the paper commented sourly. 'It is not apparent that socialist objectives and self-government are contradictory.'

Dalyell noted later: 'In retrospect, it is being claimed that had there been a fuller turnout of members, and had the Scottish football side not been encountering Yugoslavia in Frankfurt, a very different pro-assembly result would have occurred. I doubt this.' He reckoned the vote at 6–5 against supporting devolution reflected the majority feeling within the Scottish executive at the time. On a full turnout, he claimed, the vote could have been as high as 19–10 in favour of the established anti-assembly view. Others disagreed.

Judith Hart, MP for South Lanark, and Alex Kitson, of the Transport and General Workers Union, headed the charge. In later years, Dalyell defended Kitson, 'a genuine champion of civil rights when liberties were suppressed', and other left-wing activists of the period against charges that they were 'out of *Jurassic Park*'. This he described as 'ludicrous and unfair. Ancient Labour they may have been,' continued Dalyell, 'but ancient Labour had values, passionate beliefs in right and wrong, and an enormous interest in the world beyond Britain and Europe.'

To outsiders it appeared strange, however, that the main thrust for devolution was coming from the National Executive Committee in London. 'The truth was that neither had very much day-to-day contact with the Labour Party in Scotland,' Dalyell grumbled. 'But this did not prevent them from being regarded as authorities within the NEC as far as Scottish affairs were concerned.'

Dalyell, as the recently elected chairman of the Scottish group of MPs, attended his first meeting of the Scottish executive on 6 July 1974. On this occasion, there was a full attendance. Invited by the NEC to convene a special conference, the Scottish executive 'felt in no position to refuse'. If there had been 'a larger attendance and a more decisive vote' at the 22 June meeting, Dalyell believed his 'colleagues would have summoned up the muscle to refuse. But defying Transport House was a major step, rendered more difficult by the unfavourable press reaction concerning the lack of attendance at the previous meeting.'

Alex Kitson, a leading architect of the special conference convened in Glasgow's gloomy Cooperative Hall on Saturday, 17 August 1974, knew everything there was to know about the deep, dark corners of the Labour Party. Famously, when Sean Connery worked as a milkboy with St Cuthbert's Cooperative Dairy in Edinburgh Kitson was his immediate boss, driving the horse-drawn float. Dalyell, with splendid curiosity, once asked him what happened to the horse. 'Connery and I knew all about animal welfare long before there was any lobby on animal rights at the Labour Party conference or anywhere else,' the kindly and avuncular Kitson responded with a smile. 'All our horses were extremely well cared for and lived a happy life. As usual, I was before my time!'

His critics claimed archly that steering the Scottish Horse and Motormen's Union into the welcoming arms of the giant Transport and General Workers Union had been counter-devolutionary. Kitson, an arch-persuader, ignored the jibes and set about convincing other prominent figures in the trade union movement of the rightness of his cause. Arriving in Dalintober Street to attend the special conference, Dalyell and his supporters were told the vote had been 'squared'.

Earlier, when the NEC announced its support for a Scottish Assembly in advance of the conference, there was a feeling in some quarters that Scottish opinion was about to be 'bounced' into supporting the government line. In his speech to the conference, the chairman of the Scottish Council of the Labour Party, Frank Gormill, complained that 'on this most crucial issue the national executive decided to make their own pronouncements in advance of any advice they might have received from the party in Scotland'. Gormill denied that the Scottish Council had been forced to convene the special conference in response to pressure from the NEC. The possibility of convening a special conference had been discussed at their meeting on 22 June. And while it was true that the NEC 'did ask for a special conference it would have been held regardless of that request'.

Among those taking opposite sides in the devolution debate were Jim Sillars, MP for South Ayrshire, and Brian Wilson, a future Labour minister but not yet an MP. Sillars maintained that legislation affecting 'education, housing, transport, land reform and land ownership demanded a Scottish character in deciding which policies were to be applied'. Wilson warned delegates against agreeing to something they would regret in future because it could lead 'to the destruction of the Labour movement'.

John Smith, four years an MP and already PPS to Willie Ross, told the conference he believed retaining the office of Secretary of State for Scotland and 71 MPs should be a priority for the Party. According to Smith those who pressed for devolution without the loss of the office of Secretary of State and a reduction in the number of Scottish MPs at Westminster were being 'dishonest'. This was a theme the future Labour leader had been pursuing for weeks. Writing in his *Daily Record* column only days before the White Paper on Devolution appeared, Smith reminded his readers: 'Kilbrandon suggested that the number of Scots MPs should be cut and the office of Secretary of State abolished to make way for a Scottish parliament. I think that is too high a price to pay. We must seek a scheme which preserves Scottish influence at Westminster, but gives more scope for Scottish decisions on Scottish affairs to be taken in Scotland.' Before the devolution debate entered its critical phase, Smith had questioned 'the effectiveness of an assembly which does not have any real control over financial policy and trade and industry policy in Scotland'. In his view, it was unlikely that 'a voice without power would be heard, and I am even more suspicious of representation which does not carry responsibility'.

In the final vote, with one exception, all the main unions backed devolution, including some who were expected to oppose the idea. As Dalyell acknowledged ruefully, 'Alex Kitson did his job well.' Andrew Marr, in *The Battle for Scotland* published in 1992, agreed. 'Kitson,' he wrote, 'had been highly effective in bringing round the big union votes – which were not always surrendered in a mood of fervent enthusiasm.' Alex Donnett of the General and Municipal Workers Union, the first to declare his card vote, was embarrassingly honest about his motives: his union wanted no impediment to the return of a Labour government, he told the conference. And if devolution was the price, well, he supposed they would pay it.'

Dalyell described Donnett's performance: 'Then came the dagger. How Alex Donnett, believing what he does about the assembly, will be able to look at himself in his shaving mirror, I know not.'

According to Andrew Marr: 'Dalintober Street was portrayed by the Labour leadership as a return to the party's grand old traditions. But it was a victory for fix and fear, not a triumph of principle.' The conference ended with an overwhelming vote in favour of 'a directly elected assembly, with legislative powers within the context of the political and economic unity of the United Kingdom'. In his 1977 book *Devolution: The End of Britain?* Dalyell argued, strangely, that delegates attending the special conference did not realise 'they had called for a legislative assembly; most of them were under the impression that they had called for a super local authority'.

Reporters were told the proposed White Paper was in 'an advanced state of preparation and would be published within three weeks. The document is expected to amount to a declaration of intent by the government, rather than one which spells out the arrangements in detail.' Pro-devolutionists were looking forward to an assembly with 'a considerable degree of autonomy, and possibly some executive control over trade and industry'. *The Scotsman* confidently predicted there would be no change in the office of Secretary of State or the existing allocation of Westminster MPs, contrary to Kilbrandon's wishes. It also expected individual candidates to resist the Home Rule tide: some Scottish MPs who had always strongly opposed the idea of an assembly would 'appear hypocritical if they started to support it now'.

There was a distinct sense of *déjà vu* surrounding the publication of the White Paper outlining Labour's plans for Scotland and Wales. Much of it simply confirmed the recommendations made by the NEC. As predicted, there was no immediate threat to the number of MPs or the offices of Secretary of State in Scotland or Wales; although in the wake of 'major changes and a diminution in their present powers', the government conceded that 'careful thought would have to be given to their precise role'.

The speed of the operation suggested that the document had been in preparation for some time prior to the special conference, as many suspected, or that it was a rushed job, a ticking bomb awaiting the arrival of the new government, only weeks away. As if to confirm this was primarily a spoiling tactic aimed at securing the votes of all but hard-line nationalist opinion the day after the publication of the White Paper, the Prime Minister announced there would be an election on 10 October.

Dalyell told anyone who cared to listen that Scotland with 71 MPs, a dedicated seat in the cabinet, three different levels of council at local level – community, district and regional – and the promised assembly was 'in danger of becoming the most over-governed five million people in the world'. More than ever, his outright opposition to devolution made him a prime SNP target in West Lothian. Once again, Billy Wolfe commanded the nationalist guns. His vote climbed to 24,997: Dalyell's dropped slightly to 27,687, reducing his majority by more than half. Less than 14 per cent of the vote was divided between three other candidates: Tory, Liberal and Communist, all of whom lost their deposit. West Lothian was now a two-way contest in all but name.

Elsewhere, the SNP added East Dumbartonshire, Galloway, Perth and East Perthshire and South Angus to their tally in the House of Commons. Excluding Orkney and Shetland, the party now commanded a majority in constituencies virtually the length and breadth of Scotland. Significantly, most of them were located below the Highland Line, some close enough to the industrial heartland of central Scotland to justify Labour's pre-election concern.

Labour now enjoyed only a 6.4 per cent lead in the popular vote, representing a 19 per cent shift in opinion since 1970. In the course of five elections across a ten-year span, those voting SNP had risen from 64,044 in 1964 to 839,628 this time. Anyone who thought the election would put an end to the devolution argument, by killing the onward march of the nationalists, was bound to be sorely disappointed.

Harold Wilson was back in Downing Street for the fourth time, with an overall majority of three; enough, he claimed, given the divided state of the opposition, for a whole parliament. No one imagined then that he would resign within 18 months, leaving his successor, James Callaghan, never an ardent devolutionist, to face the worst of the nationalists' fire. However, even as the new House of Commons assembled, it was clear to the MP for West Lothian, attending his sixth parliament, that 'the case for the *status quo* against separation had to be robustly made, and could no longer go by default'.

FOURTEEN

SHOWSTOPPER

For a brief period following the October 1974 general election, it appeared the MP for West Lothian, its sternest critic, was learning to live with the prospect of devolution. At a press conference held at Keir Hardie House in Glasgow on the Monday following the election, several reporters heard him say he believed Labour would honour its campaign promise and that 'the Secretary of State should make haste and produce the assembly, as soon as possible'. Later Dalyell claimed he had been endorsing the 'super local authority' he thought had been agreed at the special conference in August. Somewhat artlessly, he also admitted failing to read the White Paper or 'the party manifesto, which repeated the White Paper pledge before polling day. In the 48 hours after the result of the poll, I caught up on lost sleep and had not read the White Paper by the time I faced the press on the Monday. I really imagined I was endorsing the super local authority, which I understood had been agreed to on 17 August. So did most of my colleagues.'

It wasn't until early January when he attended a meeting with Gerry Fowler, then Minister of State at the Privy Council Office, and Harry Ewing, MP for Stirling, Falkirk and Grangemouth, and minister in the Scottish Office with special responsibility for devolution, that Dalyell realised the government was 'thinking in terms of a Prime Minister of Scotland and the whole paraphernalia of a cabinet system'. Reporting this conversation back to his colleagues in London, Dalyell claimed he found them equally astonished. Their impression matched his own: that the proposed assembly would be a form of 'super local government'.

Any suggestion that Scotland would be given a parliament with an executive headed by a Prime Minister was greeted with ribald laughter. Labour's amiable chief whip, Robert Mellish, MP for Bermondsey, suggested that next thing his constituents would be wanting him to be made Prime Minister of London.

Harry Ewing acknowledged it was 'a confusing time', saying: 'There were a lot of people in government who didn't realise how far we were going. And to be fair to Tam, he has stuck rigidly to what he said then, that he didn't understand the vote. It's not a point I understand. Tam isn't the dimmest person in the world, anything but! I would be astonished if he didn't understand what the vote was all about that day.' Dalyell believed 'the confusion was easily explained. In Scotland, as elsewhere, the whole argument had been conducted up to that time in terms of over-easy slogans, trundled out as the needs of each politician's speech required. Tragically, little thought had even then been devoted to thinking the problem through, in any serious manner. Phrases and catchwords were devised: the following morning's headlines in the excitable Scottish press were the major consideration.' A separate cabinet in Scotland, Dalyell warned, would lead to a 'situation where every ill, real or imagined, will be blamed on the assembly not having enough power. The same would be true if Westminster had a power of veto and dared to use it. The appetite and pressure for more power and a separate legislature will inevitably grow.'

The job of coordinating the new policy and introducing the government's proposals in the form of a bill had been entrusted to Edward Short, Lord President of the Council and Leader of the House of Commons. Short wished to proceed with all speed, using the minimalist White Paper, published a day ahead of Wilson's election announcement, as the basis of legislation. Dalyell and other opponents of devolution, including the MP for Bedwellty, Neil Kinnock, thought differently. They wanted another White Paper, giving them a complete picture of the government's plans for Scotland and Wales. Harold Wilson, faced with a revolt inside the PLP, agreed.

A special report in *The Times* on 5 February 1975 explained: 'The anti-devolutionists believe the government is finding it increasingly difficult to prepare proposals for an assembly that will not inflame nationalist support through giving too little, or fracture 267 years of parliamentary union by yielding too much.' According to *The Times*, there would be 'no interference' with the executive powers of the new regional councils due to begin work the following May, including Strathclyde. As *The Times* explained, for the benefit of its mainly English readership, Strathclyde contained half the population of Scotland and its council would be a powerful body, with massive financial resources. 'Unless the formula for the assembly is absolutely right it could sit ill alongside that formidable new giant.' A reasoned first leader suggested the government's intention of financing devolution by way of a block grant was 'surely a recipe for chronic political conflict between the power centre at Westminster and those to be established elsewhere'.

The level of interest shown by the gentlemen in New Printing House Square suggested there was a growing awareness within the London establishment that something of historic significance was perhaps stirring in Britain's northern fastness, a far country few of them ever visited or thought much about. To *The Times* it seemed the political demand for self-government in Scotland was 'born of a revived national self-confidence, the vast extension of the country's natural resources which the appropriation of sub-marine oil reserves implies, and disillusionment with the performance of the United Kingdom and with the effect of that performance in Scotland itself'.

The paper clearly believed there was little likelihood of the government achieving its 'pious objective' of giving the people of Scotland and Wales a decisive voice in running their domestic affairs while maintaining the economic and political unity of the United Kingdom. It acknowledged that 'much ingenuity' would be expended in seeing how this could be achieved. However, it also warned that it would be as well, early in the debate, to consider the possibility that these two lines of policy response were 'ultimately compatible only in the realm of rhetoric'.

The new White Paper, *Our Changing Democracy*, reached an expectant public on 24 November 1975. *The Scotsman* reacted with disbelief: 'Politicians on both sides of the devolution argument are united in the belief that the government have bungled the biggest constitutional issue Britain has faced in centuries,' its reporter wailed. In addition to retaining control over economic and industrial matters, the Secretary of State, as the Queen's representative in Scotland, would be given formal constitutional oversight of the 142-member assembly, and the right to request Westminster to impose a veto on its actions. Far from being 'a carefully balanced piece of constitutional engineering' as the government claimed, the White Paper was 'a patchwork resulting from political expediency, concessions to trade unions and other interested parties, and security precautions against the assembly stepping out of line'.

A leading article in *The Scotsman* continued bitterly: 'There will be three governments in Scotland; Westminster, the assembly and the Secretary of State. That is one too many, and it arises from the government's desire to keep the Secretary of State as a depository of powers which they hesitate to trust to the assembly, and yet cannot remove from Scotland.'

There was general agreement among the pro-devolutionists that too much attention had been lavished on protecting the office of Secretary of State. The charismatic Jim Sillars thought his new powers would allow Scotland's man in the cabinet to 'assume the role of a controlling governor-general'. A few weeks before the White Paper appeared, Sillars had been touted by an enthusiastic Neal Ascherson, writing in *The Scotsman*, as a future Prime Minister of Scotland. Now Sillars complained: 'Running throughout the White Paper, and embodied in most of its major proposals, is the eternal verity of Westminster that the man in Whitehall knows best and always will.'

A year separated publication of the White Paper and the first reading of the no less controversial Scotland and Wales Bill it spawned. During this period of time, the political landscape at Westminster changed significantly. Less than three months into the new year, Harold Wilson astonished everyone, including his close cabinet colleagues, by resigning as Prime Minister.

Before he succeeded Harold Wilson as Prime Minister, crowning a remarkable political career as Chancellor of the Exchequer, Home Secretary and Foreign Secretary, James Callaghan had been at best cool about devolution. Visiting him during his time as Foreign Secretary, when he was chairman of the PLP Foreign Affairs Group, the highly sceptical Dalyell made several attempts to interest him in the subject, to be met with a marked lack of success. A disconsolate Dalyell noted: 'He was much more interested in knowing what the PLP thought about our policy in Cyprus.' Once in Downing Street, Callaghan's attitude didn't change. However, as Michael Foot, the man Callaghan defeated for the Labour leadership, told Arnold Kemp, 'he went with the party decisions on the matter and did his best to assist them'.

From his first few days in Downing Street, it was evident that Callaghan intended to stamp his authority on a dangerous area of legislation which threatened the government's survival. Ted Short was quickly replaced as Lord President of the Council by Michael Foot, with the young John Smith as his deputy. Dalyell later acknowledged that 'on great issues Smith did not put perceived political advantage first'. It impressed Dalyell, after nearly a decade at Westminster, that Smith could be counted among the group of Labour rebels who voted against the party and in favour of joining the European Community, in support of the Heath government, barely a year after entering parliament. Dalyell, who also defied the Labour whip on that occasion, considered the fledgling MP's decision 'the more impressive because he saw very well that such a vote might lastingly damage any hopes of a ministerial career'. It was also known to the West Lothian MP that the future Labour leader declined an invitation to join Harold Wilson's 1974 administration as Solicitor-General for Scotland to avoid being 'typecast as a lawyer-politician largely identified with Scottish affairs'.

Nonetheless, when the Scotland and Wales Bill appeared in November 1976 Dalyell decided it represented 'a surrender to the politician's most pressing temptation, which is to say different things to different people at the same time'. Scottish newspapers were told to expect 'cataclysmic' improvements in the government of Scotland, while in London ministers took the line that 'it was simply a case of altering matters pertaining to Scotland and Wales, and that the rest of the United Kingdom was not greatly affected'.

Dalyell calculated that a large majority of ministers, inside and outside the cabinet, as well as a majority of the PLP, opposed the proposals. 'Disingenuous in conception,' he thundered, 'the scheme could not fail to be dishonest in execution.' He also guessed the government would try and save its skin – and the Scotland and Wales Bill – by introducing a guillotine motion. Michael Foot wasn't allowed to forget his own anger at a Tory decision to impose a guillotine on the European Communities Bill four years earlier. 'The guillotine,' Foot had insisted on 2 May 1972, 'is the last resort of a government who know that they cannot get the full-hearted consent of parliament but are determined to have their way in any case.' It was a telling quote: evidently stung, Foot reminded his tormentor he had 'also argued that guillotines have been introduced in some circumstances so that this House can act as well as argue'.

Dalyell spent the summer canvassing support within the PLP. Seventy MPs told him they would be prepared to vote against the government if there was any attempt to introduce a guillotine motion on the Scotland and Wales Bill. Michael Foot was duly warned. Observed Dalyell: 'If a rebellion is sprung on a government out of the blue without appreciable warning, parliamentary colleagues have grounds for resentment, and the rebels have to contend with their annoyance. On the other hand, if warning is given months in advance by MPs who are known to have a serious interest in a subject, the odium that attaches itself to disloyalty tends to evaporate.'

This last view may have been inspired partly by wishful thinking. Dalyell once acknowledged that it could be difficult in the Labour Party 'to put any views strongly without being accused of factional strife', explaining that 'one of the real divisions in the Labour Party has always been that chasm between practical policy and emotional protest'. Dalyell divided opposition to the Scotland and Wales Bill into three categories. The Conservatives thought it could lead to separation; a majority of Liberals were annoyed that the assembly was to have neither tax-raising powers nor proportional representation; and 43 Labour MPs realised that the government's enthusiasm for the bill had more to do with the 'natural and not necessarily ignoble desire to remain in office than with the good government of Scotland and Wales'. He later commented: 'For Labour MPs, remaining in power is naturally a desirable object, but a substantial number of us think this should not be at the expense of the integrity of the United Kingdom.'

When the Scotland and Wales Bill passed its second reading by 292 votes to 247 on 16 December 1976, it did so, Dalyell maintained, not because those who voted in favour 'endorsed the proposals, but because they thought that it would be wrong to deny them a hearing'. It didn't escape his attention that 'during the four days of the Second Reading debate, and the 11 days of the committee stage, hardly a backbench voice was heard in favour of the Bill from either side of the House of Commons. Indeed, the ministers in charge of the devolution programme could not conceal their bitter feelings towards their own colleagues, who had demanded legislative proposals on devolution, yet had failed to turn up to speak in support of the government.'

Close to the main action, Harry Ewing believed that James Callaghan was never a great devolutionist. 'He still isn't,' said Ewing. 'But he realised we were committed to it, and he also saw it as a good issue with which to keep himself in Number Ten. John Smith dynamised the whole process. Before, with Ted Short and Gerry Fowler in charge, nothing happened. Now you had James Callaghan, Michael Foot and John Smith, all pushing it.' During its introductory stage, John Smith left no one in any doubt that the Scotland and Wales Bill would be 'formidably complex' because of its effect on existing legislation. In fact, as much as anything, it was a simple and endlessly repeated question in various forms from the resourceful Tam Dalyell which concentrated attention on a still-unanswered problem: namely, how did the government justify MPs from Scotland voting on matters affecting England, when MPs representing English constituencies were denied a similar right over subjects devolved to the proposed assembly? Equally important, what would be the role of Scottish MPs if matters of prime importance to their constituents such as education, health and housing were no longer the business of Westminster? Enoch Powell called this issue 'the West Lothian question,' and the name stuck. George Younger told Arnold Kemp it was 'an absolute show-stopper'. Dalyell himself observed: 'Like other people, MPs tend to think more clearly and urgently where their own interests are directly affected.'

Within a month of its second reading, it was clear to everyone that without a 'guillotine', the Scotland and Wales Bill was dead. Progress in the House of Commons had been worse than slow. Every clause and every line had been examined with care, bordering on tedium for some. Agreement had been reached on only four clauses at the expense of a considerable amount of scarce parliamentary time; another 111 remained, with no end realistically in sight and Dalyell, prominent among the leading prevaricators.

Other opponents of the legislation included the Tory opposition, led by Margaret Thatcher, who was approaching the end of her second year as Tory leader. At first she appeared to support the idea of devolution, telling a party meeting in Glasgow in November 1975 that more decisions affecting Scotland should be taken in Scotland. However, as Andrew Marr noted in *The Battle for Scotland*, the pro-devolutionists in her own ranks were 'not her sort of Tory'. By the time James Callaghan and Michael Foot decided to appeal to the House of Commons to let them curtail the debate, so that the legislation could progress without further needless delay, Thatcher's attitude was fixed. 'Let it be remembered,' she cried fervently, 'that we are the Unionist party.'

Dalyell believed that parliamentary notions of fair play kept the Scotland and Wales Bill alive at the second reading stage. Similar considerations didn't apply when MPs were confronted with a guillotine motion. By this time, the government was staring defeat in the face.

Throughout the critical weeks surrounding New Year 1977, Dalyell thought he detected an 'uncharacteristic reluctance to speak on the subject' among ministers with no direct responsibility for the Scotland and Wales Bill. This view of events appeared to be supported by Alan Watkins, writing in *The Observer*. He informed his readers there was no one in the government who 'is either knowledgeable or enthusiastic about the subject'. John P. Mackintosh, an ardent devolutionist, believed the Scotland and Wales Bill failed because it contained so many weaknesses that even the 'most ardent decentralisers were not prepared to fight hard for it'.

The little-loved Scotland and Wales Bill effectively collapsed with the loss of the guillotine motion on 22 February 1977. During the debate, Dalyell suggested people had been losing sight of a prime function of the House of Commons: to act as a check on the executive. With the Scotland and Wales Bill, there had been an opportunity for the Commons to perform 'its classic text-book but seldom practised role of a watchdog with teeth'. He would vote against the guillotine, 'in the belief that the more unfettered discussion that takes place in the House of Commons, the more the actual nature of the government's best attempts at a Scottish assembly will percolate through to the people of Scotland'. The reaction in Scotland if the Bill failed, he claimed, would be 'a sigh of relief that the assembly kite ever flew so high in the political firmament'.

Twenty-two Labour MPs, including Tam Dalyell, defied the whips and voted against their own side. Another 21 abstained. Of the 21 members of the PLP who joined Dalyell in voting with the Tories, only two represented Scottish constituencies: Ron Brown, MP for Leith, and the English-born Willie Hamilton, who represented Fife Central. Another dissident with strong Scottish connections and his mind set on killing the Bill was the MP for Islington South and Finsbury, George Cunningham. 'Tam had been doing a magnificent job, contesting the legislation, when many of us who got either blame or credit for torpedoing it were much less active,' said Cunningham. 'I remember Enoch Powell saying the House of Commons was educating itself to the impossibility of this arrangement. Well, it was Tam who did that, with his relentless questioning and magnificent attention to detail.'

Cunningham added: 'The West Lothian question was the issue for me. I felt it was the responsibility of every UK Member of Parliament to look at the consequences of what was being done for Scotland. If the proposal was to create Scottish independence, I believed that should be a decision for the people of Scotland alone. And I'd define that in a way even the SNP would find acceptable, as people resident in Scotland. But when you're saying the Scottish parliament will be responsible for devolved subjects in Scotland, while Scottish MPs continue to have a say in English matters at Westminster, then that makes it a subject for all MPs. If we had been proposing a federal arrangement, in which each part of the country had its own legislature, my criticisms would fall away. But nobody was suggesting a federal arrangement. So I took the view we were all entitled to look at the situation and decide whether it could last. And I argued it couldn't, because it was manifestly unfair.'

The great devolution debate didn't end with the demise of the Scotland and Wales Bill and anyone who thought it might was sorely disappointed. A rumbustious performance by the SNP in the May district elections dispelled any doubts the government may have entertained about the need for further action. A pact with the Liberals, engineered following his failure to command the House of Commons on the Scotland and Wales Bill, kept the wily James Callaghan in power. John Smith was ordered 'to redesign the Bill to please the Liberals, without making any more enemies on the Labour side'.

There was a feeling in many quarters that Smith was never wholly committed to the idea of devolution. Tam Dalyell, as one of the leading critics of the scheme he was assigned to propound, never shifted in his opinion that Smith was simply 'Mr Callaghan's attorney. He acted as a lawyer in a court.' Smith's biographer, Andy McSmith, cites a similar view, expressed from the Tory benches. He wrote: 'Norman Tebbitt suggested to him on one occasion that as a lawyer, he could be hired to say anything his client wanted him to say – a view which Smith thought unfair on lawyers.' Working alongside him on the new legislation, as the minister responsible for devolution in the Scottish Office, Harry Ewing thought that 'James Callaghan used John Smith to protect himself. As Jim was never a devolutionist, John could be his front. John was good at that – he was a professional. But his heart was never really in it. John was never a devolutionist.' Ewing added: 'When he took over as Minister of State at the cabinet office, I was told by Bruce Millan, who had succeeded Willie Ross as Secretary of State for Scotland, that John Smith and the Prime Minister wanted me to give up the devolution brief. Apparently, they thought I was too solid in favour of devolution. I asked Bruce how he felt. He said he wanted me to stay, so I told him I wasn't going to give it up willingly. If they wanted rid of me, they'd have to sack me. But I knew they couldn't do that, for the simple reason it would look bad in Scotland.'

Talking to Arnold Kemp, author of *The Hollow Drum*, the future Labour leader defended himself strenuously against the charge that he was 'never emotionally committed to devolution but was a master of its complexities and an able parliamentary advocate of it'. Smith maintained he was 'very committed to it, very committed indeed'. As he said in the House of Commons on 13 January 1977, with the Scotland and Wales Bill in terminal decline: 'It is my firm judgement that the unity of the United Kingdom will be strengthened by recognising the diversity of its different parts.'

However, Ewing claimed that: 'James Callaghan and John Smith were playing both ends against the middle. They would do their best, but if the legislation failed, they wouldn't have been too worried. John knew that as soon as the devolution bill was either on the statute book, or we'd lost the referendum, the Prime Minister would have to give him another job. John thought he might become Secretary of State for Energy. Then Edmund Dell resigned, and there was a ready-made opening at the Department of Trade. The rest, as they say, is history.'

Given the task of resuscitating the ailing legislation Smith, with the Prime Minister's consent, produced separate bills with different powers for Scotland and Wales. It was hoped this tactic would eliminate some of the opposition from his own side. He also tried, as Arnold Kemp recorded, 'to contain the Labour rebellion by making sure that the devolution proposals were at all points endorsed by the party conference'.

The main result of his labours, the Scotland Bill, arrived in the House of Commons for its second reading on 14 November 1977, with the amount of time on offer for debate already fixed. There were two issues facing MPs, said Smith. First, there was 'a need to decentralise decision-taking and increase accountability in both Scotland and Wales'. Secondly, by 'recognising that need and desire, we shall effectively strengthen, not weaken, the unity of the United Kingdom'. In his view, 'just to put up the shutters of the *status quo* and say nothing' to people in Scotland, Wales and other parts of the United Kingdom who wanted more control over their own affairs was 'no intelligent way to preserve the unity of the United Kingdom'. To those who suggested there would be no meaningful role for Scottish MPs at Westminster following devolution, Smith listed 'the conduct of international affairs, including our developing partnership within the European Economic Community; policies for national security and defence; trade and industry; employment and industrial relations; the management of the economy; energy; social security; and a great many other matters. That is a great deal,' said Smith.

To Dalyell, it appeared the devolution coach was 'now on a motorway without exit roads to a separate Scottish state'. He continued to oppose the legislation on the grounds that 'it provides not the remotest chance of a lasting settlement between Scotland and England'. He maintained there was a 'basic design fault in the steering of the devolutionary coach, which will cause it to crash into the side of the road before it has gone 100 miles'. Among his reasons for this belief was 'the inevitable frustration of the assemblymen being unable to honour the promises that they have made, on account of what they would claim are lack of powers over the economy from Westminster and lack of money from a parsimonious English Treasury that is unwilling to allocate oil revenues'. He predicted: 'Within weeks of arriving at the High School, they will be clamouring for more.'

On more than 100 occasions during the following few weeks, Dalyell defied a three-line whip to vote against his own side. 'There was a mixed group of MPs who continued to believe it was a bad bill,' he said. 'Whenever we said so, however, the response from those in favour of devolution never varied. They kept telling us an overwhelming majority of people in Scotland wanted devolution, and we were wrong to oppose it.'

With the guillotine already in place, and the support of the minority parties, the legislation was virtually guaranteed – or so it seemed to those who insisted that an assembly meeting in the former Royal High School on Calton Hill, Edinburgh, was the will of the Scottish people. In fact, after nearly four years of bitter argument, the most controversial stage of the entire devolution process was about to begin.

On 31 July 1978, the government's proposals for Scotland and Wales received the Royal Assent, normally the last stage in the legislative process. An amendment to the Scotland and Wales Bill, proposed in its original form by the future Labour leader Neil Kinnock, committed the government to a referendum. A subsequent amendment passed on Wednesday 25 January 1978 (Burns Night!) ensured it would be a referendum unlike any other in British parliamentary history. Tabled by the Dunfermline-born MP for Islington South and Finsbury, George Cunningham, it required at least 40 per cent of those entitled to vote to accept devolution before an assembly could be introduced.

That evening, amid extraordinary scenes in the voting lobby when the Sergeant-at-Arms was summoned by the Deputy Speaker, Sir Myer Galpern, to restore order, MPs also voted to accept an amendment proposed by Jo Grimond, which permitted Orkney and Shetland to opt out of a devolved Scotland if a simple majority of people living there so wished. To the nationalists especially, this was a noxious mix of cynicism and perfidy, considering the main location of the country's known oil deposits.

Far from the chaotic scenes at Westminster, those who wanted an assembly in Edinburgh reacted with fury. A leading article in *The Scotsman* struggled to comprehend the enormity of the deed, and decided that 'the extraordinary referendum amendment is the greatest insult so far to the intelligence of the Scottish people'. Entry into the EEC was a bigger constitutional change, the paper noted, and the referendum was held on the normal basis of a simple majority. Similarly, a majority of one was good enough for decisions of parliament. Viewed from North Bridge, 'the wrecking amendment for the Scottish referendum' was so 'blatantly unfair that the jubilant anti-devolutionists may live to regret their shabby manoeuvre'.

More than 20 years after the event, George Cunningham, author of the 'wrecking amendment' which so incensed large numbers of his countrymen, explained: 'There was no magic about 40 per cent. I simply didn't feel a third, which had been suggested, was enough. The normal turn out at parliamentary elections in Scotland is about 60 per cent, which would have meant a simple majority of one would secure an assembly. But we had been told there was an overwhelming demand for devolution in Scotland. One-third doesn't represent an overwhelming demand. I also thought we were entitled to expect a higher turn out in a referendum.'

Dalyell's reaction to the idea of a requirement amendment was 'tepid at first. It didn't seem to me the British way of doing things. But people who supported the government line kept saying there was an overwhelming demand for an assembly in Scotland. Those of us who opposed it decided we were entitled to know if this was true.' George Cunningham admitted: 'I think it's fair to say that devising that amendment wasn't Tam's style. The originator of the concept of the 40 per cent amendment was Robin Cook. As a Scottish MP, elected on a manifesto which promised an assembly, he felt obliged to support the bill. But he also felt the legislation should be subjected to a requirement of support from the electorate. During the long summer recess, Robin had been able to find only one person in his constituency who gave a damn about devolution. He thought a third of those entitled to vote would be enough. And an amendment to that effect went forward in the name of Bruce Douglas Mann. I did two things: first I changed Robin's figure, with a sub-amendment, to 40 per cent, then I got the bloody thing passed.'

With the country hopelessly divided over the merits of the proposed legislation, the debate in Scotland was a bad-tempered affair. Labour Party policy discouraged loyalist MPs from debating the issues with any of the dissidents, unlike the Britain-wide referendum on Europe, when umbrella organisations ensured those who disagreed with official policy could put their case without fear of reprisals. Barely a year later, the resourceful and combative Helen Liddell, secretary of the Labour Party in Scotland, set a different tone. 'We will not be soiling our hands by joining any umbrella Yes group,' she announced firmly.

Dalyell, who was a leading figure in the Labour Vote No campaign alongside Robin Cook and Brian Wilson, complained at the time: 'Some of us in the Labour Vote No campaign are beginning to wonder where all the pro-devolutionists, outside the SNP, have gone.' He also claimed: 'Overwhelmingly, Labour Party activists think it is high time the case for and against was deployed in public and in depth, in the interests of democracy.'

Dalyell was clearly sure of the merits of his case, and he was not the only prominent figure from the Labour side who criticised the devolution proposals. Robin Cook believed the assembly, with 150 more politicians, would add an unnecessary layer of government and lead to a loss of Scottish influence at Westminster. Cook, according to his biographer John Kampfner, dismissed devolution as 'irrelevant to the real problems we face. Given the present situation, to go ahead with devolution seems to be like fiddling while Rome burns.'

Still, no one representing the Labour Vote No campaign could find anyone in the party willing to debate the issue in public. In search of a suitable opponent, Dalyell turned to the seriously-out-of-favour Jim Sillars. Harold Wilson's last government was barely a year old when Sillars and John Robertson, MP for Paisley, stunned the PLP by defecting to form the short-lived Scottish Labour Party. Sillars had been a fast-ascending Labour star, on the brink of a glittering parliamentary career. Five years in parliament left him sorely disillusioned with Labour's attempts to deliver meaningful devolution. As a newly elected MP, he had been a ferocious critic of the SNP. Within a decade, Dalyell would claim he 'puts the pro-Assembly case better than anyone else I know, although his real aim is a separate Scottish state'.

Dalyell was aware that some of his colleagues opposed the idea of him 'taking on rebel Jim Sillars' on the grounds it might do 'a little to revive Mr Sillars' political fortunes'. With characteristic single-mindedness, however, Dalyell stuck rigidly to his opinion: 'Assuming people agree the future of Scotland should be debated, seriously and courteously, there ought not to be undue vexation that I have chosen Jim Sillars as a sparring partner.'

This held an uncommon appeal in the new media age, reaching beyond the contrived comfort of the television studios, and the restricted column inches of the daily newspapers, to confront people direct. Encountering them at Jordanhill College of Education in Glasgow, one disappointed reporter, Murray Ritchie, found their performance 'friendly and polite almost to the point of tedium. In the case of Jim and Tam, friendliness has bred philosophical accommodation. Never did an angry word pass.'

In an unequalled three-month-long slog through Scotland the pair visited 16 different centres. Sillars argued mainly that the consequence of a No vote in the referendum would be that 'all the institutions and distinctive character that makes Scotland what she is will be undermined and diminished in importance. No one in Westminster or the Common Market will ever again listen with respect to a Scottish voice, if we ourselves deny that any such thing exists.'

To those who feared that devolution could encourage separatism, Sillars asserted: 'The fact is that not once in the world has devolution ever led to separation, although there are countless examples where people, totally frustrated by a denial of some self-government, have been driven into the extreme of separation. Devolution, in practice, is the opposite of separation.' Dalyell countered by likening the Scotland Bill to 'the Sultan of Turkey's battleship, ingenious in many ways except that it would not float'. He also maintained that the proposed legislation raised expectations 'that neither this assembly nor anything remotely like it could do much about'. To him it continued to appear self-evident that since only a small number of people wanted the assembly for its own sake, 'the only logical reason for voting Yes is to get a stepping stone to a Scottish state separated from

England. If, however, you do not want a Scottish state separated from England, then you must make the effort to get to the polling station on 1 March and vote no.'

Meeting them as they approached the end of their self-imposed marathon, Murray Ritchie offered the view: 'Jim narrowly won on the clapometer, but Tam cornered the market in lapel stickers.'

As the day of the referendum approached, it worried Dalyell that the Prime Minister might suddenly appear in a Party Political Broadcast on the eve of the referendum and advise people to vote yes. In an appeal to the House of Commons a few months before polling he insisted: 'Just as in a general election, when things have to be done on balance, so they must be in a referendum. Both sides of the argument must be given fair treatment in the run up.' Later he said: 'Jim Callaghan was never convinced about the merits of devolution. My campaigning in a straightforward way against the legislation didn't bother him. What he didn't like, however, was the idea of us appealing to the Court of Session over TV access.' Callaghan's sole contribution to the referendum campaign was a fleeting visit to Glasgow on 12 February 1979. By then, as his biographer Kenneth O. Morgan noted, 'The polls in Scotland showed the majority in favour of devolution slowly sinking and the entire campaign poisoned by the bitter antipathy of Labour and the SNP.'

By having their case for equal access on television upheld in the Court of Session, the Labour Vote No team scuppered any plans which might have been hatching in Keir Hardie House for a last-minute emotive TV appeal, using allocated Labour Party time and featuring the Prime Minister. It also guaranteed their case would be heard in discussion programmes, which proliferated on all the main Scottish channels in the weeks immediately preceding the vote.

The absence of soothingly persuasive referendum broadcasts during the final stage of the campaign could have been a factor in helping to reduce the number of people voting yes. Hardline opposition to the idea expressed by leading members of the business community, alongside a well-funded Scotland Says No campaign, was another. Those who didn't vote didn't vote; although it was claimed many people who voted no or abstained had been lulled by Lord Home's cunning assertion: 'I should hesitate to vote no if I did not think the parties would keep the devolution issue at the top of their priorities.' This quite ignored the Prime Minister's blunt warning to Scotland that it was 'now or never.' Although it took some issue with him over the use of the word 'never' in politics, even *The Scotsman*, in urging its readers to vote yes, acknowledged the

Prime Minister was 'right in saying that Westminster would not touch devolution again for many years'.

Harry Ewing thought three main factors crippled the Yes campaign. 'One,' he said, 'was the 40 per cent amendment. Two was the Dalyell–Sillars circus going round Scotland. They did a lot of damage, playing to packed audiences from Inverness to Dumfries, saying the same things to each other, night after night. It's true they raised the profile of the referendum. But they also ensured a lot of other people with constructive arguments to make found themselves talking to empty halls. And lastly, of course, there was the SNP, saying vote for this and it will lead to separation. Every time one of them said that it cost the Yes campaign another 10,000 votes.'

Others argued that the government's appeal had been tarnished beyond repair by the events of the previous few weeks, known ever after as 'the Winter of Discontent'. Andrew Marr, writing in *The Battle for Scotland*, insisted: 'The devolution referendum result cannot be isolated from the general unpopularity of the Callaghan government during that winter of closed schools, piled rubbish, furious public sector workers, unburied dead and a general sense of drift.'

Snow on the day of the referendum probably didn't help. More than a third of those entitled to vote didn't turn up, and the rest divided almost equally, with 33 per cent in favour of the legislation and 31 per cent against. It was the worst possible result. Judged by two different sets of rules, two sides won. The yes vote won the day, but it failed by a wide margin to meet the conditions set by the Cunningham amendment. The narrowness of the vote, and the general lack of interest, was reflected in Lothian, part of which Dalyell represented at Westminster. On a 66 per cent turn out, the second-equal highest recorded on the day, the yes majority was 800 votes.

A retired Church of Scotland minister from Whitburn attacked Dalyell bitterly, claiming he was 'now a discredited politician'. However, Dalyell clearly believed he had been vindicated by the result. Before the referendum, people had been told by government ministers, the STUC, the Co-op Party and the Yes for Scotland campaign that 'an abstention equalled a no vote. In that case,' he declared, 'the result was a decisive no.' Dalyell added: 'Let's get on the with the real problems of Scotland, such as low pay. One cannot take care of these things by tinkering with the machinery of Scotland.'

Andrew Marr mused: 'It is quite clear that the 40 per cent hurdle was, in the context of a country that regularly elects Westminster governments on a minority of votes actually cast, an unusual stratagem, advocated by people who wanted to destroy devolution. But, given the actual result, it is hard to feel a sense of outrage that an assembly was not established because less than a third of the electorate wanted it.'

More than 20 years after the events of 1 March 1979 – in Wales, devolution had been rejected by a majority of four to one – Dalyell is convinced that the Cunningham amendment was a mistake. 'I thought it looked all right at the time,' he said, 'and I agreed to go along with it, to test whether or not support for devolution was really overwhelming. In retrospect, it was a dreadful blunder.' Harry Ewing thought the 40 per cent amendment was 'dishonest in the sense they knew it could never be achieved. Robin Cook's fingerprints were all over it. During the referendum, I got myself in hot water for saying publicly that anyone who stayed at home and didn't vote would be counted as a no vote. But that was the purpose of the 40 per cent rule. And not only was it the purpose, it was the direct effect. R.P. Fraser the Returning Officer for Scotland, told me I was right: anybody who stayed at home and didn't vote was a no vote, and would be counted as such. Tam came to regret it, because whatever else Tam does, he does not play unfairly. But he came to realise that what George Cunningham had done, promoted by Robin Cook, was downright unfair.'

Dalyell observed: 'It looked like a trick, a bit below the belt. There was a widespread perception that Scotland had been cheated out of an assembly. I should have seen it coming and didn't – my political antennae were pretty faulty. If we hadn't introduced the 40 per cent amendment, I am absolutely sure we would have obtained a decisive no vote. It's my biggest regret of the whole devolution exercise.'

Those who wanted devolution, regardless of the unconvincing nature of the vote, entertained the forlorn hope that the government could be persuaded to find the means. The Prime Minister showed himself unwilling to oblige. What followed was bloody. Following the repeal of the Scotland Act, the government lost a no-confidence motion, inspired by the SNP and finessed by the Tories, by a single vote. Roy Hattersley, a member of the outgoing cabinet, blamed Dalyell. 'He told me one of the side-effects of my 47 days on the floor of the House of Commons, opposing devolution, had been to bring down the Labour Government.' Dalyell thought the charge was 'preposterous and unfair'. Michael Foot, who carried the burden of the Scotland Bill in cabinet, acknowledged: 'Everyone knows Tam makes up his own mind in these matters and he's not going to be shifted. I discovered that during the whole of the devolution argument. I didn't agree with what he was saying but I respected the way in which he put his case.' Added Foot: 'If you are going to hold the United Kingdom together, you need a proper parliament working in Scotland. I don't think Tam has ever appreciated that fact, and he has always thought his objection was absolutely over-riding. I don't blame Tam for the failure of the Scotland Bill, but if we had been able to carry through the devolution scheme way back in 1979, we might have saved ourselves a lot of trouble, including the whole era of Thatcherism and all the wretchedness that involved.'

FIFTEEN

HUNTING THE BELGRANO

There was now a widely held view, inside and outside parliament, that Tam Dalyell's days as an MP could be numbered. Roy Hattersley wasn't alone in blaming him for the chain of events which ended with the no-confidence motion defeat of the Callaghan government on 28 March 1979. Large numbers of his constituents also held him personally responsible for the loss of the assembly. Although it would have been fair to remind them that the strategic amendment which brought about the end of the devolution process was in the name of an English-based MP, it was widely expected that Dalyell would suffer in West Lothian as a result. 'No doubt about it,' he said, 'the SNP were gunning for me right up until the polls closed. I was the one scalp they wanted above all others.'

That Dalyell's principal opponent in West Lothian was William Wolfe was by now routine. When the pair first met at the by-election in 1962, Dalyell had been defending an inherited majority of 9,371, and won comfortably. Ever since, however, apart from a backwards lurch in 1970, Wolfe had been steadily gnawing away at his electoral hide, moving from a 27.6 per cent deficit in 1962 to 4.4 per cent in October 1974. This last figure represented nearly a six per cent improvement from February. 'Did I ever think Tam would lose?' his constituency chairman, Allister Mackie, demanded with a chuckle. 'Oh, aye!' Dalyell responded matter-of-factly. 'I thought I would be defeated in both the 1974 elections. And five years later, because of my bloodymindedness over devolution, some of my own supporters thought I couldn't really expect to win. A poll commissioned by the Labour Party showed I was going to lose.'

By any calculation and assessment of the political runes, it appeared Dalyell was about to face his biggest test at the polls, outside his hopeless assault on the Borders in 1959. Allister Mackie agreed. 'His majority was under 3,000. Things were going badly for Labour, due to the Winter of Discontent and the loss of the assembly. Tam was really up against it.'

During the campaign Dalyell didn't let anyone forget how the SNP, the party represented by his main opponent, 'combined with the Tories to bring down a Labour government'. He also stressed that 'people in industrial Scotland have to understand that should Mrs Thatcher become Prime Minister – and this is the issue on 3 May – we would be in for a government of right-wing prejudice the like of which we have not seen since 1945'. Slogans about confrontation with the trade unions might sound attractive to some people, Dalyell conceded. However, as a past member of the TUC–Labour Party Liaison Group, he 'understood better than most the disastrous nonsense of such slogans in practical terms'.

The result of the vote in West Lothian surprised many people. Dalyell's winning margin of 20,082 over Billy Wolfe – seen by Allister Mackie as 'an excellent person, of very strong personal worth' – represented a 25.7 per cent swing against the nationalists in favour of Dalyell. Amazingly, the man from The Binns now enjoyed the highest majority in Scotland. 'Some of my colleagues were less than pleased,' Dalyell chuckled. 'It was absolutely against the trend. In my opinion, the reason it happened was because people decided, well, I might be right or I might be wrong about devolution, but I had a great deal to say on the subject. And I said it honestly.'

Other assessments of the final result (Dalyell 36,713 votes, Wolfe 16,631, the Conservative candidate J.R. Whyte 13,162, and the Communist candidate William Sneddon 404) suggested that in a largely working-class con-stituency, more lasting blame attached to the SNP for siding with the Tories to bring about the fall of a Labour government than against Dalyell for his stand on devolution. Billy Wolfe admits: 'Voting against Callaghan was a very bad mistake for the SNP to make.'

With Margaret Thatcher beginning her long tenure of Downing Street, the previous occupant, James Callaghan, waited until well into the following year before resigning his leadership of the Labour Party. Dalyell supported Michael Foot in the election for his successor. His wife wanted his vote to go to Denis Healey. Dalyell's reservations about the former Chancellor dated from Healey's days as Secretary of State for Defence. 'I am seldom upset by insult,' Dalyell explained, 'but I was jolly angry with him for saying that those of us who opposed the government's East of Suez policy had tiny minds. In 1976, when Healey was a candidate for the leadership, his campaign manager, Joel Barnett, pressed me to vote for Healey. I told him, "Joel, I've had only one serious conversation with Denis Healey in my life." And Joel Barnett said, "Well, that's one more than I've had." Denis Healey would not talk properly to his colleagues.' Dalyell confessed: 'My wife was very angry with me. She thought it was pusillanimous to vote for Michael Foot against Denis Healey. She believed Denis was electable and Michael wasn't.'

More than 20 years after the event, Denis Healey responded cheerfully: 'I thought his wife was a very nice woman and much more sensible than Tam. I mean, there was this element of the upper-class maverick about Tam. I am not particularly surprised he didn't vote for me; nor would I be worried, really. I am surprised he thought Michael would be a good leader of the Labour Party. I can't be sure we would have won in 1983, because we had so many problems then. But I think we would have won the elections after that. It's luck, a lot of it. It's being in the right place at the right time.'

Dalyell's reward, when Foot succeeded Callaghan, was a place on the opposition front bench. Neil Kinnock, appointed Shadow Spokesman on Education and Science, suggested: 'Science policy and science issues justified specialisation. I also thought Tam was best equipped to take on the role. Michael agreed. Tam was good,' Kinnock added, 'and, as intended, built on the reputation and contacts he'd made over his several years as a columnist on *New Scientist.*'

Said Foot: 'One of the great weaknesses of the House of Commons is its weakness in knowing about scientific subjects. Tam was one of the few MPs with an interest in science. I don't think Tam was always right in his scientific judgements, but it's good to have a minister who is in touch with the scientific world and who can talk to them and understand what they're saying. I think he could have been a very good minister, and he would have been especially good as Minister of Science.'

Dalyell's front bench career ended on 24 May 1982, fatally holed by his unremitting opposition to the Falklands War. Four days earlier, at the end of a long debate, Dalyell attempted to prolong the argument by forcing a vote on the adjournment. Labour MPs were ordered to abstain. Dalyell, along with 32 other members of the PLP and two Welsh nationalists, voted against the government. 'The main purpose of the vote,' Dalyell explained, 'was to demonstrate to the country and to the world that the oft-repeated claim by government ministers and others, such as Sir Nicholas Henderson, Ambassador in Washington, that the British parliament was united behind the sending of the task force was not true.'

Dalyell had been working to ensure this was the case from day one of the

Falklands crisis, Friday 2 April 1982, when the cabinet met in emergency session and the world learned about events in the South Atlantic. In his view, the government's response was dangerously mistaken. The fact that the task force sailed with Labour's blessing didn't alter his opinion. 'How, after the endless party agonising on the general principles of accountability,' he later complained, 'did it happen that the most crucial decision by a British government in a quarter of a century came to be endorsed by the parliamentary leadership of the opposition, with a minimum of consultation?'

That the PLP and the National Executive, together with 'other senior ruling councils in the trade union movement' later endorsed the leadership's stance failed to satisfy the MP for West Lothian. He believed there should have been a meeting of the PLP and the National Executive, to discuss the terms of Labour's reaction, before Michael Foot committed the party to action in the South Atlantic. Dalyell remained convinced that 'without the support of the official opposition in the House of Commons, I do not believe that even a Prime Minister of Mrs Margaret Thatcher's mulish obstinacy would have felt able to despatch the task force and still less inclined to persistently sabotage the various peace initiatives'.

Tony Benn compared Michael Foot's reaction to the Falklands invasion with 'Gaitskell on 2 August 1956, at the time of Suez. He made a very pro-Eden speech, and then such pressure was brought to bear on him by Alf Robens and myself that he reversed his line. Michael Foot made a very pro-Thatcher speech. The task of a backbencher who is active is to question. If you get a bit of flak, you have to live with it. Tam wouldn't be deflected by that kind of criticism in any way at all.'

It was an essential part of Dalyell's argument that 'once the approval of the House of Commons had been given to the task force, it was difficult for those who either had not been present, or who had not voiced their objection, to criticise the decision to send it'. Others acknowledged the truth of this. 'Michael Foot and various other people took a decision to support the government and we were bounced into it,' said one minister. 'But to rescind that decision would have meant Michael Foot and a whole host of other senior people having to resign. There would have been no option. We were in a bad enough state as it was at that time, but Michael Foot resigning would have made it a million times worse. Everybody knew the day the Falklands war started that it would be followed very quickly by a general election. I think if Tam made a mistake at all, it was in failing to take account of that possibility.'

Dalyell believed that 'had the debate lasted six hours, the normal time allotted on a routine parliamentary day, it would have been neither so tightly packed with MPs nor so highly charged. The hysteria, acknowledged by seasoned parliamentary observers in the press gallery as unique in their experience, would not have become so combustible.'

In fact, Dalyell was barely heard during the emergency debate on the Saturday morning immediately following the invasion: the first weekend sitting of the House of Commons since Suez, a quarter of a century earlier. The Prime Minister had been at the despatch box for nearly 20 minutes when Dalyell rose to inquire: 'Have we any friends in South America on this issue?' Mrs Thatcher replied firmly: 'Doubtless our friends in South America will make their views known during any proceedings at the Security Council. I believe that many countries in South America will be prepared to condemn the invasion of the Falklands by force.' It was Dalyell's one contribution to the proceedings: later, when he asked David Owen to give way, he was rebuffed with a short, sharp 'No.'

Earlier, Dalyell had listened with growing alarm as Michael Foot insisted: 'There is no question in the Falkland Islands of any colonial dependency or anything of the sort. It is a question of people who wish to be associated with this country and who have built their lives on the basis of association with it. We have a moral duty, a political duty and every other kind of duty to ensure that is sustained.' There was also, according to the Labour leader, 'the longer term interest to ensure that foul and brutal aggression does not succeed in our world. If it does, there will be a danger not merely to the Falkland Islands, but to people all over this dangerous planet.'

Dalyell had been interested in the apparently intractable question of what post-colonial Britain should do about the Falkland Islands for years before President Leopoldo Galtieri despatched his invasion force to South Georgia. In 1974, as chairman of the PLP foreign affairs group, he had been invited to attend a meeting with representatives of the islanders arranged by the Foreign Office. 'Foreign Office men who wanted the representatives of the Falkland Islanders to be reasonable and accommodating towards Argentina were near despair,' claimed Dalyell. 'There was no hope of a meeting of minds. They were more British than the British.'

According to Dalyell's account of the meeting, the islanders' demands included the provision of a decent airfield to make them less dependent on Argentina. 'They were clearly irritated and hurt,' he noted, 'when I suggested that I could not believe airport facilities for Port Stanley were a greater priority for the British taxpayer than improvement of the then primitive facilities at Edinburgh airport, which served thousands of times as many passengers.' His usual good temper evidently stretched, Dalyell left his listeners in no doubt that he thought it was 'high time they came to terms with the twentieth century and took positive steps to develop a warmer relationship with Argentina in general, and the Argentinians in South Patagonia in particular. After all, the South Patagonians lived in conditions very similar to their own rural, maritime surroundings.'

Dalyell 'refused to concede that territorial rights could ultimately be decided by 1,800 people, an implanted population, the majority of whose members were dependent on landowners resident in Britain, in particular the Coalite Company. In other words,' he argued, 'numbers do make a difference. It is also important whether the population is indigenous or not.'

There had been a number of attempts by successive UK governments to try to resolve the future of the islands. The last of these had been as recent as 1980, with Mrs Thatcher in Downing Street. One of her most trusted colleagues, Nicholas Ridley, then at the Foreign Office, attempted to broker a 'lease back' deal with Buenos Aires, similar in concept to the agreement reached with China over Hong Kong in the last years of the previous century. Dalyell thought Ridley, whom he had known since Eton, was 'surely the most undiplomatic man ever to be a Foreign Office minister'. But he also thought Ridley's proposals offered a real chance of achieving a lasting solution to the problem. The case Ridley made for recognising the reality of the need for negotiations with Argentina particularly impressed Dalyell, who claimed: 'Ridley's plan came unstuck because he was like a red rag to the bull of the Falkland islanders. Then, during a ministerial statement, he upset the House of Commons, as only he could, by offhanded and offensive disdain, even for those of us who agreed with him.'

On the morning of the first Falklands debate, Dalyell and his old friend George Younger, then Secretary of State for Scotland, travelled to London together following a chance meeting at Edinburgh airport. 'Talking about it on the way down, Tam said nothing to indicate he was passionately opposed to the idea of us recovering the Falklands by force,' said Younger. 'I think that when he got there, and saw it was obviously rather a dicey operation, he couldn't resist the opportunity to knock hell out of everybody.'

The following day, at a scheduled meeting of his local constituency party, a motion was passed giving Dalyell 'a free hand in opposing the sending of the task force.' Earlier, he'd telephoned Allister Mackie to discuss the crisis. 'I felt he wasn't sure which way to go,' said Mackie. 'We had our constituency meeting in the afternoon and he was swithering. But the constituency came out against sending the task force, and Tam went along with that view. Whether he very cleverly saw what the party wanted, or whether it was his own view, I don't know.' Dalyell later recorded: 'I do not pretend that I would have changed my mind on the task force if the West Lothian CLP had reacted differently. Their backing, however, was of enormous psychological importance. It gave me, as it would any MP, confidence to campaign within the party in the knowledge that I was voicing the views of those without whose work I would not be a Member of Parliament at all.'

The next day, with the task force preparing to sail, there was talk in the bars and tearooms of Westminster that Dalyell might be obliged to resign as a front bench spokesman due to his outright opposition to the government's action. Dalyell later claimed he made it clear he was prepared to resign, and that Michael Foot 'had only to give the word'. The fact he was able to continue openly opposing the war throughout April and most of May, while remaining part of Michael Foot's shadow team, convinced him that 'the Labour leadership, like most people in Britain, believed that it would never come to any kind of battle and that the dispute with Argentina would be solved peacefully through diplomatic negotiation'.

On Wednesday, 7 April, two days after the first vessels in the task force left port, Dalyell warned a meeting of the PLP that the further south the Armada went, 'the more impossible it would become for the Prime Minister to cry halt'. He didn't doubt Mrs Thatcher had the will to fight and he declared that any of his colleagues who thought otherwise were kidding themselves. But he also realised there was little support for his views within the PLP. Dennis Skinner told him bluntly as they left the meeting: 'Don't kid yourself that a majority of the PLP is on your side. Most of them simply don't agree with you.'

A meeting with the Prime Minister in her room at the House of Commons on 21 April 1982, two days after MPs returned from the Easter recess, did nothing to purge his concern. It followed an offer Mrs Thatcher made to Roy Jenkins in the House of Commons, saying she would give an interview to any MP who wished to see her. Few accepted the challenge – Dalyell did. 'To her credit, she saw me at 9.30 p.m., the same day my request reached her. Most courteous she was too.'

Thatcher greeted him with the offer of a drink and the disarming pronouncement: 'I've always got time to see the awkward squad!' Dalyell quickly learned 'the crux of the government's case was that the use of armed force must not be seen to be rewarded'. He left the meeting convinced that Mrs Thatcher 'would not compromise in giving Argentina even the most minimal of concessions that it needed'. As he later noted, however: 'The lady I saw in her room on 21 April was worried sick about what might happen to many young Britons in the task force. My judgement was that she was genuinely appalled. And any MP who observed her at close quarters on that dreadful night of 4 May, sitting dressed in black beside the Defence Secretary John Nott while he told us that HMS *Sheffield* had been sunk with losses, must have sensed that there was a genuinely distressed soul. Whether she was distressed about the loss of life or potential military defeat, I shall never know. My instinct tells me that Mrs Thatcher was, in her private moments, more deeply touched by the deaths, burns and maiming than she felt it prudent to publicly reveal.' Writing several months after the war ended, Dalyell also acknowledged: 'My complaint about Mrs Thatcher relates not to her private person, but rather to her public actions as Prime Minister and her general warlike demeanour.'

His conviction that the Prime Minister used the war to strengthen her grip on power, at a time when her opinion poll ratings were dangerously low and there was speculation she might be replaced as leader of the Conservative Party, brought angry denials from her admirers. Speaking in the House of Commons on 13 May 1983, more than a year after the first shots were fired, Cranley Onslow, Minister of State in the Foreign Office, suggested that 'his disgraceful vendetta against the Prime Minister' came close to being 'a gross abuse of the procedures of the House'.

One of the defining moments of the war, the sinking of the *General Belgrano* by the British submarine HMS *Conqueror*, with the loss of 368 lives in the freezing waters of the South Atlantic, was less than two weeks away. Two vintage Mark 8 torpedoes did the damage. The *Belgrano* went down stern first. Reporting to MPs on 4 May 1982, the Defence Secretary John Nott claimed the *Belgrano* and two accompanying destroyers had been detected at eight p.m. London time, two days earlier. According to Nott: 'This heavily armed surface attack group was close to the Total Exclusion Zone, and was closing in on elements of our task force, which was only hours away. We knew that the cruiser itself had substantial fire power, provided by 15 six-inch guns, with a range of 13 miles, and Seacat anti-aircraft missiles. Together with its escorting destroyers, which we believe were equipped with Exocet anti-ship missiles with a range of more than 20 miles, the threat to the task force was such that the commander could ignore it only at his peril.'

Next day, following the loss of HMS *Sheffield*, Nott emphasised that 'every action by our forces in the South Atlantic is taken within strict political control and authority. The actual decision to launch a torpedo was clearly taken by the submarine commander, but that decision was taken within very clear rules of engagement, which had been settled in London and discussed by the government.'

When he first rose in the House of Commons on Tuesday, 4 May 1982 to ask if the cruiser had been sunk with the Prime Minister's authority, Dalyell made no criticism of the action. He acknowledged: 'War is unpleasant. Unpleasant things happen, whether hostilities are declared or not.' Dalyell's later claim that the *Belgrano* was sunk in order to scupper a peace initiative by Peru continued to make headlines around the world long after the Falklands were recovered. On three separate occasions, he was ordered to leave the chamber of the House of Commons after he accused Mrs Thatcher of lying. He later wrote: 'The charge is not that Mrs Thatcher manipulated Galtieri into a military adventure against the Falklands. It is that, given the knowledge of a likely attack on the Falklands, the Prime Minister was quite content to let the situation run and, by seeming inaction, to lure the Argentines on to the punch. A little war, deemed to be righteous by public opinion, might restore the domestic political fortunes of a Prime Minister who sat lower in the opinion polls than any Prime Minister had done since political polling began.'

Three days before his meeting with the Prime Minister on 21 April 1982, it appeared to Dalyell that 'the cheerful confidence shown by many MPs before the recess had begun to fade. It had now become evident that the Argentines were not going to cut and run simply because the British fleet was on the distant horizon.' Five weeks later, Dalyell warned the House of Commons that Britain could be in danger of suffering 'a defeat of great magnitude'. He also insisted: 'It is not a matter of cowardice. The real cowardice of people like myself would be not to tell the truth as we saw it. It does nothing but honour to our forces to say that they are up against highly professional forces, whatever we may think of the Argentine regime. Should we not therefore say, faced with the stark reality of a war with unforeseeable consequences on a continent where we are friendless, that we advocate withdrawal of the task force to home ports?'

Dalyell worried that, faced with defeat, the government might resort to using nuclear weapons, despite being treaty-bound not to do so in the South Atlantic. Others discounted that danger, on the grounds that it would alienate the United States, and cause unimaginable trouble for Mrs Thatcher. Tony Benn thought 'the Americans would have punished her terribly because of the hostile public reaction'. Dalyell, however, took the view: 'Politicians and proud naval officers, facing possible humiliation and defeat, could resort to mad and immoral decisions.'

Dalyell continued to oppose the war for as long as the fighting lasted. However, it wasn't until early July 1982, and the return to Faslane of HMS *Conqueror*, that his particular interest in what happened to the *Belgrano* quickened. Asked why he sunk the *Belgrano*, Commander Christopher

Wreford-Brown told reporters he was acting under orders from Northwood. 'This,' Dalyell, observed darkly, 'was significantly different from what parliament, the press and the British people had been told.'

Later the same year, in a history of the war written by the *Sunday Times* Insight team, officers from the stricken vessel claimed they were on patrol outside the exclusion zone, and sailing west towards the Argentinian mainland, when the attack occurred. 'Whatever she was doing when the *Conqueror* first found her,' commented the Insight team, 'it was clearly of no immediate threat to the submarine, or the rest of the task force, since the decision as to what action to take was referred to Northwood and, in turn, to Mrs Thatcher's war cabinet. It was the war cabinet that gave the order for her to be attacked.'

Dalyell's formal campaign to learn the truth about events surrounding the sinking of the *Belgrano* began on 29 November 1982, with a question to the Secretary of State for Defence asking 'what course the *Belgrano* was steering when she was torpedoed'. As Clive Ponting, the civil servant put on trial at the Old Bailey in 1985 under Section 2 of the Official Secrets Act for passing *Belgrano*-related documents to Dalyell, remarked: 'It was the start of a long, lonely campaign to get at the truth. He was to be opposed every step of the way by the government, who were determined to try and ensure that he did not undermine what they had said earlier in 1982.' However, as Ponting also noted in his 1985 book *The Right to Know*, written following his sensational acquittal by a jury at the end of an 11-day trial, 'Dalyell had a reputation in Whitehall as a great campaigner who, once started on a subject, did not let go until he was satisfied. The *Belgrano* campaign was to turn out to be one of the longest, even by his standards.'

Dalyell piled question on question, to the undoubted irritation of many of his parliamentary colleagues with shorter attention spans concerning events in the South Atlantic than the MP for West Lothian. Indeed, between starting his campaign to establish the truth about the destruction of the *Belgrano* and the time it took before the government finally acknowledged, bit by bit, that the information originally given to MPs in early May 1982 was wrong on three important counts, his constituency changed to Linlithgow.

Slowly but surely, the facts of the matter emerged. Crucially, it was established that HMS *Conqueror* detected the Argentinian warship on Friday, 30 April, moving to within periscope sight of the *Belgrano* and her escorting destroyers, *Piedra Buena* and *Hipolito Bouchard*, the following day. *Belgrano* was sailing away from the task force at the time she was torpedoed.

The fatal order had been issued from the naval HQ at Northwood, with the approval of the war cabinet meeting at Chequers.

Dalyell then began his relentless pursuit of the Prime Minister. Why, he wanted to know, did she continue to maintain that HMS *Conqueror* 'sank the *Belgrano* immediately upon encountering it, when in fact the submarine tracked the cruiser for 30 hours before sinking it?' Dalyell believed 'had the *Belgrano* not been sunk, there would have been no retaliation against HMS *Sheffield*, HMS *Coventry*, and the supply ships of the British fleet'. Parliament, he claimed, had been 'grossly deceived'.

On 13 May 1983, more than a year after the event, Tory junior minister Alan Clark counter-claimed in the House of Commons that the decision to sink the *Belgrano* 'saved more lives than any other, because, after the sinking of the *Belgrano*, the Argentine fleet scuttled to port and did not emerge again'. A self-congratulatory note in his *Diary*, written two days later, records how he knocked 'poor dear Tam around as he ploughed on with his batty arguments about the *Belgrano*. So what does it matter where it was when it was hit? We could have sunk it if it'd been tied up on the quayside in a neutral port and everyone would still have been delighted. Tam is too innocent to see this.'

Dalyell worked tirelessly to project his case. His constituency neighbour Harry Ewing recalled a meeting in Grangemouth: 'Tam was due to speak on the subject of the *Belgrano*,' said Ewing. 'We'd booked a hall that holds 200 people. The meeting was due to start at half past seven. At half past six, the hall was full. So we asked the caretaker for another hall. That one seated 400 people. Before the meeting started, that hall was full. We finished up in a hall seating 800. It was packed, with people standing round the edges. Tam came down off the platform and walked up and down the centre aisle, talking without a single note. When he started, I'd say 90 per cent of the audience were against him. By the time he finished he'd completely reversed that, with 90 per cent on his side. I have never seen such a performance. Even people who went there to attack him finished up praising him. It was brilliant.'

George Younger, a senior member of the government outside the war cabinet, thought the delay between HMS *Conqueror*'s first sighting and ultimate destruction of the Belgrano could be traced to natural caution in Whitehall. 'You'll always find someone there who'll say, whatever you do, for God's sake don't do that!' said Younger. 'I thought Tam put two and two together and made seven. To me, it was plain as a pikestaff. If you have a huge and very vulnerable fleet in the area, there's only one option: eliminate the danger. The direction the ship was steaming at the moment it was hit may be of some rhetorical interest, but it is of no fundamental interest at all. Tam is wholly, enormously, switched on and quite intelligent enough to see that. In my view, he simply couldn't resist the wonderful role of hammer of the *Belgrano*.'

From his own side of the divided green benches, George Robertson, NATO secretary-general, and Secretary of State for Defence in Tony Blair's first government, thought it was significant that there was no complaint from the Argentinian government following the sinking of the *Belgrano*. 'You'd have thought the Argentinians would have been the ones making a fuss, going to the international court, raising war crimes actions against the UK government,' said Robertson. 'But they didn't. They seemed to think it was part of the price of war. The *Belgrano* wasn't out there on some sort of school cruise, remember. She had been ordered out to sea to sink British ships. It doesn't really matter which way she was headed: she was not out there for peaceful purposes.'

Writing in her own defence in *The Downing Street Years*, the former Prime Minister disdained from mentioning the troublesome Tam Dalyell by name. But he was almost certainly in her thoughts when she wrote: 'A large amount of malicious and misleading nonsense was circulated at the time and long afterwards about the reason we sank the *Belgrano*. These allegations have been demonstrated to be without foundation. The decision to sink the *Belgrano* was taken for strictly military, not political, reasons: the claim that we were trying to undermine a promising peace initiative from Peru will not bear scrutiny. Those of us who took the decision at Chequers did not know anything at that time about the Peruvian proposals, which in any case closely resembled the Haig plan, rejected by the Argentinians only days before. There was a clear military threat, which we could not responsibly ignore.'

Among those close to Mrs Thatcher, her official spokesman Bernard Ingham thought Dalyell 'had a prejudice about the *Belgrano* which was totally unreasonable. He objected to its sinking, and he objected to the loss of life. In other words, he quarrelled with our work at war. I don't think the *Belgrano* did him any credit whatsoever, except in the eyes of the trendy lefties.' In his view, Mrs Thatcher didn't suffer any embarrassment over the *Belgrano*; an opinion at serious odds with her unhappy appearance on a BBC *Nationwide* programme during the 1983 election campaign, in which she faced questions from 'ordinary' voters. Mrs Diana Gould, described as a housewife from Cirencester, asked her why the *Belgrano* had been sunk when it was outside the exclusion zone and sailing away from the Falklands. Mrs Thatcher explained it had been 'in an area which was a danger to our ships and the people on them'. Mrs Gould resolutely dismissed the Prime Minister's calm and practised rebuttal. 'She knew her facts and stubbornly stuck to them,' said Dalyell. A poll of memorable TV moments conducted in 1999 placed the Thatcher–Gould confrontation at number 19. Commenting for the programme, Ian Hislop, editor of *Private Eye*, remarked: 'This was the only time I ever saw Mrs Thatcher rattled in any interview and it was by a member of the public. It was a great demonstration, I think, of the limits of the professional media and the power of the general public, which is why politicians try to avoid the general public whenever possible.'

Diana Gould denied she had been coached by Dalyell in advance of her appearance on *Nationwide*. 'I wrote to him for information about the *Belgrano*,' she said. 'He sent me a list of all the important dates and referred me to Hansard. That was the extent of my contact with him before the programme. It isn't true, as some people suggested, that he used me to attack the Prime Minister. I didn't know him then. Later, though, I attended a meeting at Clive Ponting's house, when he agreed to support the campaign for a citizens' inquiry into the war. I also wrote a book on the subject and he contributed a foreword.' Dalyell added: 'Diana Gould wasn't exactly a housewife. She was a Cambridge graduate, a former naval officer, who taught geography at a huge girls' school. During the interview, she treated Mrs Thatcher as if she was a rather obstinate, wayward senior schoolgirl!'

Dalyell offered two reasons why the Prime Minister's discomfiture over the *Belgrano* failed to make any impact on the election. 'Most of the people who might have made something of it were out canvassing or at meetings, and missed the programme. In addition, the Labour Party was nervous about the whole issue of the Falklands and did not wish to harp on about the subject. The mind boggles at what the press would have done to a Labour Prime Minister who was exposed on television as Mrs Thatcher was by Mrs Gould.'

For the doggedly conscientious Dalyell, the Falklands war is 'unfinished business.' Seventeen years after it ended, he headed a parliamentary delegation to Peru. Fernando Belaunde Terry, former President and architect of the Peruvian peace plan, agreed to see him. The two men had last met in 1984 when Dalyell visited Lima at his own expense to inquire into the mystery surrounding the peace plan. Belaunde suggested then it would have been very odd if the British government did not know what his country was doing since 'the Peruvian peace proposals were on the international press tapes'. A decade and a half later his opinion hadn't altered. He felt 'certain that the Peruvian peace proposals had been conveyed to Mrs Thatcher before she made the decision to sink the *Belgrano*'.

Dalyell's account of his last meeting with the former President appeared in *The Scotsman* on 30 June 2000, more than 18 years after the task force sailed. It had been prompted by the news that the families of men drowned on the *Belgrano* were seeking damages from the UK government. Their action failed in the international court. Dalyell was never involved, but he couldn't resist the opportunity to disinter his campaign for the umpteenth time: 'If the object of sinking the *Belgrano* was to protect the British task force, it would surely have been deemed essential to sink the cruiser on first contact, when she was refuelling at sea, rather than waiting 30 hours and following her in a west-north-west direction, when each hour she was becoming less of a threat to the British task force.'

Writing in November 1982, Dalyell maintained: 'The most damaging charge against the politicians of the last two decades is one of cowardice, of recoiling from the effects of British public opinion, from confronting the Falkland Islanders with the naked truth – that Britain had neither the resources nor the will to guarantee them protection from Argentinian aspirations indefinitely, and that they would have to get used to that disagreeable fact.'

To those who questioned the cost of the original operation, Mrs Thatcher insisted on putting principle before money. In the 18 years that followed, according to the government's own 'best estimate', the cost of maintaining a British presence in the Falklands exceeded £4.1 billion. Money spent on the war alone, allied to the expense of maintaining a garrison on the islands throughout the following year, amounted to 'some £1,780 million'. The figure between 1983 and 1999, including the cost of constructing Mount Pleasant airfield, was 'some £2,263 million'. There were 'out-turn costs' in the 1999–2000 financial year, totalling £71.1 million. However, as Dalyell carefully established, these figures do not include the costs of the RAF air bridge to the Falkland Islands, or the cost of naval deployments to the South Atlantic, which fall to other budgets and cannot be identified separately.

Whether or not Britain will continue to sustain a military presence in the Falklands indefinitely is a question few dare raise. 'Our commitment to the Falklands over all these years has seen this country haemorrhage money,' said Dalyell. 'And since then, we have taken on other commitments in Kosovo, Bosnia and Sierre Leone. No one knows how long these will last. In the end, it will all depend on what we can afford.' As chairman of the all-party Latin American group at Westminster, he detects a feeling within other major South American countries, such as Brazil, Chile and Uruguay, that the islands remain an anomaly. 'I don't believe Argentina will try to recover the Falklands by force,' he mused. 'But it is possible there could be a diplomatic solution. This would mean a reprise of all the old arguments. But the pressure from other countries may be such that we can't avoid it. It's all very untidy.'

SIXTEEN

SUPPING WITH A LONG SPOON

Dalyell fought hard to keep his place in Michael Foot's front bench team. In the event of Labour winning the 1983 election, he desperately wanted to be a minister. Two days after he voted against the adjournment he wrote to Michael Foot, 'gently suggesting that it was not a good moment for the party to conduct shadow bloodletting'.

Dalyell identified a difference between the level of collective responsibility required in government and that which applied in opposition, when a party did not 'suffer the constraints of wielding power on a day-to-day basis'. He could recall occasions when opposition spokesmen ignored shadow cabinet instructions without suffering any penalty. In opposition, he argued, there were situations, when it was 'not unreasonable' to defy the principle of collective responsibility.

He also believed there had been a serious shift in opinion about the Falklands issue within the Labour Party, between 5 April 1982, when the task force sailed and he offered to resign, and 20 May 1982, when he defied the whips over the adjournment. It could be shown, Dalyell reasoned, that there was now 'a substantial amount of support' for his view at grassroots level. 'Out of 66 resolutions received from constituency parties at the party headquarters in Walworth Road,' he later wrote, 'no less than 60 were critical of the position adopted by the official opposition.'

In fact, it caused little surprise within the ranks of the PLP when Dalyell, together with Andrew Faulds, spokesman on Arts, and John Tilley, spokesman on Home Office Affairs, were sacked for not abstaining on the adjournment motion as instructed. It demonstrated to many observers, as

Tony Benn noted in his published *Diaries*, that Michael Foot was not prepared to tolerate 'any intra-parliamentary activity, let alone extra-parliamentary activity'.

Foot commented: 'We had to make up our minds what we thought about the whole situation. Tam urged me very strongly not to support any action to recover or protect the Falklands. He held that view absolutely and he pursued it through the whole of the controversy. But if we'd followed his policy, Galtieri would still be in control of the Falklands and Argentina. I told him we couldn't allow fascist dictators to get away with it. Tam put his case with absolute sincerity,' added Foot. 'And he had a good case to put. But I thought he was fundamentally wrong in his analysis.'

Dalyell responded: 'If he'd accepted my advice that Saturday morning before the task force sailed, then a Labour government might have been in Downing Street soon afterwards, and he might have been leading it. It was catastrophic for Michael Foot to make a statement endorsing Thatcher's action. If he hadn't done so, the whole political set-up in Britain would have been very different.'

Foot added: 'People who were against the whole expedition, and voted against it in the House of Commons, didn't get expelled from the Labour Party. In my day, they were perfectly respected for their views. But they couldn't expect to be holding positions inside the party at the same time they were opposing the party on one of its main policies.'

Dalyell had noted at the time: 'Getting rid of ministers or shadow ministers, who are old friends and supporters, is a painful part of the job of any Prime Minister or opposition leader. With me, the exchange was wholly civilised and friendly.' Years later, he revealed how when they met, Foot said, 'Tam, I'm very concerned about you.' He retorted, 'Michael, I'm concerned about you, which is much more important!'

Foot said: 'Tam never made any complaint to me about what I did then. Tam wouldn't object to me sacking him.'

Dalyell admitted: 'I knew in my bones that having left, I would never get back. It wasn't simply because I disagreed with the leadership over the Falklands. There was a widespread belief within some sections of the PLP that Tam Dalyell was hassle.' His old ally, Neil Kinnock, supported Foot. 'Tam knew the rules of voting responsibility related to a position on the front bench,' said Kinnock. 'He made his voting decisions conscientiously. But he knew they implied removal from the front bench. Michael's decision was therefore just.' Described by Margaret Thatcher as one of the 'awkward squad', Dalyell agreed: 'I am bloody awkward!' However, he denied emphatically that he enjoyed being difficult for its own sake. Dalyell insisted:

'Some people enjoy being awkward, but I'm not one of them. People are entitled to ask questions. But, no, I am never awkward just for the sake of it.'

Tony Benn, a close friend from his earliest days in the House of Commons, thought it significant Dalyell hadn't 'looked for promotion or abandoned a position in the hope of promotion. That's the key test,' said Benn. 'Very often people like that are given jobs on Harold Wilson's crude principle which he used to describe to me as: You're better having him inside the tent pissing out than outside pissing in. Tam would have been a brilliant minister. The fact he never achieved office means he has never been corrupted in any way by the temptation of promotion. And that gives him great strength.'

George Robertson, who arrived in the House of Commons 16 years after Dalyell and spent a large part of the following two decades as an opposition front bench spokesman before achieving a place in Tony Blair's first cabinet, offered the view: 'I think he could have been an effective front bench performer if he had taken that enormous talent and focused it on constructive things. But he's not a team player, and he never wanted to be one. In fact, he wanted to be an anti-team player. So his ability to focus on science, for example, was always going to be overwhelmed by a wish to dash off and do something else.'

Robertson's sentiments were echoed by his old mentor at Westminster, Denis Healey. 'Tam never showed any real signs of wanting office,' said Healey. 'He certainly didn't behave in a way which suggested he wanted office. A minister, as the word suggests, does have to administer, as well as decide policy. I don't think Tam would ever claim he had administrative ability. He had a good mind but a very flighty one.'

Viewed from the Conservative benches, George Younger thought him 'one of those chaps who hasn't got the capacity to trim his views to work as a committee man with his colleagues. He would be a nightmare in a cabinet. Whatever cabinet it was, and whoever else was in it, it would be about ten minutes before Tam was in fundamental disagreement about something, possibly something quite minor.' Dalyell's constituency chairman, Allister Mackie, denied that his failure to obtain a lasting place on Labour's front bench disappointed local activists. 'I don't think we ever had any aspirations that Tam would achieve high office,' said Mackie. 'He was always too honest – the idea of an honest politician may be a joke to some people, but Tam really is one.'

In fact, it was years before Dalyell abandoned all hope of a return to the front bench. As he once explained: 'In British politics, if an MP is seen as no longer to be fighting for a political future, colleagues reckon that it is a sign of slipping down the greasy pole. If an MP does not have a future, that MP does not have much of a present either. Reducing one's ambitions diminishes one's effectiveness.'

He steadfastly refused to apologise for maintaining a tough stance over the Falklands. 'When people ask me how I felt about being sacked from the front bench, I tell them I was right on the issue. The trouble is, if you leave the front bench over an issue, people automatically think, the bugger will do it again. I happen to think this is a very complex matter. People complained I wasn't a team player and it was claimed, in order to run a government or an opposition, you need people who are prepared to work as a team. You can't have people who are going to create trouble. On that, I'd say they've got me wrong. I wouldn't make a fuss about trivial matters.' Asked if he would have been prepared to find a place for Dalyell in his government team, Michael Foot declared, 'You bet! We had arguments, but we never had deep quarrels.'

In the end, it was Margaret Thatcher's long occupancy of Downing Street which destroyed Dalyell's hopes of ever holding office. Her landslide victory in the 1983 general election owed much to the huge wave of xenophobia which the Falklands war unleashed in England, and to a Labour opposition in almost total disarray. Dalyell, unsurprisingly, blamed Labour's sick state on events in the South Atlantic. His interpretation of events reflected three of his strongest personal prejudices, namely his dislike of Mrs Thatcher, his support for Michael Foot as leader of the Labour Party and his opposition to the war. With unabashed conviction he maintained: 'Before the task force sailed, Margaret Thatcher was struggling in the polls and in danger of being replaced as Tory leader. Michael Foot, on the other hand, generated tremendous enthusiasm among Labour Party activists. Without the Falklands factor, the whole scenario would have been different.'

Dalyell's own position as an MP wasn't seriously threatened. Boundary changes meant that after 21 years representing West Lothian, he would be contesting a new constituency with an ancient name: Linlithgow. The number of electors he was required to woo had been considerably reduced from 85,645 in 1979 to 58,111. Those he lost had been assigned to a new name on the political map, Livingston New Town. There the first time candidate was Robin Cook, previously MP for Edinburgh Central.

At one stage, the selection process for Livingston promised an intriguing clash between the future Foreign Secretary and another Labour heavyweight, Tony Benn. Said Benn: 'My constituency of Bristol South East had been abolished and redistributed in a way that made it a Tory seat. A lot of people said you should go somewhere else, because we want you in parliament. I was approached by six different constituencies, one of which was Livingston.'

Another was Sedgefield, Tony Blair's constituency which, if he'd had taken it, mused Benn, 'would have changed history a little bit'.

Writing in his *Diaries*, Benn recorded that Dalyell offered the opinion in his 'Tammish' way that Robin Cook had 'no special claim' on Livingston and that Alex Eadie, another neighbouring MP, would be friendly. Anyone tempted to accuse him of carpet-bagging was firmly disabused with the argument: 'On my birth certificate my father's occupation is given as Member of Parliament. He was MP for Leith. My grandfather was MP for Govan. My mother was a Paisley woman. Her grandfather was the Provost of Paisley. So, you see,' said Benn, 'I'm only half-English.'

A contest between Benn and Cook for the Livingston nomination was avoided when the veteran left-winger decided to stay and fight Bristol South East. 'I'm really pleased I did it,' said Benn. 'They'd supported me for 33 years. I didn't think I'd get back. Nine months later, Chesterfield came along. So it wasn't too bad.'

On safer ground, Tam Dalyell's chances of winning Linlithgow always looked good. For the first time since 1962 he didn't have to face Billy Wolfe, whose place as SNP candidate had been taken by D.H. Ramsay. In seven previous parliamentary contests it had been Dalyell and Labour first, Billy Wolfe and the SNP second, with the Tories usually a distant third. This time the race for second place was won by the Conservative candidate, C.I. Jones. Less than 1,000 votes separated him and the fourth placed candidate, P.P. Cockroft of the SDP, with the Communist Party, represented by Dr Morag Parnell, in their customary position a long way back, fifth. In the newly drawn constituency, Dalyell could no longer claim he was the first choice of more than half the people who had troubled to vote. But 45.1 per cent of the votes cast and a majority of 11,361 meant he could return to the House of Commons in good heart, knowing he continued to command the trust of a large majority of his mainly working-class constituents.

A good deal less appealing to Dalyell was the prospect of several more years of Conservative Party government with Margaret Thatcher as Prime Minister, supported by a majority of 144 in the House of Commons. Dalyell deplored the idea of either side enjoying a massive majority. A majority in excess of 50 allowed MPs too little control over the executive and was the enemy of good government, he argued. A decade and a half later, when it was Labour's turn to command the House of Commons with a majority of 179, his opinion hadn't changed. 'Large majorities are unhealthy,' he said. 'They were unhealthy for Mrs Thatcher and they're unhealthy for Tony Blair. He would have been a far better Prime Minister if he'd had a parliamentary majority of 30.'

Having finished one election, Labour quickly entered another when Michael Foot resigned as party leader. Dalyell supported Neil Kinnock against Roy Hattersley. 'I voted for Kinnock,' said Dalyell, 'first of all because it was a foregone conclusion. But I also thought, if I didn't vote for Kinnock, he would regard me in a way he didn't other people, as treacherous.' Considering he was in almost daily pursuit of the Prime Minister over the *Belgrano*, and was an unceasing embarrassment to large sections of the PLP, there was no chance Dalyell would be offered a front bench post, whoever won. His opportunity, he thought, might come at the next election, under Kinnock. 'I would have been loyal to him,' said Dalyell. 'We'd campaigned together against devolution. I used to send him rolls of Vote No stickers to use in his campaign in Wales. Then, when he was shadow education spokesman, he made that speech about laying down blood in the Falklands. That was cooked up after a lunch in Bathgate. In a curious way, I believe Neil Kinnock might have been a very good Prime Minister,' Dalyell continued. 'I'm not sure he would have been good at any other ministry. But as a Prime Minister, I do think he would have been rather good.' Said Kinnock: 'All is speculation. I would say, however, that his experience, his nose for smelling out nonsense, and his huge capacity for hard work would have made him a good minister. Whether he would have found himself able to accept the obligations of collective responsibility for an extended period is, however, a different matter. If the issue had ever arisen in the wake of a Labour victory,' Kinnock continued, 'I would have put the requirements of collective discipline to him fairly and squarely. He would then have made the choice. And, being Tam, honoured it.'

As well as badgering the government over the *Belgrano*, Dalyell's attention was fixed on the growing battle of wills between the National Coal Board and the National Union of Mineworkers. He represented a constituency with mining at its heart. He owed his position at Westminster to the fact that he had been nominated, in the first instance, all those years ago, by NACODS. He recognised that his debt to the mining community was incalculable. He once wrote: 'I have always believed that there is indeed something special about miners. Ever since my father arranged for me to go on a visit down a coal mine as a fourteen-year-old boy, I have had nothing but respect for those who win coal for the rest of us.' Allister Mackie maintained: 'He felt personally hurt by the miners' strike. Tam has nothing in common with a man living in a miners' row, but he perceives the constituency as a kind of extended family. He never forgave Mrs Thatcher for the way she treated the miners.'

In *Misrule*, written when the violent scenes and prolonged suffering which characterised the last great miners' strike were still fresh in the public mind, he wrote feelingly: 'I remember a score of men, once tough and strong, unable to mount their own staircase for want of breath. The price of coal was pneumoconiosis, and too often life itself. If people romanticise the coal industry, I just recollect attending too many funerals of young and middle-aged miners, killed in pit accidents or withering away through dust in the lung, to entertain these kinds of hallucinations.'

It was her approach to the 1984 miners' strike, as much as the Falklands, which finally turned Dalyell completely against Margaret Thatcher. As a junior minister in the Ministry of Pensions and National Insurance between 1961 and 1964, she attracted favourable comments from his old boss, Richard Crossman, then at work on his own scheme to improve the national pension system. Crossman found her tough, able and competent, one of the few Tories he bothered to greet in the lobby of the House of Commons, and , as he told his PPS, 'rather a pal of his'. He also thought she was 'as likely to lead the Conservative Party as Shirley Williams was to lead the Labour Party, but more likely to be the power equivalent of Barbara Castle'.

Dalyell, in his biography of Crossman published in 1989, went some way towards endorsing his old friend's warm opinion of the lady from Grantham. 'I too had a favourable view of Mrs Thatcher,' he conceded, 'until some months after she became Prime Minister.' In an interview with Kenneth Roy published the same year, Dalyell continued to maintain there had been a period when he wished Mrs Thatcher well, as the first woman Prime Minister. He also admired the 'gut courage' she displayed following the Brighton bomb attack by the IRA. But he couldn't forgive her handling of the miners' strike – he believed it was her duty to 'heal the situation in the coalfield' and instead, he alleged, she made it worse. 'Macmillan was a healer. Alec Home was a healer, even Heath was a healer. But not this bloody woman,' Dalyell thundered.

Dalyell was withering in his criticism of 'all those old Etonians' in the Tory ranks who failed to keep Mrs Thatcher under control. According to Dalyell, his former schoolmates had been 'absolutely gutless in dealing with the woman'. He thought she should be 'stuck up to, and confronted. Bloody well treated like a man.'

Elsewhere, he suggested it was important to remember that Mrs Thatcher had been 'a member of Edward Heath's cabinet, which had been brought down by the circumstances surrounding the miners' strike of 1974, and the three day week. Above all else, it mattered in life to Mrs Margaret Hilda Thatcher that she should be seen to be "different from Ted Heath".' Allister Mackie believed that representing a mining constituency, Dalyell 'inherited the problems of the miners, and the attitudes of the miners, even the prejudices miners have. He still has them. It wasn't an intellectual decision. It's something he absorbed – he can be quite malleable at times. It's just fortunate, with the miners, that it was the right environment.'

There were many people, including some on his own side, who thought Dalyell went a long way too far in his criticisms of Mrs Thatcher. His language, despite the quiet civility of its delivery, was often brutal. It was possible to disapprove of the Prime Minister and her policies and still object to hearing her called 'a bounder, a liar, a deceiver, a cheat and a crook'. This outburst, delivered in the House of Commons on 29 October 1986 during a debate on the Westland affair, was his measured response to an order from the Deputy Speaker, Harold Walker, to withdraw a previous remark in which he claimed the 'Prime Minister is a sustained, brazen deceiver now hiding behind cynical performances'.

When he refused to withdraw his remarks, suspension followed; a parliamentary rebuke delivered against his person on five separate occasions. Dalyell defends himself stubbornly: 'I have not particularly enjoyed being thrown out of the House for abusing long-standing rules of conduct which are central to the continuance of an effective parliament. But if heeding these rules means that falsehoods flourish unchecked and a vigorous institution becomes an empty parody, what other course is open?'

At the time of the Westland affair, according to one prominent Tory backbencher, Julian Critchley, the Prime Minister's 'own position was more vulnerable than the leader writers of our largely foreign-owned newspapers were willing to admit. Imperious and unpopular in the country, she was sustained by her party's instinct for self-preservation, the inertia of her backbenchers and the absence of an obvious successor.'

The crisis over Westland, a small helicopter manufacturing company based at Yeovil, began in December 1985. The company, though short on orders, was attracting the attention of two rival bidders, the American-owned Sikorsky company and a European consortium. The Prime Minister wanted the American bid to succeed. The Secretary of State for Defence, Michael Heseltine, favoured the European option. What might have been a disagreement between the Prime Minister and one of her senior colleagues, to be resolved in cabinet if necessary, erupted into a full-scale government crisis.

Within a few weeks Heseltine was gone, gathering his papers and striding purposefully from the cabinet room, to the astonishment of his colleagues and the great surprise of the usual media corps gathered outside. Leon Brittan, Secretary of State for Trade and Industry, also resigned, believing he had 'lost the confidence of his colleagues'. Even the Prime Minister, by her own admission, came close to losing her grip on power.

At issue was Heseltine's insistence that an American-owned Westland would be denied European military orders. A letter from the Solicitor-General, Sir Patrick Mayhew, to Heseltine dated 6 January 1986, copied to the Prime Minister and the Secretary of State for Trade and Industry among others, warned there were 'material inaccuracies' in the correspondence between him and the consortium's bankers. Westminster was stunned when selected passages from Mayhew's letter appeared in the afternoon edition of that day's evening papers. Law officers' letters were rarely leaked: their advice to ministers was considered sacrosanct.

There was general agreement that the Solicitor-General's letter had been selectively leaked in order to inflict maximum political damage on the 'shamelessly and honourably ambitious' Heseltine. Mayhew and the Attorney-General, Sir Michael Havers, wanted an inquiry. At one stage, Downing Street appeared to resist. Sir Michael threatened to call the police. 'Here,' Dalyell observed drily, 'was the senior law officer of the Crown returning from his sickbed and threatening to send the constabulary to the doorstep of Number 10. Hardly an everyday occurrence.' Denied an inquiry, he claimed, 'the Attorney at that point in time would have resigned on a matter of principle, taking the Solicitor-General with him. It would have been one thing to lose a Defence Secretary – another to lose a Trade Secretary – but to have the Law Officers resigning as well on a matter of principle would certainly have portended a change of Prime Minister, if not a change of government.'

Dalyell's role in the affair was simple and straightforward: he named the source of the leak as Colette Bowe, Chief Information Officer at the Department of Trade and Industry. 'I had a bad night afterwards,' Dalyell admitted. 'I don't like dumping people in the mire. But I needed to show the story for precisely what it was, an attack on Heseltine. I'd discovered that the person who wrote the report was Chris Moncrieff of the Press Association. It was inconceivable to me that this particular journalist would quote selectively from a law officer's letter. I also knew he would only accept the story from someone who was in a position to know. I learned that person was Colette Bowe, but the person who told me wasn't Chris Moncrieff.'

As the row rumbled on accusatory fingers pointed in several directions, not least at Mrs Thatcher and her staff, before blame for the leak attached itself to Leon Brittan. Interrupted at lunch by a telephone call from a civil servant, he agreed to the release of the letter, 'subject to the agreement of Number 10'. Telephoned by Colette Bowe, the Prime Minister's hugely experienced press secretary, Bernard Ingham, refused 'point blank' to let the letter come from Downing Street. 'At no time was I asked to approve of the disclosure,' he later insisted. 'I could not have done so without seeking Mrs Thatcher's specific permission, and I would not have been prepared to put such an idea to her.'

Dalyell said: 'It was civil servants allowing themselves to be used by the politicians that caused the trouble. Colette Bowe was given immunity from prosecution. She acted very sensibly and correctly, from her own point of view. She disapproved strongly of the action she had been forced to take and was determined not to be made the scapegoat. I took the view that she didn't deserve protection, although I did have qualms about doing what I did, as anyone would. I don't think she was unduly harmed in the civil service,' Dalyell added, 'not by the permanent secretaries. The senior civil service were absolutely shocked at the selective use of a law officer's letter. In fact, as far as I'm aware, her career flourished. She wasn't my source, she was Chris Moncrieff's source. I haven't knowingly spoken to her in my life.'

Dalyell, the Prime Minister's most persistent critic, and Bernard Ingham, her principal protector, were never likely to agree about anything involving Mrs Thatcher. 'I've said repeatedly we were very fortunate to have him as an enemy,' said Ingham. 'I think he damages his good qualities by his lack of control. On most of the issues he didn't have much credibility. I took the view that if I'm being attacked by Tam Dalyell, I must be doing something right.' According to Dalyell, the bluff Yorkshireman who served as Mrs Thatcher's high-profile press secretary during the whole of her time in Downing Street was no ordinary press officer. Ingham, he once claimed, was 'arguably the most important man in the government'.

Ingham, a former *Guardian* journalist, complained none-too-bitterly: 'Mr Dalyell will believe anything if it accords with his prejudices. Is this, I wonder, the definition of a dangerously happy man?' He added: 'I think he is to be congratulated on his consistency in attacking government. If he espouses a cause, such as the *Belgrano,* he never lets go. And he shows very considerable political courage in pursuing it regardless of whether or not it is popular. But I think he is his own worst enemy, because he isn't taken seriously.'

Dalyell, according to Ingham, was 'a wonderful conspiracy theorist. He really is quite comical on conspiracy theories.' He dismissed Dalyell's claim that a 1987 police raid on the headquarters of the BBC in Scotland, described by the local MP, Roy Jenkins, as the work of 'a second-rate police state' was authorised from Downing Street. In his 1991 account of his career, *Kill the Messenger,* and on the lecture circuit for years afterwards, Ingham insisted with dry good humour: 'I suspect that I have a singular lack of influence over

Her Majesty's constabulary. I have never put it to the test. I am just grateful that they have got me safely through life this far.'

During the 28-hour-long night search of Broadcasting House, Glasgow, over the weekend of Saturday, 31 January and Sunday, 1 February 1987, police and Special Branch officers from London required three vans to transport film, video tape and documents to the headquarters of Strathclyde Police in Pitt Street. Reports indicated the material was removed after BBC staff were wakened from their beds and ordered to assist the search. Two previous attempts to obtain warrants under Section 9 of the Official Secrets Act failed when it was ruled in the Court of Session that the first warrant was 'too far-reaching and vague' in its demands; while the second applied to the wrong address. BBC assistant director general Alan Protheroe observed later: 'It's quite clear the police are determined to get hold of this material. However careful, however precise, however dramatic the legal arguments may be, warrants will keep on coming back until a warrant that is entirely waterproof is produced.'

The raid on BBC Scotland was the latest evidence of acute government anxiety over the contents of a controversial six-part series, *Secret Society*, involving investigative journalist Duncan Campbell. The Zircon programme centred on a secret satellite which Campbell claimed could eavesdrop on half a continent, or only on a single building. Earlier, when the BBC bowed to government pressure and announced it wouldn't be shown, Campbell published his findings in the *New Statesman*. The authorities responded with police raids on the magazine's office and Campbell's home.

Commenting on the raid on BBC Scotland, the *Glasgow Herald* presented its readers with a disturbing scenario: 'Having thoroughly searched the offices of a dissident magazine, the secret police then worked through the night removing documents from the headquarters of the broadcasting organisation.' Added the right-wing-leaning *Herald*: 'It is not of Eastern Europe that we write, but of our own dear free country. The actions of the government in the Zircon affair began by seeming merely incompetent. They now appear incomprehensible and, worse, sinister.'

When he first learned the Zircon programme had been banned by the BBC on security grounds, Dalyell characteristically looked for deeper reasons. 'When it emerged that the source of the commotion was some geostationary satellite that we were proposing to hoist up over the Indian Ocean,' he commented soon afterwards, 'scepticism spawned more scepticism. Geostationary satellites are not nowadays really very special creatures.' He also claimed that as soon as a satellite appeared over the Indian Ocean, it would be picked up by Soviet satellites. The fact the Zircon programme featured contributions from two establishment heavyweights, Sir Frank Cooper, ex-permanent secretary, and Professor Sir Ronald Mason, Chief Scientist of the Ministry of Defence throughout the Falklands war, helped to heighten his suspicion that security was not the real reason for the ban. A report in *The Observer*, dated 18 January 1987, suggested 'half a billion pounds had been kept from the scrutiny of parliament, through the Public Accounts Committee'. 'Having served in the 1960s on the PAC under three chairmen,' Dalyell observed, 'I am alert to anyone who attempts to mess around with that body.' He was soon convinced that whatever the Zircon affair was about, it was certainly 'not about the technology of geostationary satellites'. From his personal viewing of the programme, Dalyell decided 'political embarrassment' was the reason the government wanted it buried. On costs, he alleged, 'there has been a flagrant breach of promise to parliament'.

During one Commons exchange, Dalyell had been attacked by Malcolm Rifkind, the Secretary of State for Scotland, when he suggested police officers would not have initiated such a raid 'unless they were very clear they had ministerial authority'. Dalyell also wanted to know if the Prime Minister's press secretary, Bernard Ingham, had been involved in any way. His remarks angered Rifkind, who dismissed them as insulting and irresponsible.

Later, Dalyell found 'answers to legitimate questions became terser and terser, walls set up in order to gain time and create conditions whereby other matters engage public attention, and awkwardnesses vanish through boredom'.

But in one matter relating to Zircon at least, Dalyell's vision of the will of parliament prevailed. As he reported in *Misrule*, a government move to have 'the House of Commons ban itself from seeing material the government had managed to ban elsewhere' was frustrated by 'an unlikely combination' of Tony Benn, Enoch Powell and former Prime Minister, Sir James Callaghan. Dalyell believed that if passed, the motion would have been 'a remarkable curtailment of the rights of the House. Fortunately, it rose to the occasion and party divisions were, for an historic moment, set aside. It was a galling experience for Mrs Thatcher,' Dalyell added with unconcealed satisfaction, 'no less so for being uncommon in these last eight years.'

Dalyell's first contact with the dark underside of Britain's secret world happened without his knowledge when he was just 15, on a visit to the Courtauld Institute. Taken on a tour of the gallery, as part of a group from Eton, he was given, as he recalled half a century later, 'an understanding of Poussin and the French Impressionists which enriched our lives'. His guide, Anthony Blunt, was the son of a clergyman, a Cambridge graduate, former

MI5 officer, Director of the Courtauld Institute and Surveyor of the King's Pictures. Three decades passed before Margaret Thatcher revealed in the House of Commons, on 15 November 1979, that Blunt had been a long-serving Soviet spy. It also emerged that his activities had been known to the authorities since 1964 when it was agreed, in return for his confession, that he could 'continue with his Royal appointment, retain his knighthood and pursue his life and career normally'.

Mrs Thatcher's announcement had been prompted by a question from the Labour MP, Ted Leadbetter. In an obituary of Leadbetter, published in *The Independent* on 27 December 1996, Dalyell appeared to condone Blunt's wartime activities on the grounds that 'the Soviets were allies and the intelligence comings and goings of the Second World War were exceedingly complex matters, to be seen in various shades of grey'. Having put this view of things to Leadbetter following the announcement of Blunt's treachery, according to Dalyell's own account of their encounter, his fellow Labour MP exploded: 'Bloody elitist! Why the hell should there be special treatment for Blunt and his ilk? It's my responsibility as a Member of Parliament to deal with these upper class spies.'

Two years later, a full account of Blunt's activities appeared in *Their Trade is Treachery*, written by the distinguished Fleet Street correspondent Chapman Pincher. Famed for his high-level contacts inside the security service and throughout Whitehall, Pincher sensationally alleged that Sir Roger Hollis, a postwar head of MI5, was a Soviet agent. People puzzled that nothing was done to prevent publication of the Pincher book – yet not long afterwards, the government went to what proved disastrous lengths to stop *Spycatcher* by the former MI5 officer Peter Wright from appearing. Among his allegations was the claim that during the period of the first Wilson government, MI5 officers burgled and bugged the offices of leading Labour Party figures, including the Prime Minister, in an effort to determine if Wilson or any of his close political associates were communists, or even Soviet agents.

On 26 March 1987, Dalyell challenged the Prime Minister to 'refer to the Security Commission allegations of security services operations against Ministers of the Crown in the 1970s; and if she will make a statement'. Mrs Thatcher replied, 'No.'

Dalyell accepted that a very respectable case could be deployed against 'the thesis that we all have an absolute right to know absolutely everything. In my view, contrary to that of some of my best political friends,' he explained when the Wright case was at its height, 'we do not and should not have any such right. Nor should ex-employees of the state, working in the security services, believe that it is acceptable to break their oaths of confidence, and publish what they will, either for money or to advance their own views or their vendettas against former colleagues, alive or dead. Reluctantly, I concede that the nation needs a secret service and that it needs to know that its activities will remain secret.' However, he also believed, equally strongly, that 'when politicians mount their high horses in public, involving this sacred principle or that, it is wise to sup with a long spoon'.

Dalyell claimed 'one of the Prime Minister's main motives in launching the prosecution of Wright stemmed from the frenetic pressure of MI5. If Wright's revelations were to be made public, officials feared that a future Labour government would be tempted to purge, or even disband, the existing Intelligence services and start afresh. This would not be the cosily anti-Labour world of MI5 that Mrs Thatcher wished.'

It figured in Dalyell's calculations that Wright had been the subject of a *World in Action* programme broadcast on ITV on Monday 16 July 1984. 'What conceivable logic is there,' Dalyell demanded, 'in doing nothing about a television programme featuring an ex-employee of the security services, seen by eight million-plus people, and then making a mountain out of a relative molehill by attempting to stop his memoirs being published? None whatever.'

Dalyell sympathised with Sir Robert Armstrong, the cabinet secretary, who was ordered to Sydney to defend the government's position before the Supreme Court of New South Wales. 'Mrs Thatcher bounced Sir Robert Armstrong into a task which he did not want, which was none of his business, which was a perversion of the age-old niceties, and which he knew from an early stage was a certain loser,' Dalyell declared. 'Mrs Thatcher sent him, in the full glare of worldwide publicity, to defend a case which was indefensible.' During his evidence, Sir Robert confessed that in his job it was sometimes necessary 'to be economical with the truth'. The phrase wasn't original, although there were few who recognised that at the time. Delivered by Sir Robert Armstrong in the Supreme Court of New South Wales, it attached itself firmly to the British cabinet secretary. Wherever English was spoken, Dalyell remarked, it would 'last for a thousand years'.

SEVENTEEN

AN HONOURABLE MAN

Like a good many other people on both sides of the House of Commons, Tam Dalyell's hopes of a ministerial career vanished with Mrs Thatcher's long tenure in Downing Street, followed by John Major's surprise victory in the 1992 general election. 'I certainly can't blame Tony Blair for not making me a minister,' said Dalyell. 'By the time he won in 1997, age had overtaken me. My ministerial sell-by date,' he vouchsafed gloomily, 'had been passed!'

Ten years earlier, in the 1987 election, he had been obliged to resist a fierce challenge from Jim Sillars, representing the SNP. His old debating chum from the devolution roadshow a decade earlier was well-known and popular throughout Scotland, despite the failure of his short-lived Scottish Labour Party. When the two men faced the voters in Linlithgow memories were stirred of the 17-year-long battle between Dalyell and Billy Wolfe to win the hearts and minds of West Lothian. There, as history recorded, Labour always won, with the SNP second. At the previous election, following boundary changes, the SNP had been relegated to third place behind the Tories in Linlithgow. Four years later, Sillars added 6.5 per cent to the SNP vote and finished second. Tory hopes, forlorn before but raised at the last election, slipped again, due, at least in part, to the Prime Minister's failure to convince voters in Scotland that her social and industrial policies would bring lasting benefit to everyone in Britain.

The final voting figures for Linlithgow on 11 June 1987 were: Dalyell 21,869 votes; Sillars 11,496 votes; T.C.R. Armstrong-Wilson, representing the Tories, 6,828 votes; Mrs H.A. McDade, from the SDP, 5,840 votes. The Communist Party, undeterred by a long succession of poor returns in the area, were also represented. Their candidate, John Glassford, received 154 votes. Dalyell's majority: 10,373.

Nearly a full five years later, with Mrs Thatcher despatched from Downing Street in a flurry of tears, it was John Major's turn to appeal to the electorate. The new Premier considered Tam Dalyell 'an honest, courageous man whom I respect'. It hadn't escaped his notice that by raising the West Lothian question during the devolution debates, Dalyell had been 'rewarded with abuse, intimidation and threats from his fellow party members'. The same cruel treatment awaited John Major in the years ahead – and this despite his unexpected triumph at the polls on 9 April 1992.

Kenny McAskill, the third candidate in as many elections to shoulder the SNP challenge against Dalyell, was rewarded with a near four per cent swing in the 1992 election. Those voting for McAskill totalled 14,577 against 21,603 for Dalyell, reducing his majority to 7,026. Miss Elizabeth Forbes registered the highest Tory return in the new constituency to date, with 8,424 votes, with M.G. Falchikov, representing the Liberal Democrats, attracting 3,446 votes.

Following another long parliament, and more boundary changes, Dalyell restored his lead over the SNP on 1 May 1997 with a notional swing of 4.1 per cent and a majority of 10,838. The figures then were: Dalyell 21,469 votes, Kenny McAskill 10,631 votes, Tom Kerr, for the Conservatives, 4,964 votes, Andrew Duncan, Liberal Democrats, 2,331 votes, and Kenneth Plomer, representing the Referendum Party, 259 votes.

Almost 35 years earlier, Dalyell had made his way to Westminster for the first time, the surprising upper-class choice of an essentially working-class constituency. Following the vote in Linlithgow on 1 May 1997, the man from The Binns would be attending his eleventh parliament. And the credit for this, Dalyell acknowledged gratefully and repeatedly, belonged to 'a whole lot of people who sweated their guts out tramping the streets of the constituency in order to get me elected'.

In large sections of the public mind, and, probably to worse effect, among many of his contemporaries at Westminster, his reputation was firmly fixed: Tam Dalyell was there to give governments, whatever their colour, a bad time. In particular, it appeared, he required a good deal of convincing before British troops were deployed in dangerous situations abroad. Those who complained about his opposition to the task force, the war in the Gulf and the NATO-led action in the Balkans also believed, as a prominent and long-serving MP, that his firmly stated opinions provided propaganda for the enemy. It troubled George Robertson and Bernard Ingham, for example, that Buenos Aires, Baghdad and Belgrade had all used Dalyell's name and seniority in the House of Commons to undermine Britain's position during the Falklands campaign, at the time of the Gulf War and in Kosovo. 'On most of the big things he has been more wrong than right,' Robertson claimed. 'In some cases badly wrong, on other occasions dangerously wrong.' Robertson, Secretary of State for Defence in Tony Blair's first cabinet, and now Secretary-General of NATO added: 'A lot of people in the Labour Party were unhappy about having the war. But Saddam had invaded Kuwait and was threatening to extinguish it. There was no point pretending diplomacy would get him out. But Tam kept saying don't do it, you can't do it, it's wrong to do it and taking his side. It irritated me because I was bearing the brunt of it and I kept saying to him, answer me this question: When Hitler invaded Poland would you have been in favour of war? But he never answers the question.'

Dalyell reacted angrily. 'Tony Benn and I deeply resent cheap and sly attacks of this kind from people who have never been in the forces themselves when we criticise their wars,' he declared. 'I would have volunteered the moment Hitler entered the first non-German territories, that is, when he crossed the Sudetenland into Czechoslovakia. I might have gone along and not asked for war when he went into Austria, because he was obviously welcomed in Vienna. And he was welcomed in the Sudetenland. But when he wasn't welcomed in Czechoslovakia, that was a different story.'

Tony Benn was equally blunt. 'Claire Short implied we were pro-fascist because we were against what was being done in Kosovo,' he said. 'These charges are made all the time. It's a form of scapegoatism and smearing that Tam wouldn't allow himself to be affected by. You are told, you must always support our troops, our boys. All that means is the politician is shielding behind the troops he's sent to war. When the war is over and our boys come back, gravely injured or with Gulf War Syndrome, nobody's interested in them at all. They turn up at the DSS and they're told they've got to have a means test before they get the disability allowance.'

A hugely unrepentant Dalyell also insists: 'When people say I was wrong about the Falklands, wrong about Iraq and wrong about the Balkans, I ask them to explain in what way I was wrong. The Falklands War was fought for domestic political reasons. And the injury to Britain in Latin America was absolutely appalling. There is a consensus in South America that the generals would have gone anyway. If I had won on this, there would have been a settlement of the Falklands problem. It is still a problem.' He continued: 'If I had won on Iraq, we wouldn't be sending planes over Iraq, day and night. The second biggest, and what is likely to be the third biggest, oil reserve in the world wouldn't be denied to us. There wouldn't have been 500,000 dead Iraqi children. And the whole situation in the Middle East might have been a good deal more stable. I thought much of what was said about the clever northern Arabs, namely the Iraqis, was unjustified – black propaganda, like the story of Iraqi soldiers upending babies' cots in a hospital in Kuwait which was the work of a US public relations firm, as an investigation by *The Guardian* and Channel 4 revealed. When I went with Albert Reynolds, the former Irish Prime Minister, to Iraq and we met Saddam Hussein's foreign minister Tariq Aziz, he told us, "You may think that Saddam and I are extremists. We are nothing compared to what will follow if this sanctions business isn't sorted out".'

Dalyell went on: 'I said the bombing of Belgrade would achieve nothing, at party meetings and to the Prime Minister privately before it happened. And I was right. Without the Balkans war the biggest drug traffickers on the planet, namely the Albanians, wouldn't be operating to the same extent. The Danube wouldn't be blocked. Great sections of Serbia wouldn't have been laid low. The monasteries wouldn't have been destroyed. Society there wouldn't be about to implode. And the situation in Kosovo itself would be a bit different.' He recognised, after the event, having argued against UK involvement in Bosnia and Kosova, that a British presence was essential to prevent a bloodbath. 'Without us there, they would be at each other's throats,' he conceded.

However, this concession didn't stop him worrying that, with the country's forces already stretched, Britain could be engaged in a never-ending commitment to the Balkans. On a four-day visit to the Royal Scots Dragoon Guards stationed near Podujevo, he asked a group of Albanians how long they expected the British to remain. 'Forever!' he was told. When he reported this experience at a meeting of the European Standing Committee in the House of Commons a few days later, he also disclosed he'd detected 'a thirst for revenge in Serbia. That is why we need to adopt a long-term view and establish what can be done to stop Armageddon from breaking out again. The next time,' Dalyell warned, 'the Russians might be rather less helpful. The situation is fraught with danger.'

Writing in *The Spectator* on 29 July 2000, the former tank crewman complained: 'It is deeply unsatisfactory that an armoured regiment should be asked to perform an infantry role – or, more accurately, a police role.' He also noted: 'NATO allegedly went to war to bring an end to ethnic cleansing by Serbs; what has occurred, with a vengeance, is ethnic cleansing of Serbs by Albanians.'

Occasionally, Dalyell finds it necessary to remind everyone he isn't a pacifist. 'I have served in the army,' he said. 'I have seen the effects, though never in anger, of modern weapons.' Addressing the general question of

Britain's military involvement in events which might be considered someone else's business, Dalyell insisted, 'I am against becoming involved in military situations where you don't have an exit. It's always a damned sight easier to put an army into a situation than to pull it out.'

✧ ✧ ✧

Neil Kinnock's mixed, but finally disappointing, spell as leader of the Labour Party ended with his defeat in the 1992 election. It was now John Smith's turn to step centre stage, as Leader of the Opposition. Dalyell, who voted for Smith in the leadership contest against Bryan Gould, explained: 'I was coloured against Bryan. John Smith was of the party. I'd also noted he hadn't done anything about devolution. It's true he talked about unfinished business, in his West Highland way. But did he give his mind to it? No, he didn't!'

Dalyell didn't doubt Smith would have made 'an effective and, with luck, a great Prime Minister'. Among the qualities Dalyell admired was his well-developed 'forgettory' about past political disagreements and the manner in which he would 'unerringly latch on to the weakest point in a political opponent's argument, or a verbal ambiguity, and flog it for what it was worth to his own advantage'. The fact that John Smith was 'a tremendous gossip' also attracted Dalyell. 'I could gossip to him very easily,' he said. Smith's kindness in visiting him in hospital, following a hip operation, and ordering him to 'stay away from the House of Commons, whatever the vote' also impressed the veteran MP. 'He knew my operation needed time to heal.' Dalyell added: 'I am not saying John Smith was an admirer of my political judgement. We were totally different political creatures. I was an issue politician. John Smith was absolutely careful about doing nothing that was not about power: obtaining power and exercising it. Donald Dewar was a passionate believer in the whole idea of devolution and talked about "John Smith's unfinished business". It was nonsense! John Smith never really gave his intellect to the nuts and bolts of devolution from the day of the referendum in 1979 to the tragic morning he died.'

Dalyell's vote in the leadership contest which followed John Smith's death was kept from Tony Blair. His preferred choice from the three names available – Margaret Beckett, Tony Blair and John Prescott – was Prescott. 'I regret now that more of us within the PLP didn't try to dissuade Gordon Brown from taking the decision not to run,' he said. 'I am sure he bitterly regrets it. Brown certainly believes he was deceived over the business of who should run, him or Blair. Maybe there can't be friendship at the top of British politics. I am sure when they both leave office it will all come out.' Before the 1997 general election which swept New Labour to power, Dalyell had visited the chancellor-in-waiting, Gordon Brown, and 'pleaded with him to do two things: one, to give the Bank of England its head, two to join the Euro'. Dalyell believed 'not joining the Euro at the first possible opportunity was a historic mistake'.

Dalyell's commitment to the idea of European union has been unswerving, starting with his support of Britain's entry into the European Economic Community, when he was one of a large group of Labour rebels who voted against the whips, followed by his appointment as deputy leader of the first Labour delegation to the European Parliament in 1976. Dalyell suspected this appointment wasn't unconnected with the leadership's determination to distance him from the devolution legislation taking shape at Westminster. With Michael Stewart, a former Foreign Secretary, as leader, the Labour contingent also included a future deputy Prime Minister, John Prescott, and a future Speaker of the House of Commons, Betty Boothroyd – 'Miss Boothroyd being at that time the least important of the politicians on the UK delegation,' remarked Dalyell. 'The pendulum swings!' Dalyell, in his new role, was 'very much for making friendships and liaisons with other Europeans. We worked very hard and did our country a lot of good,' he claimed.

He also learned something about *realpolitik à la Roma*. 'I was a member of the Budget sub-committee, which was the Public Accounts Committee of the European parliament,' Dalyell explained. 'There had been a terrible earthquake in Italy and it was said European funds were being misused. When the delegation was chosen to visit the disaster area, it didn't include an Italian. I thought this was wrong. So I went to see the Italians and said it would be awful if we didn't have one or two of their number as part of the delegation. The Socialist group made all sorts of excuses. My next stop was the Christian Democrats. Their leader looked at me as though I was mad. He told me I must be very wet behind the ears, to use an Anglo-Saxon expression, to imagine an Italian would visit the earthquake area on that particular subject, the misuse of public funds. He told me I must be very naive. In fact, he said, with the words delivered in guttural Italian, "Don't be a silly little boy!" My accuser's name,' Dalyell added, laughing loudly, 'was Giulio Andreotti, six times Prime Minister of Italy.'

Dalyell spent more than a year as the appointed deputy leader of the Labour delegation to Strasburg before a rules change within the PLP required him to face an election. 'There was a coup against me from the critics of the market and they replaced me with John Prescott,' he said. 'John at that time was anti-market and I was vehemently pro-market. Later, when Michael Stewart retired, John became leader. The last thing a majority of the PLP wanted then was an ardent marketeer as leader of the Labour group in the European Parliament. John beat me by one vote. But there was no personal aggro between him and me and we've remained friendly ever since, to the extent that I voted for him as leader of the party against Tony Blair.' He also claimed, 'I think that original group was rather useful. We helped ease Britain into the European community. Many of the commissioners were very forthcoming if one treated them properly.'

His experience then convinced Dalyell that, instead of introducing direct elections, Europe might have been better served by continuing with a nominated parliament, recruited from 'elected people' in each of the member states. 'In a sense,' he claimed, 'under the old system, the European Parliament was much more influential. We were all members of our own national parliaments, dealing with very real problems in Europe, such as Spain's application to join the community. In our case, as members of the UK Parliament, we were able to report back to the House of Commons. A directly elected parliament doesn't have the same input.' He believed, in particular, that if things had continued in that way the United Kingdom would 'have been part of the single currency by now'.

Given the chance to put the clock back, Dalyell would 'stick with the old system' and have a rotational basis for membership, lasting three or four years. He was unimpressed – and indeed felt 'uneasy' – when the parliament succeeded in removing the entire commission. 'I thought they were posturing a bit,' Dalyell complained. 'All that particular episode demonstrated was that the parliament should have had the power to remove one commissioner.'

His response is less assured when questioned about the performance of the Scottish Parliament, having worked hard for years to stop it happening, and failed. 'I have bitten my tongue on the Scottish Parliament partly because any criticism I made in its early stages, people would say, he would say that, wouldn't he?' Dalyell explained. 'But what I always found impossible to believe was that there was going to be consensus and light, because that was not the nature of political life. I also wonder how they got themselves into a number of issues that are not high on most people's list of priorities, such as Clause 28. I was annoyed with Donald Dewar in particular, over the way I was ridiculed at the time of the referendum for going on about the cost of the building. I was called irresponsible and alarmist, and a lot worse beside, when I pointed out that the Standard Life building in Edinburgh cost more than £100 million. And that was without replenishings. So how much more was a parliament going to cost? Donald Dewar assured me it wouldn't cost a penny more than £40 million. Now we learn from a report by the Auditor General that the £195 million which MSPs approved earlier this year might not be enough – and no one is certain when the building will be finished'

Musing on what will happen at the next general election in Scotland, he arrives at the conclusion: 'It will be an extremely odd election. One is often asked questions about health, education, housing. What am I to say to people who have waited a quarter of an hour and travelled some distance to see me? Write to your MSP! I have been meticulous about not interfering in other people's patches. But I've got to do something for them. Fortunately, relations between me and Mary Mulligan are perfectly civilised. In some areas they are not very civilised and there are turf wars. Well, I am not going to spend my life engaged in turf wars.'

Allister Mackie revealed: 'Tam makes a point of never criticising the local authority and he would never dream of interfering in areas which are the responsibility of the Scottish Parliament. Our group leader wanted a meeting to discuss the fact we were having our grants cut from the Scottish Executive. Tam responded by telling him he had been advocating devolution for Scotland for years and now he had it, he should just get on with it. He wouldn't allow himself to be part and parcel of criticism of the Scottish Executive, even although it was on a confidential basis.'

On the future governance of the United Kingdom, Dalyell continues to await the expected English backlash over devolution, while rejecting any idea of federalism. 'You can't have one part of a federal state having 86 per cent of the population,' he said. 'So a parliament for England isn't the answer.' Since the opening of the Scottish Parliament in Edinburgh, and the reaction to it in England, Dalyell has not changed his mind over devolution. 'We are on a motorway without an exit to independence,' he said simply.

Dalyell forecasts there will be a reduction in the number of Scottish MPs at Westminster. Asked to predict their future role, he responded cautiously: 'I am on extremely weak ground if I am asked to justify a large number of Scottish MPs in the House of Commons, as I am the man who has been asking these questions for 20 years. It sounds terribly like being unco' guid,' Dalyell admitted, 'but a number of my colleagues are in real difficulty over this. I am particularly lucky in that for 35 years, I have interested myself in international affairs and general affairs of major economic policy. There are others who have confined themselves to purely Scottish local affairs.'

Dalyell discounts any suggestion that Scottish MPs in London could act as 'a pressure group, to argue for an extended Scottish budget. That is a recipe for trouble,' he declared. 'The idea that the Scottish Executive will ask the Secretary of State for Scotland to act on its behalf is preposterous. Scottish ministers will want their own bilateral relations with Downing Street and the Treasury.'

In fact, unknown to many people, shortly before he agreed to stand again at the next election, there was a question mark over his own future parliamentary career. Allister Mackie disclosed: 'He was actually swithering over whether or not he should continue in Parliament. I was being pressurised into saying it was time for him to go. Not officially, but the word was coming out from Glasgow, although it probably started in London. I got the impression Millbank would have been happier without him. We're happier with him.' Dalyell himself once ruminated that it was a 'strange experience' being a long-serving MP, working over the years within a constituency party, first with an older generation, then with people of the same age, until finally a new generation appeared 'who had no part in the original selection conference'.

Mackie continued: 'If we hadn't had Tam then the vacancy would have been advertised, certain people would have applied, the selection panel would have been vetted. We could have finished up with someone we didn't know. That wouldn't have been a good situation. We could have lost the seat. I spent two hours with him, talking him into standing again. I told him it was for our sake as much as his. If there was ever any question of Tam being forcibly de-selected the nationalists would enjoy a field day,' Mackie added. 'His adoption was unopposed. Not one single person in the party voted against him. Considering the number of enemies he made in his approach to the Scottish parliament, that's quite amazing. He goes out of his way to be controversial and yet that happens. Afterwards, we simply issued a statement saying he had been re-selected and informed London of the outcome.'

According to Mackie there was only one occasion when Dalyell came close to seriously falling out with his constituency party, over devolution. 'Tam was obstinate in his opposition to a Scottish parliament, 'Mackie explained. 'We told him he would have to come and go a bit. So he promised that he wouldn't oppose the Scottish parliament at the time of the 1997 election. But, of course, he did oppose it. He didn't vote against it but he opposed it in public debate. In that sense, he deluded us into supporting him for re-selection. It's possible he could have been selected without making any promises. It was in the balance. I was the one who told him straight that before we considered his position we needed certain commitments. He gave us those commitments and it was on that basis he was selected. I thought he dishonoured himself by this approach and told him so, which hurt. Tam likes to think everything he does is honourable. It's a conscious thing with Tam. He tries hard to be honourable.'

At an early stage in his political career, Tam Dalyell expressed the hope: 'I am more concerned with doing something than being somebody.' Nearly 40 years on Michael Foot thought 'he'd done wonderful service to the House of Commons just by being there'. Neil Kinnock suggested: 'I don't think that valiant for truth is too dramatic or sentimental a title to give Tam Dalyell.' Tony Benn argued: 'What he does is to uphold the right of free thought which is as important as free speech.' George Younger maintained: 'He's a one-off, one of the rich products of the British parliamentary system and should be treasured.'

Dalyell considers the 1980s, which included a spell on the National Executive Committee of the Labour Party, as his best period in parliament. It was his misfortune that he was at his prime during a long period when Labour was denied office. Dalyell himself admits: 'I regret not being a minister. I think I would have been rather a good minister. But one can't go through life moping and sulking. If anyone asks me, as a former school teacher, how would I mark my career, I'd say it had been worthwhile, could have done better, could have been luckier. The ill luck was timing.'

SELECT BIBLIOGRAPHY

Tony Benn, *Office Without Power* (London, 1988)

Vernon Bogdanor, *Devolution in the UK* (Oxford, 1999)

David Butler & Michael Pinto-Duschinsky, *British General Election 1970* (London, 1971)

James Callaghan, *Time and Chance* (London, 1988)

G.B. Carter, Porton Down 1916–1991' (in *RUSI Journal*, 1991)

Barbara Castle, *Fighting all the Way* (London, 1993)

Alan Clark, *Diaries* (London, 1993)

Bill Coxall & Lynton Robins, *Contemporary British Politics* (London, 1998)

Michael Crick, *Heseltine* (London, 1999)

Julian Critchley, *Heseltine* (London, 1994)

Richard Crossman, *Diaries of a Cabinet Minister* (London, 1975–77)

Hugh Cudlipp, *Walking on the Water* (London, 1976)

Tam Dalyell, *The Case for Ship Schools* (Glasgow, 1960):

Tam Dalyell, *Devolution: The End of Britain?* (London, 1977):

Tam Dalyell, *One Man's Falklands* (London, 1982):

Tam Dalyell, *A Science Policy for Britain* (London, 1983):

Tam Dalyell, *Thatcher's Torpedo* (London, 1983):

Tam Dalyell, *Misrule* (London, 1987):

Tam Dalyell, *Dick Crossman: A Portrait* (London, 1989)

Tony Geraghty, *Who Dares Wins* (London, 1980)

Christopher Harvie, *Scotland and Nationalism 1707–1977* (London, 1977)

Denis Healey, *The Time of my Life* (London, 1989)

Lord Home, *The Way the Wind Blows* (London, 1976)

Bernard Ingham, *Kill the Messenger* (London, 1991)

Thomas Johnston, *The History of the Working Classes in Scotland* (Glasgow, 1920)

Jack Jones, *Union Man* (London, 1986)

John Kampfner, *Robin Cook* (London, 1982)

Arnold Kemp, *The Hollow Drum* (Edinburgh, 1993)

John P. Mackintosh, *The British Cabinet* (London, 1968)

Andy McSmith, *John Smith: Playing the Long Game* (London, 1993)

John Major, *The Biography* (London, 1999)

James Margach, *The Abuse of Power* (London, 1978)

Andrew Marr, *The Battle for Scotland* (London, 1992)

Lt. Col. Colin Mitchell, *Having been a Soldier* (London, 1969)

Kenneth O. Morgan, *Callaghan: A life* (Oxford, 1997)

James Morris, *Farewell the Trumpets* (London, 1968)

Anne Pagan, *God's Scotland?* (Edinburgh, 1988)

Ben Pimlott, *Harold Wilson* (London, 1992)

Chapman Pincher, *Inside Story* (London, 1978)

Chapman Pincher, *Their Trade is Treachery* (London, 1981)

Clive Ponting, *The Right to Know* (London, 1985)

John Prebble, *The Lion in the North* (London, 1971)

Desmond Rice & Arthur Gavshon, *The Sinking of the Belgrano* (London, 1984)

Gareth Boyd Roberts, *Ancestors of American Presidents* (California, 1995)

Kenneth Roy, *Conversations in a Small Country* (Ayr, 1989)

Trevor Royle, *The Best Years of their Lives* (London, 1986)

Sunday Times Insight Team, *The Falklands War* (London, 1982)

Margaret Thatcher, *Downing Street Years* (London, 1993)

Phillip Whitehead, *The Writing on the Wall* (London, 1985)

Harold Wilson, *The Governance of Britain* (London, 1976)

Billy Wolfe, *Scotland Lives* (Edinburgh, 1973)

Peter Wright with Paul Greengrass, *Spycatcher* (Australia, 1987)

Woodrow Wyatt, *Journals of Woodrow Wyatt* (London, 1999)

Hugo Young, *One of Us* (London, 1989)

Philip Ziegler, *Wilson* (London, 1993)

INDEX